IMAGES
of America

Hawthorne Works

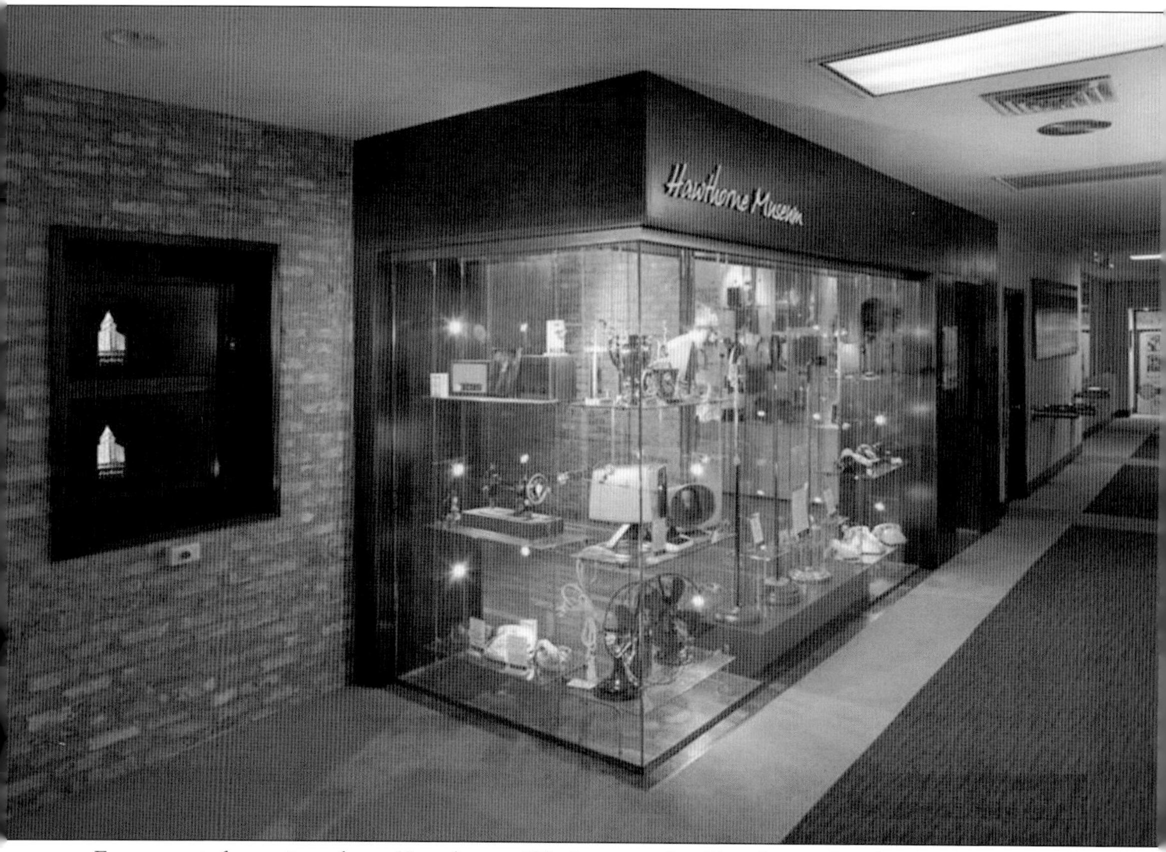

For more information about Hawthorne Works, visit the Hawthorne Works Museum, located on the Morton College campus, at 3801 South Central Avenue in Cicero. (Courtesy of the Hawthorne Works Museum.)

On the Cover: It is quitting time in the spring of 1924 as crowds of Hawthorne employees leave through Entrance No. 1, along Cicero Avenue. (Courtesy of AT&T Archives.)

IMAGES
of America

HAWTHORNE WORKS

Dennis Schlagheck and Catherine Lantz

ARCADIA
PUBLISHING

ISBN 978-1-4671-1135-5

Published by Arcadia Publishing
Charleston, South Carolina

Printed in the United States of America

Library of Congress Control Number: 2013943909

For all general information, please contact Arcadia Publishing:
Telephone 843-853-2070
Fax 843-853-0044
E-mail sales@arcadiapublishing.com
For customer service and orders:
Toll-Free 1-888-313-2665

Visit us on the Internet at www.arcadiapublishing.com

*To Tess and Emily: your smiles inspire me, your love uplifts me;
to my sister Luisa: ikaw ang aking bayani!*

Contents

ACKNOWLEDGMENTS

We would like to express our thanks to the many people who said *yes* to us during every step of this project—yes to our requests for time, stories, images, and input. This book would not have been possible without their enthusiasm and support. We really appreciate the patience and talents of our Morton Library colleagues. A special thank-you goes to Jennifer Butler, the director of Morton College Library and Hawthorne Works Museum, for allowing us to take on this project.

The Hawthorne Works veterans, living witnesses to that special, long-lost time and place, added deeply personal touches and vivid details to our story. Our thanks go to Tom Brandsness, a Hawthorne employee from 1965 to 1985, for his devotion to preserving the memory of the Works and for sharing its positive influence on his life. We are also grateful to John Diaz, a Hawthorne Works fireman and security officer and the creator of the website www.westernelectric.weebly.com. John shared the "Countdown" tribute, a perfect and touching epitaph for the old Works. Tom Bell shared his memories of the cable plant. Many thanks for explaining the process so even we could understand it.

During our research, few things moved us as deeply as our discovery of the story of Virginia "Ginny" Brouk Davis. The real lives lived at Hawthorne need no embellishment, by Hollywood or otherwise, and we are honored that she has allowed us to tell another generation about her courage and resilience. Our gratitude also goes out to genealogist Jennifer Holik, the author of *To Soar With the Tigers*, for connecting us with Ginny and for providing generous advice and encouragement.

Marian Manseau Cheatham, the author of the novel *Merely Dee*, set in the era of the *Eastland* tragedy, offered honest and professional critiques to a novice writer. Thank you for your helpful suggestions and uplifting support.

George Kupczak of the AT&T Archives and History Center in Warren, New Jersey, lent his time, talent, and resources to the project. His guidance and hospitality are greatly appreciated. The archives' website, techchannel.att.com, is a priceless treasury of the history of telecommunications.

Unless otherwise noted, all images are courtesy of the Hawthorne Works Museum.

INTRODUCTION

About six miles southwest of downtown Chicago, there is a shopping center at the corner of Cicero Avenue and Cermak Road. Its only unusual feature is a five-story stone tower just behind the storefronts. With its decorative brick arches, slit windows, corner turrets, and steeple, the tower looks like it would be more at home in a medieval fortress or a Disney theme park. Few realize they are looking at the last vestige of an American historical landmark. These 200-plus acres were the home of the Hawthorne Works, a vast industrial complex of over 100 buildings with five million square feet of workspace. Known as the Electrical Capital of America, it was where the Western Electric Company kept pace with the nation's demand for communications equipment. At its peak, over 40,000 workers passed through its gates each day. When Pittsburgh and Gary meant steel and Detroit reigned as the Motor City, the Hawthorne Works in Cicero stood for telephones. In its heyday, the Western Electric brand and the Hawthorne Works name were synonymous with cutting-edge telecommunications. The Hawthorne Works is worth remembering because it was more than just another factory. Its story is nothing less than the story of the rise and fall of urban industrial America in the 20th century.

When Hawthorne opened in 1905, its shops were filled by immigrant workers struggling to secure a place in a strange new homeland. The Hawthorne Works exerted a powerful influence over their lives. With its own hospital, railroad, power plant, athletic fields, fire department, and night school, the Works functioned as a modern industrial commonwealth. Its workforce bought homes with loans arranged through the employee-run club, joined company-sponsored sports teams, drove automobiles on paid vacations, and planned for retirement on a company pension. Instead of squalid housing or company-owned towns, solid working-class communities sprang up. Hawthorne employees worked together, played together, lived together, and, at times, tragically, died together.

Year after year, Hawthorne's workers turned out an endless stream of complex communications apparatus, engineered by the sharpest minds in the field and assembled by skilled craftsmen. The company's accomplishments won the admiration of business leaders around the globe and inspired pioneering research in industrial psychology and labor relations. The Works' bustling shops provided the perfect setting for testing new manufacturing methods, and company officials gladly served up employees as subjects for groundbreaking studies whose results are still debated by psychologists and sociologists.

In its time, the Hawthorne Works exemplified the "virtuous circle:" a win-win proposition whereby corporate success forged a bond of loyalty with its employees. Today, when "cradle-to-grave" care is often scorned as a soft-hearted and soft-headed business model, when labor struggles to be heard and management looks only to downsize and outsource, Hawthorne's decades of prosperity stand as a model of a workable middle ground, somewhere between class antagonism and plutocracy. This carefully crafted partnership left a permanent imprint on American society.

Curiously, America's privately owned telephone system, a showpiece of free enterprise, owed much of its success to the government-sanctioned monopoly of the nation's telephone service for much of the 20th century. The Bell System's vertical configuration—long distance (AT&T), research (Bell Labs), manufacturing and supply (Western Electric), and service (regional Bell companies)—assured its dominance. But as the technological landscape changed, newcomers clamored for a piece of the telecommunications pie and drew the Bell System into the swirl of downsizing and breakups that characterized American business in the last decades of the 20th century.

As the century closed, the heavy industries that fed generations of Americans and built a bridge to the middle class disappeared with alarming speed, the Works along with them. Hawthorne's very size, which allowed it to function on such a vast scale, became impractical. Tasks were dispersed to other plants, the payroll shrank, and the imposing red brick edifice looked like a relic of a past age. But the end came not because its employees became complacent or less efficient, not because its engineers ran out of ideas, but simply because its time had passed. The very technologies its workers had done so much to make a part of everyday life rendered it obsolete.

Today, precious little is left of the Hawthorne Works. Only a handful of artifacts in a small museum, along with the memories of a dwindling number of veteran employees, remain as reminders of its existence. This book is an attempt to preserve in words and images the history of an important place and time, to pay tribute to the lasting contribution made by the many thousands who worked there over nine decades.

One

Beginnings

Electrical Capital of America

Founded in 1869 by Enos Barton and Elisha Gray, Western Electric manufactured telegraph equipment for Western Union. In 1882, Alexander Graham Bell's company bought Barton's firm and made it their sole supplier of telephone apparatus, a partnership that would last for a century. In the 1890s, the number of telephones in the United States jumped from 285,000 to over three million, overwhelming Western Electric's factory near downtown Chicago. Enos Barton convinced his board of directors to construct an enormous new factory just outside the city.

In 1902, Hawthorne was little more than undeveloped land in the town of Cicero. Hawthorne's location, straddling the urban-rural border, made it ideal for Western Electric; there was plenty of room to expand; access to rail, street, and water transportation; and proximity to a willing workforce. Western Electric purchased nearly 300 acres in Hawthorne, and construction began in April 1903. In February 1905, the 600,000-square-foot Hawthorne Works opened its doors. It continued to grow from day one, reigning as the world's largest and most modern telephone factory.

On Saturday, July 24, 1915, the *Eastland*, an excursion boat preparing to take Hawthorne employees on a lake outing, capsized in the Chicago River. The disaster devastated the tight-knit Hawthorne Works community. A total of 22 entire families were lost. The death toll rose to 844. To read the victims' obituaries is to begin to grasp the depth of the tragedy. Story after story tells of lost loved ones, of solitary survivors left without family, of households left without a breadwinner, or of twists of fate that placed unlucky souls on the *Eastland* that morning. But the demands of the fast-growing telephone industry allowed little time for grieving. The vacant jobs were filled by applicants who lined up at the employment office even before the funerals began. In the coming years, Hawthorne would face new challenges and new losses as it and the nation were drawn into world events.

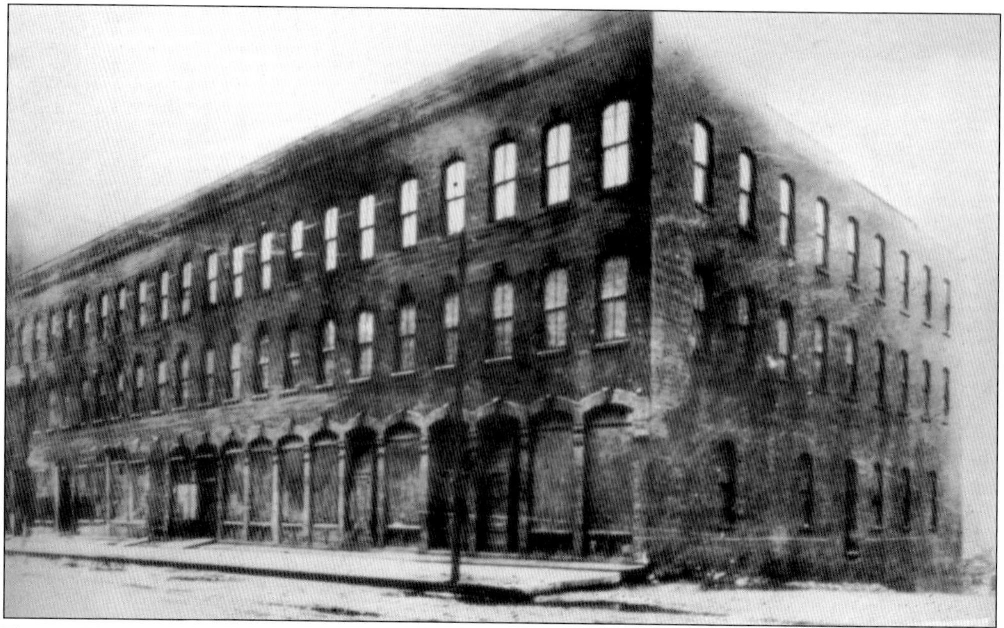

From 1872 to 1884, Western Electric's headquarters were at 20 West Kinzie Street in Chicago. The factory produced telephones, switches, and fire alarms. Rapid growth forced the company into a larger facility on South Clinton Street. By 1900, growing demand prompted the company to construct the Hawthorne Works. (Courtesy of the Simak collection.)

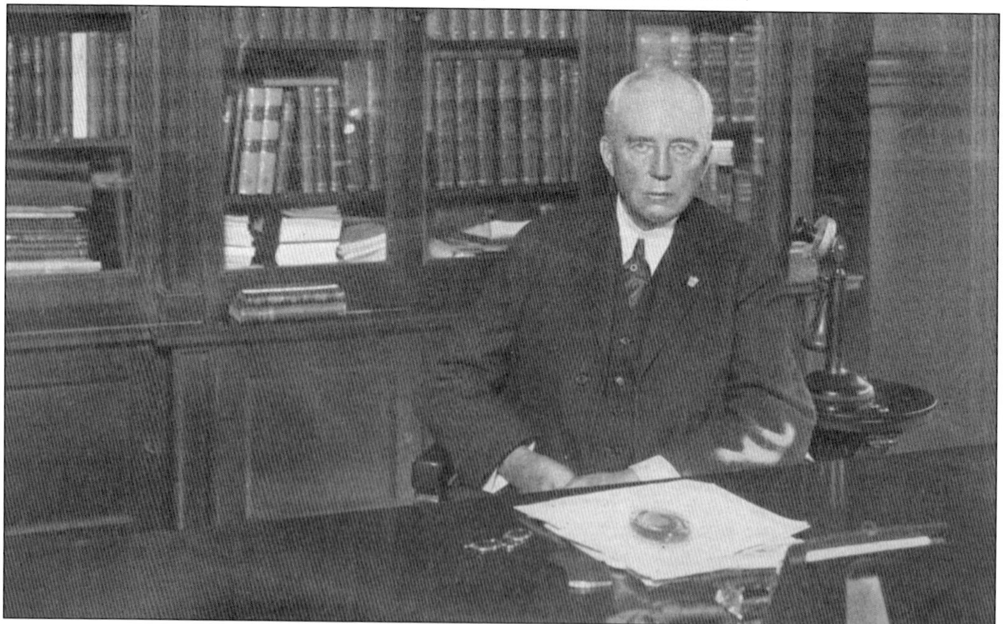

Enos Barton (1844–1916) cofounded Western Electric with Elisha Gray in 1869. Western Union, their primary customer, used Gray's telephone patent to compete against the American Bell Company. When Bell's patent was upheld and Western Union withdrew from the telephone business, Bell found a reliable supplier in Western Electric (WE). Their partnership lasted a century. Construction of the Hawthorne Works stands as Barton's crowning achievement. (Courtesy of the *Western Electric News*.)

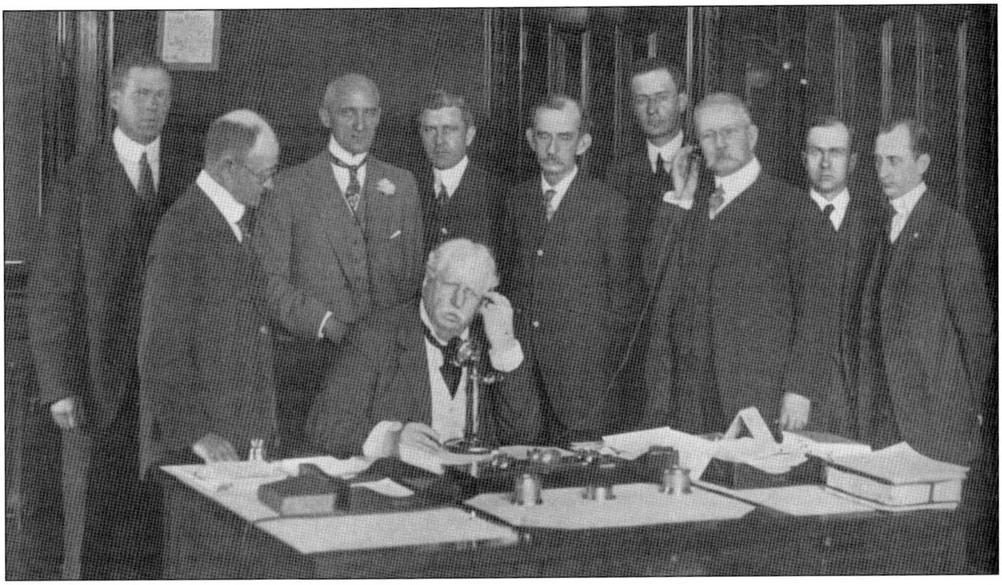

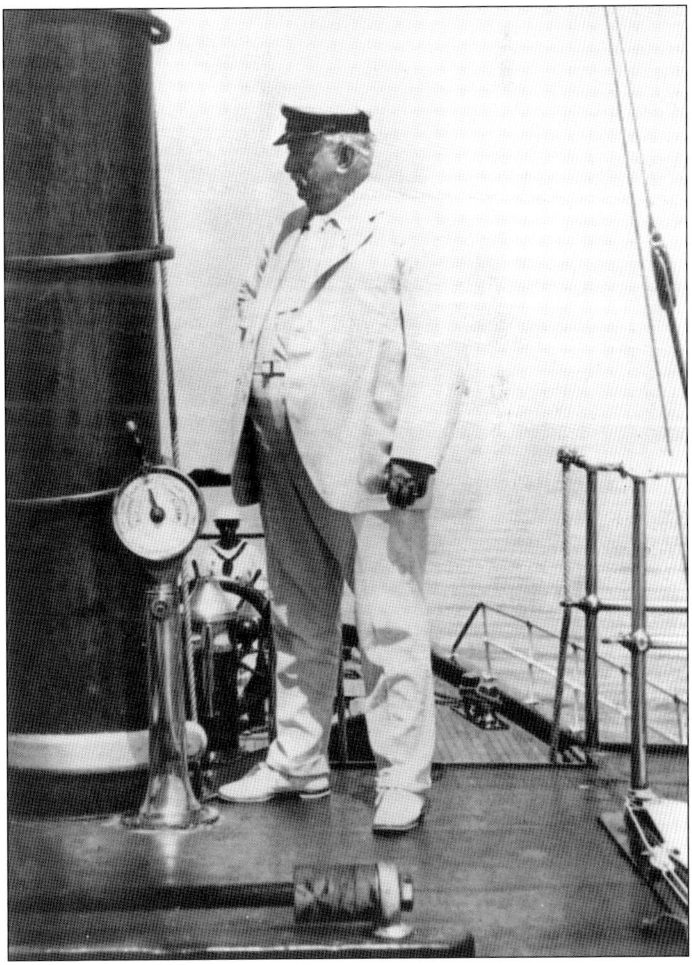

Above, AT&T president Theodore N. Vail takes the first phone call from San Francisco to New York in 1915. At right, he enjoys a day aboard his yacht *Speedwell.* Vail, AT&T's chief from 1907 to 1919, established the Bell System as a nationwide, integrated telephone service, dominated, of course, by AT&T affiliates. Vail bought up independent telephone companies and urged Western Electric to make telephone production its priority. AT&T acquired a majority interest in Western Union, prompting an antitrust suit in 1913. Facing a breakup, Vail sold AT&T's interest in Western Union and agreed to submit to government approval of any further acquisitions. Vail's pragmatism allowed the Bell System to remain intact. (Both courtesy of the *Western Electric News.*)

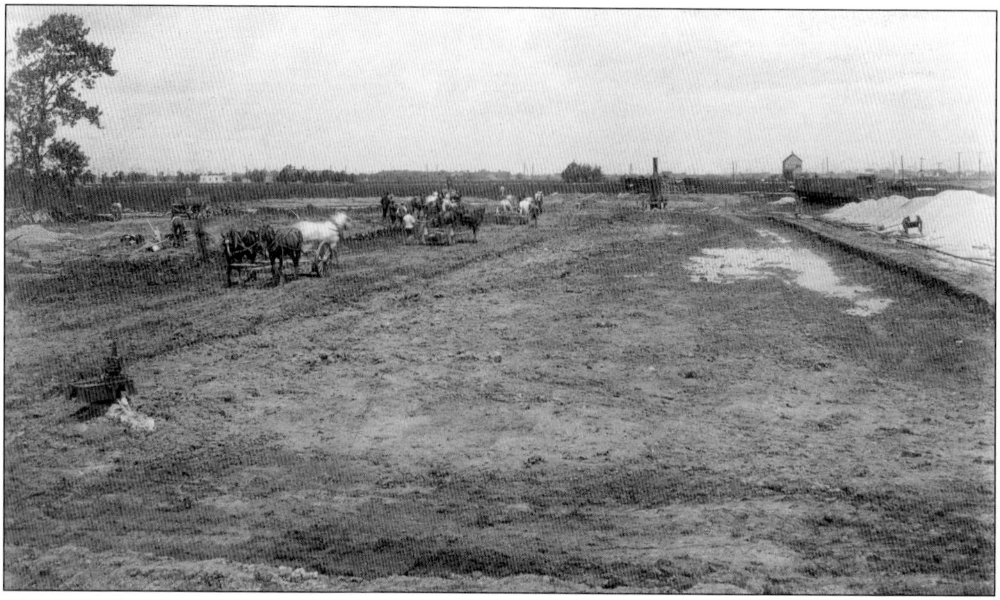

The town of Cicero was little more than a few scattered dwellings when construction of the Hawthorne Works began in 1903. Here, horse-drawn graders clear areas soon to be occupied by shops and mills. Despite its apparent isolation, the property held many advantages: room to expand, proximity to transportation, and access to Chicago's vast labor pool. (Courtesy of AT&T Archives.)

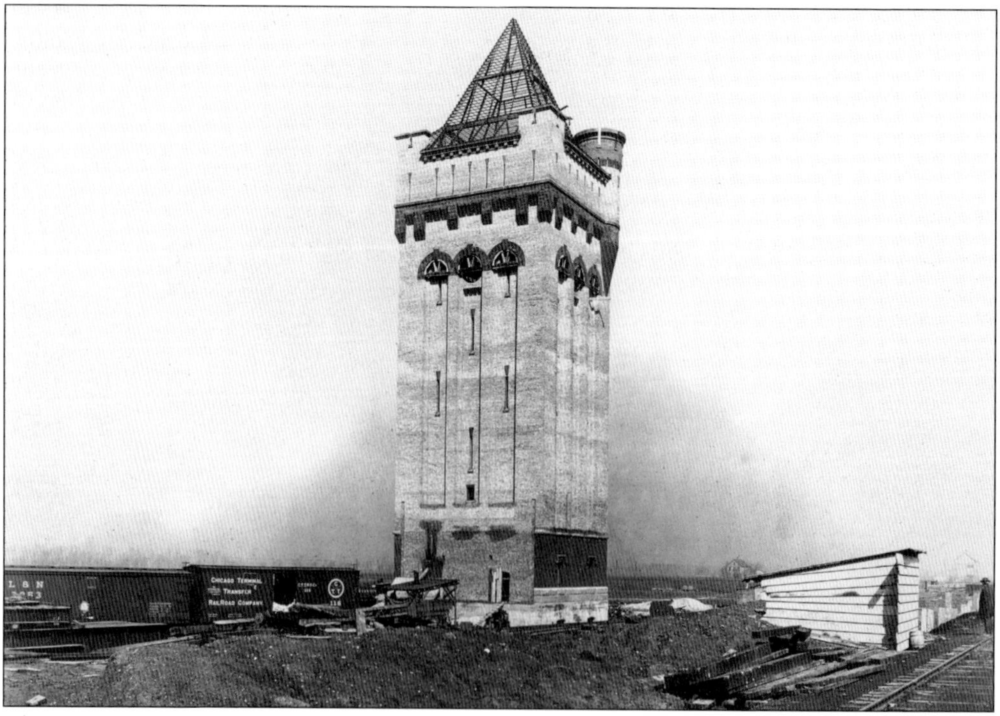

The Hawthorne Works water tower, the first structure completed, rises over the tracks of the Manufacturers' Junction Railroad in this 1904 photograph. By 1905, the powerhouse, the cable plant, the foundry, and the telephone apparatus buildings were completed and the 600,000-square-foot Hawthorne Works was open for business. (Courtesy of AT&T Archives.)

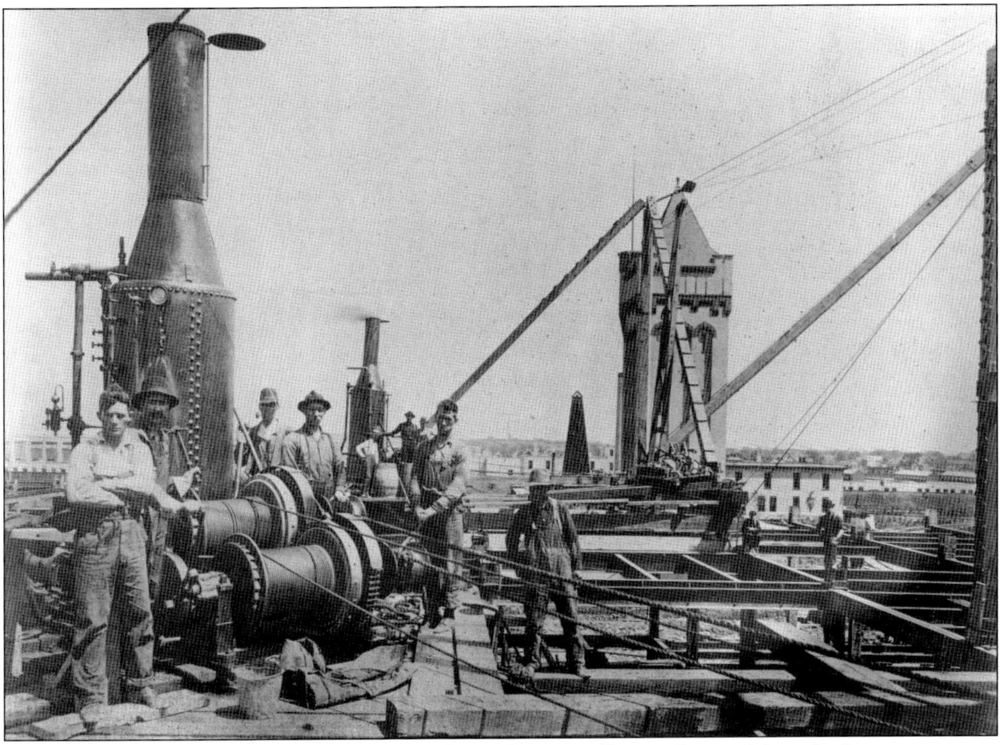

A construction crew takes a break from work on the upper floors of one of the telephone apparatus buildings in 1904, with the completed water tower in view just beyond. Western Electric spent $310,000 to purchase nearly 300 acres at Hawthorne and laid out an additional $1.1 million to construct the first group of buildings. (Courtesy of AT&T Archives.)

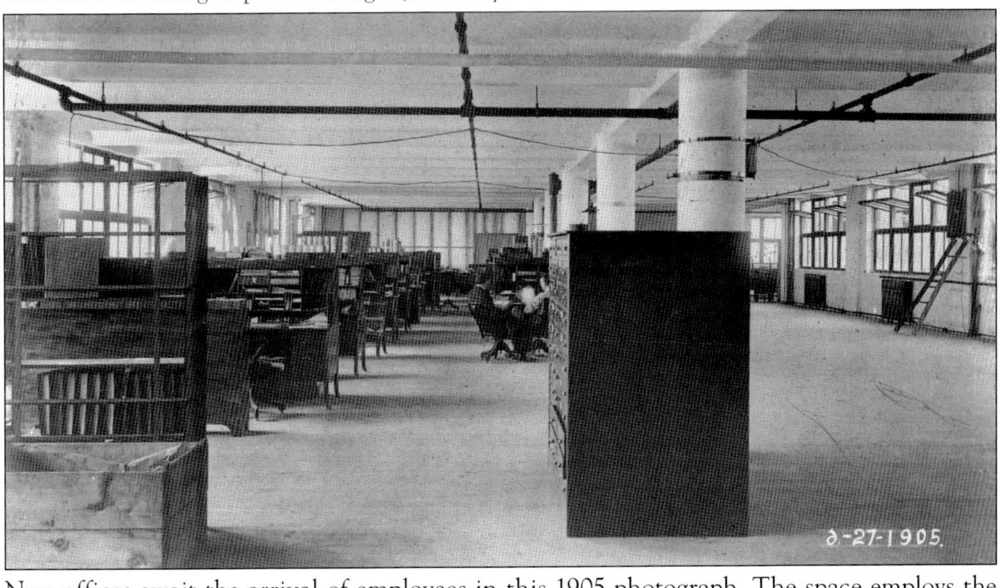

New offices await the arrival of employees in this 1905 photograph. The space employs the latest in early 1900s office equipment: wooden desks and file cabinets, swivel chairs, and climate control (opening or shutting the windows). Generations of clerks, draftsmen, and engineers kept the Hawthorne Works running smoothly for over 75 years.

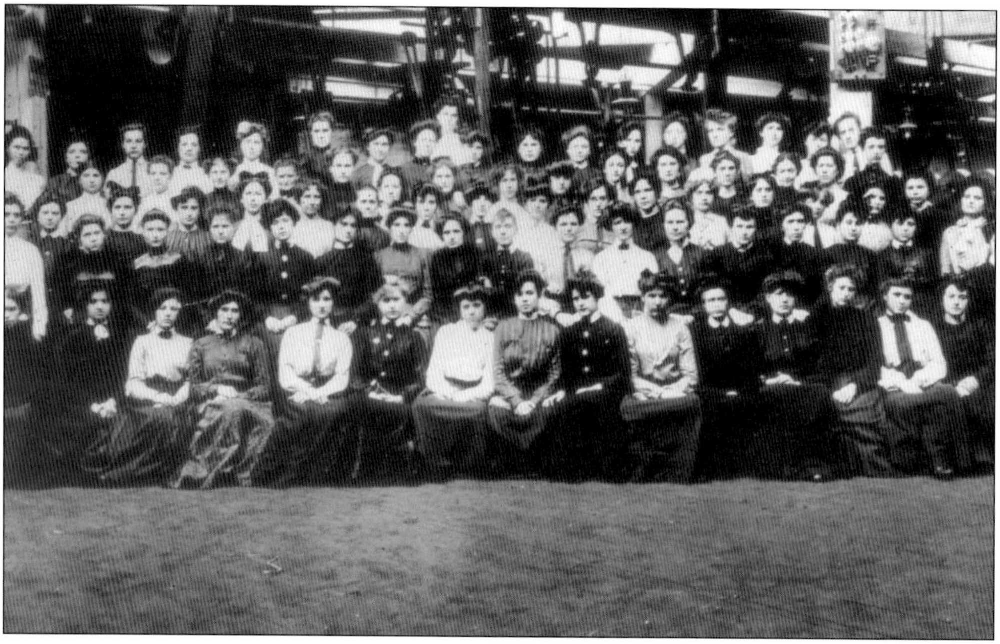

The young ladies pictured here, from the Clinton Street plant, were among the first employees to transfer to the new Hawthorne Works, in February 1905. They worked 51 hours a week, Monday to Saturday, and earned an average of $13 a week. In the first year, Hawthorne turned out 700,000 telephones. (Courtesy of the *Western Electric News.*)

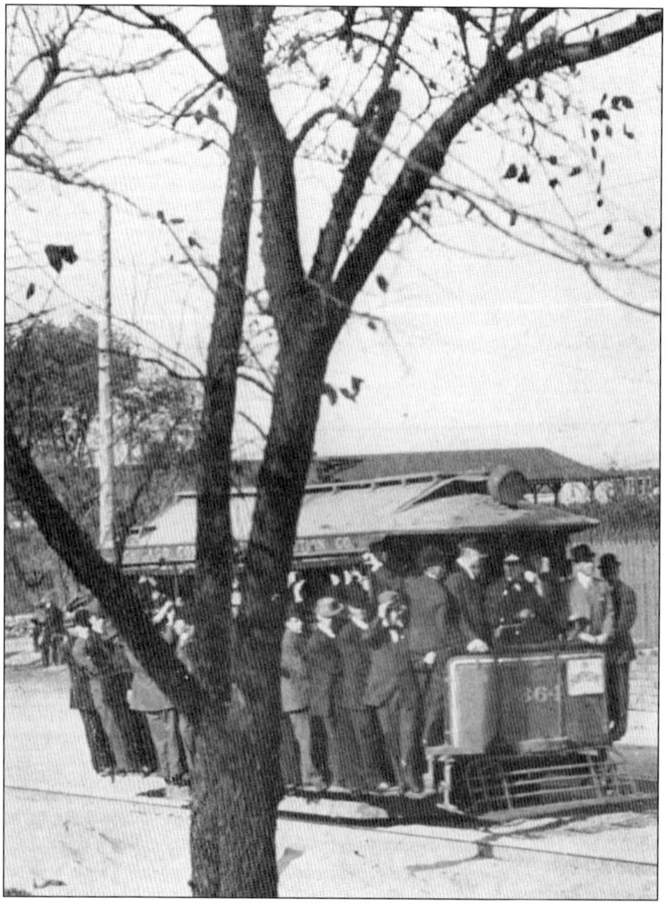

When Hawthorne opened, Chicago streetcar lines ended a mile from the plant, and early employees waited on muddy corners for rickety company "dummy" cars to complete their trip. The city extended the lines in a few years to accommodate Hawthorne's thousands of commuters. (Courtesy of the *Western Electric News.*)

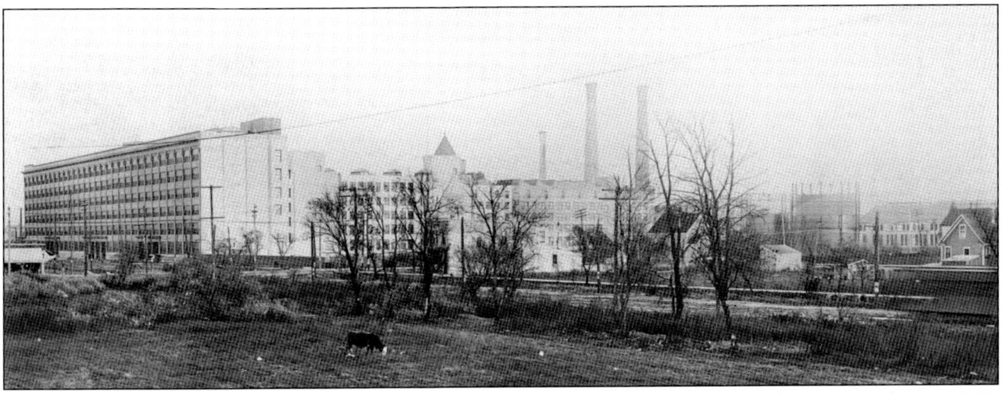

A cow grazes contentedly just across Twenty-second Street from the Hawthorne Works in 1914. Viewed from the northwest, one of the original telephone apparatus buildings is on the left. Beyond the trees, the peak of the water tower and the powerhouse are visible. By 1914, the Works already dominated the local landscape, as it would for decades to come. (Courtesy of AT&T Archives.)

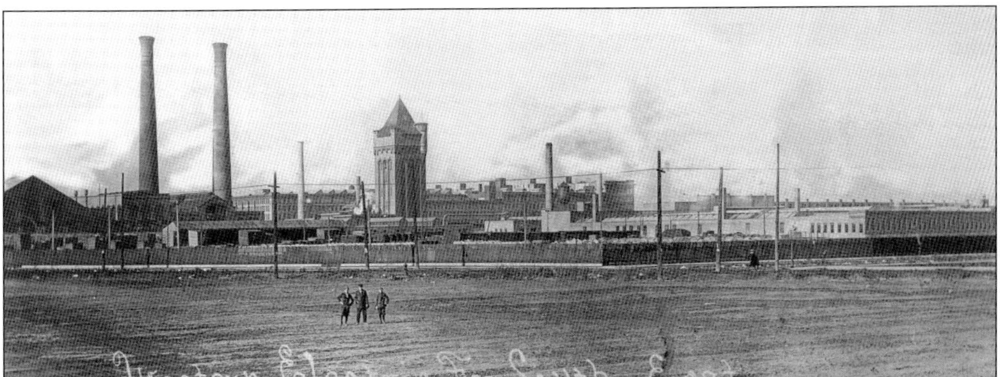

A view from the opposite side of the complex shows the fenced-in storage yard in front of the cable plant. As always, the stylish water tower is the dominant feature. Within a few years, every vacant lot for miles around would be filled by residences, stores, and more industry attracted by the Hawthorne Works. (Courtesy of AT&T Archives.)

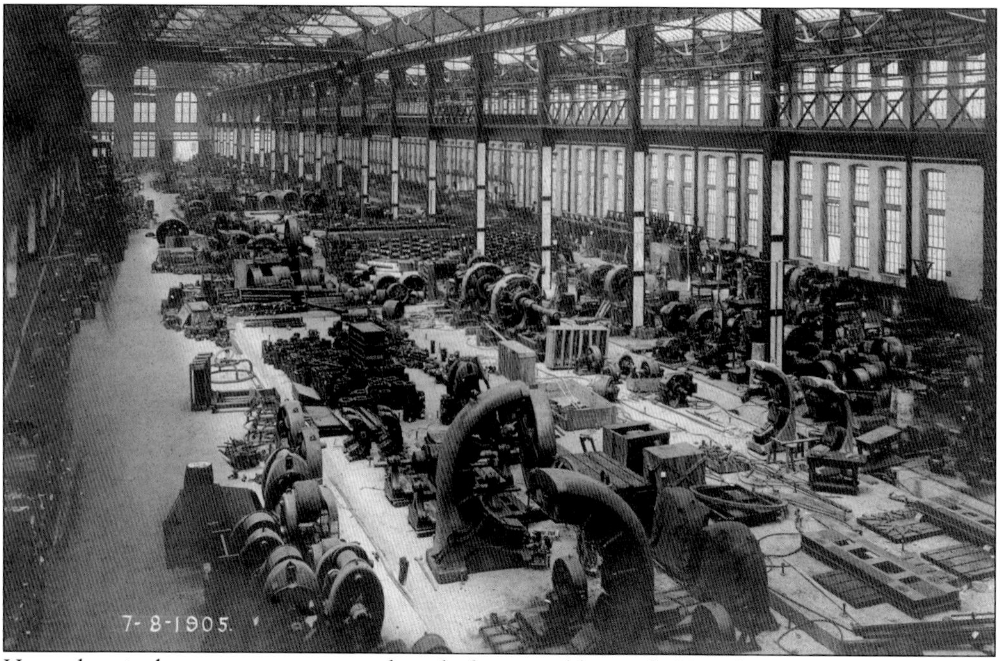

Huge electrical generator parts stand ready for assembly inside Hawthorne's cavernous power apparatus building in 1905. Just four years later, Western Electric stopped manufacturing power-generating equipment to focus on the production of telephone equipment. This structure later became the main merchandise warehouse. (Courtesy of AT&T Archives.)

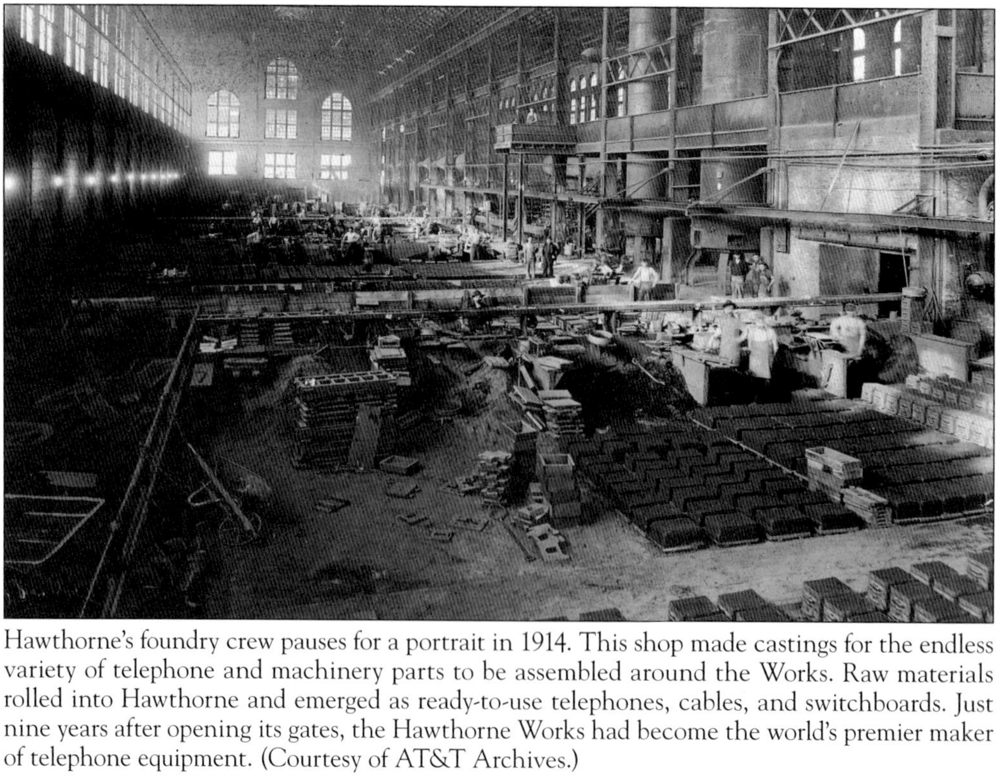
Hawthorne's foundry crew pauses for a portrait in 1914. This shop made castings for the endless variety of telephone and machinery parts to be assembled around the Works. Raw materials rolled into Hawthorne and emerged as ready-to-use telephones, cables, and switchboards. Just nine years after opening its gates, the Hawthorne Works had become the world's premier maker of telephone equipment. (Courtesy of AT&T Archives.)

Western Electric also served as the Bell System's parts supplier. In this 1917 photograph, Hawthorne packers fill some of the 11,000 daily orders. An overhead conveyor system transported order forms to the warehouse, where items were retrieved, packed, shipped, or special-ordered from Hawthorne's shops. (Courtesy of the *Western Electric News.*)

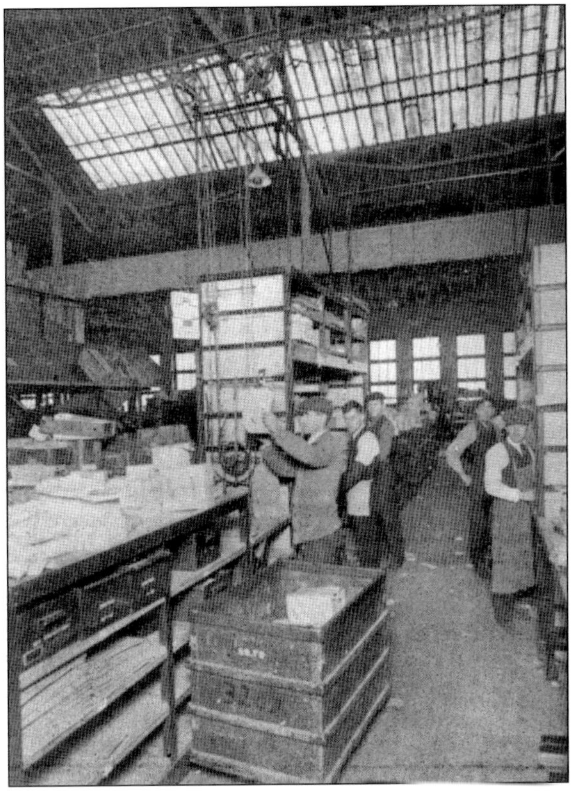

Just 12 years after opening, the Hawthorne Works needed more space to handle the ever-growing volume of orders. Below, ironworkers erect the frameworks of nine new buildings that would add 319,000 square feet to the telephone and coil assembly shops. The project was completed in 1917, just in time to meet the rush of military orders. (Courtesy of the *Western Electric News.*)

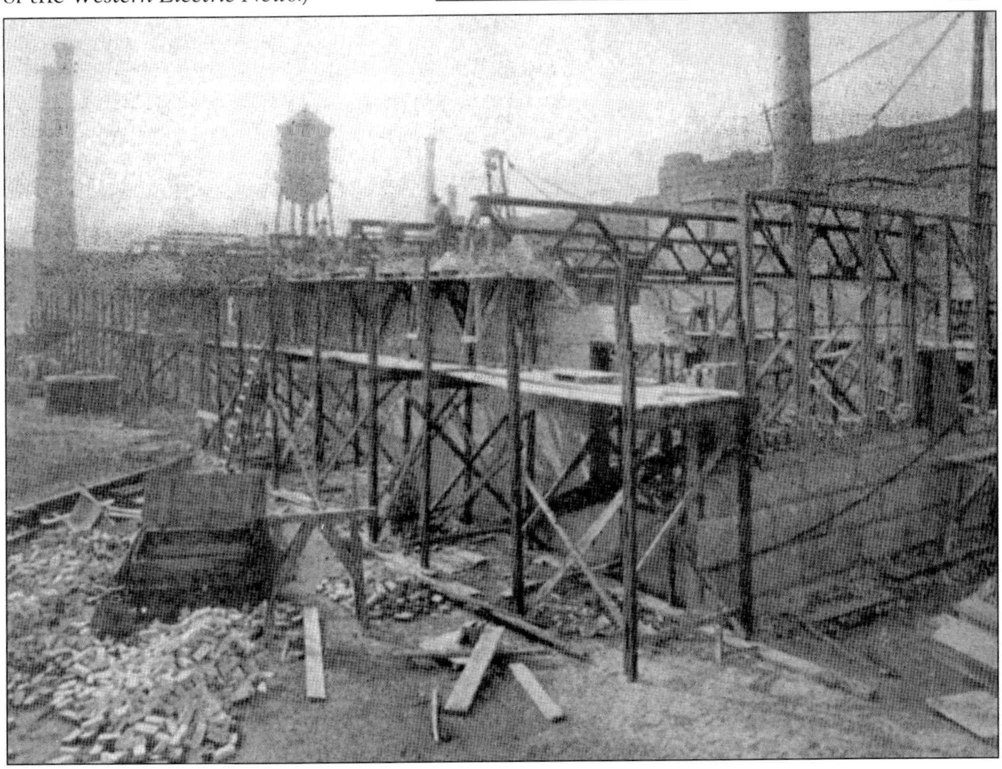

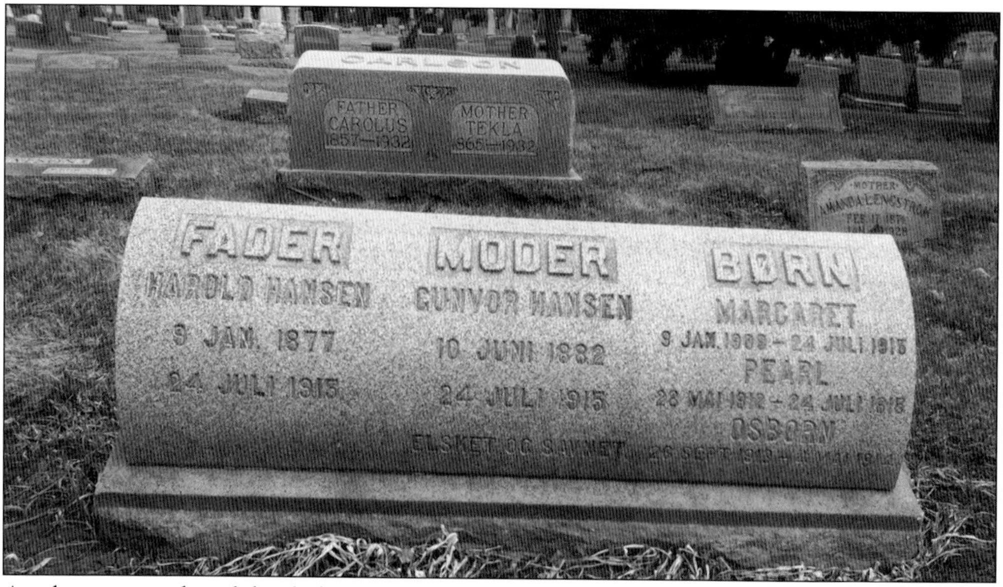

A solemn reminder of the darkest day in Hawthorne history is this gravestone of the Hansen family, at Chicago's Mt. Olive Cemetery. After arriving from Norway in 1906, Harold Hansen was hired by Hawthorne. By 1915, the family was living in a comfortable apartment in Chicago's Logan Square. On that fateful Saturday, July 24, 1915, the Hansens boarded the *Eastland* for a pleasant outing. Instead, they were one of 22 families to perish in the disaster.

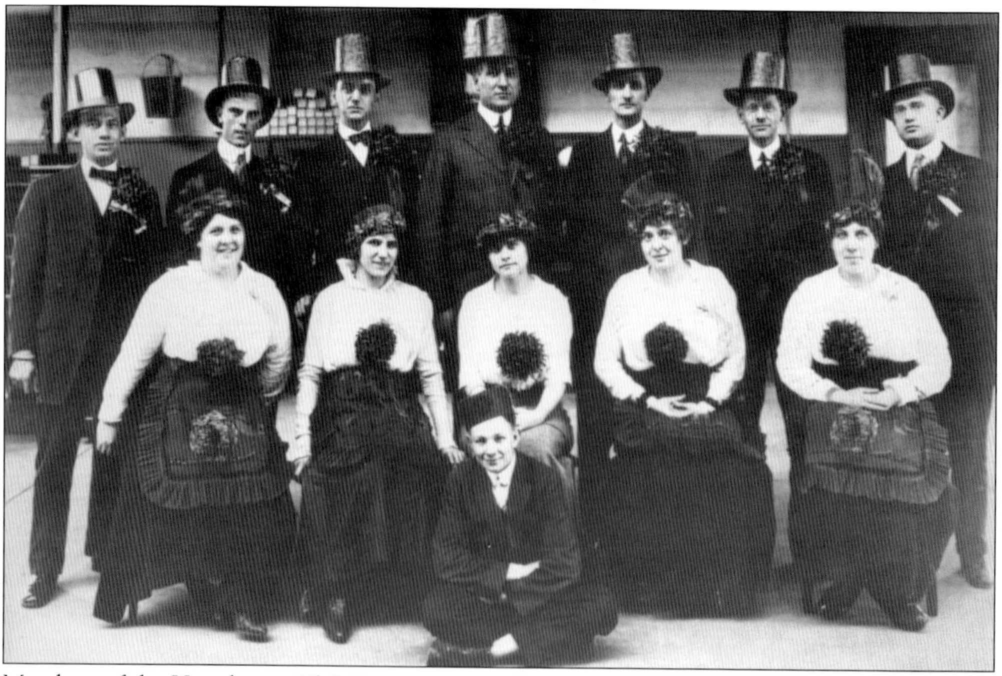

Members of the Hawthorne Club Entertainment Committee attempt to strike a festive pose for the camera during the 1915 holiday season. Life went on at the Works that Christmas, even in the wake of the *Eastland* tragedy four months earlier. Social activities were always a prominent part of the Western Electric culture. The Hawthorne Club leadership coordinated the entertainment, athletic, hobby, and educational programs at the plant.

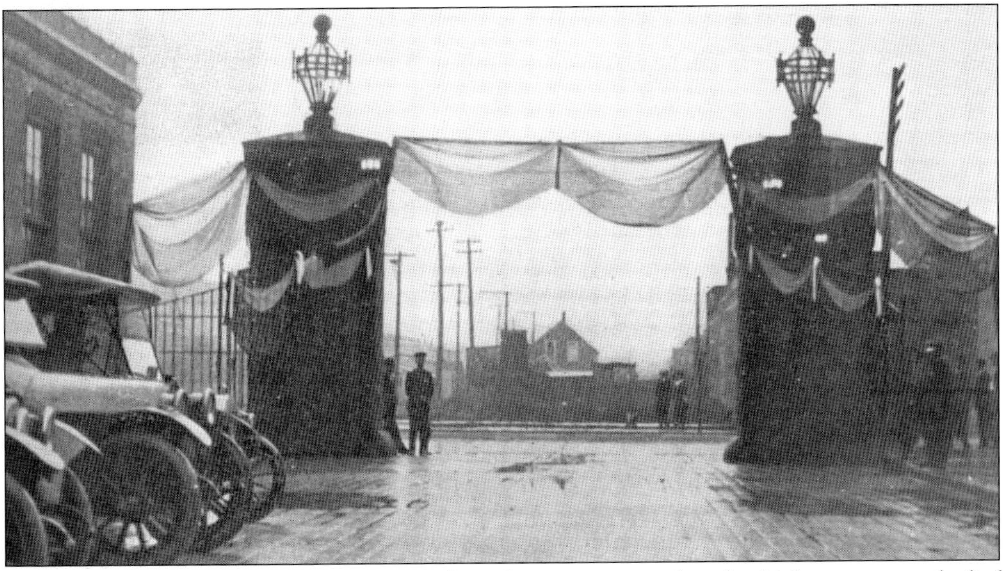

Entrance No. 1, along Cicero Avenue, was draped in mourning as hired vehicles transported relief workers to victims' homes in the days after the *Eastland* tragedy. The Hawthorne Club planned the *Eastland* outing with all the fanfare of a holiday. Excursion boats were to ferry fun-seekers to Michigan City, Indiana, for a day of swimming, games, music, and dancing. For Hawthorne's 14,000 employees, especially the young and single, the outing had become the biggest social event of the year. Many arrived early to find a place on the *Eastland*, the first of five boats docked along the Chicago River, only to be lost when the boat capsized. Sadly, the Hawthorne Works, ever a leader in fairness to its employees, will always be associated with that day's terrible death toll. (Both courtesy of the *Western Electric News*.)

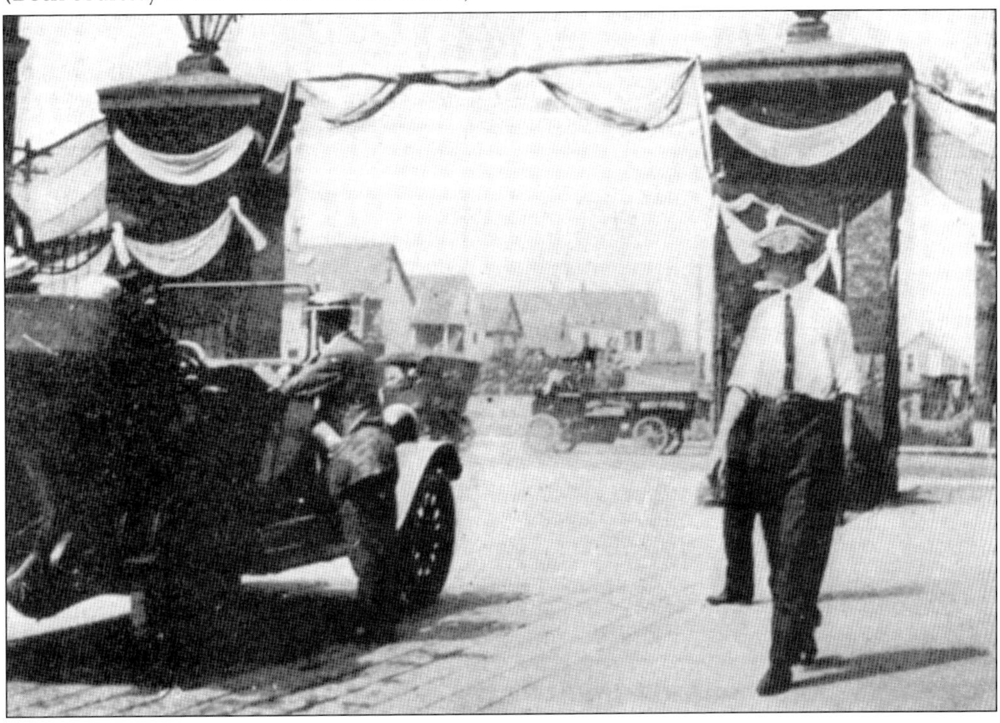

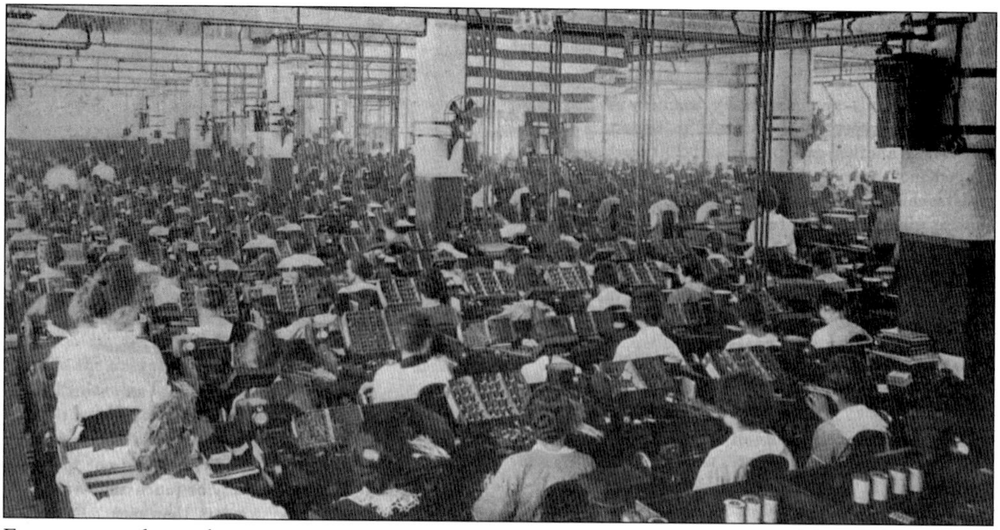

Every piece of sound-transmitting apparatus needed winding coils—electromagnets that helped maintain signal strength. The coil-making process involved over 1,000 Hawthorne employees, from wire winders to insulators to inspectors. Machine operators wound the copper wire like fishermen taking in line, carefully applying pressure on their footpad to maintain tension on wire moving at 5,000 revolutions per minute. Broken wires were spliced with finger-blackening rosin powder. Additional parts streamed in from other Hawthorne shops. Finally, one of the 175 inspectors scrutinized the finished product. By 1918, the Works had produced between 10 and 12 million coils. (Both courtesy of the *Western Electric News.*)

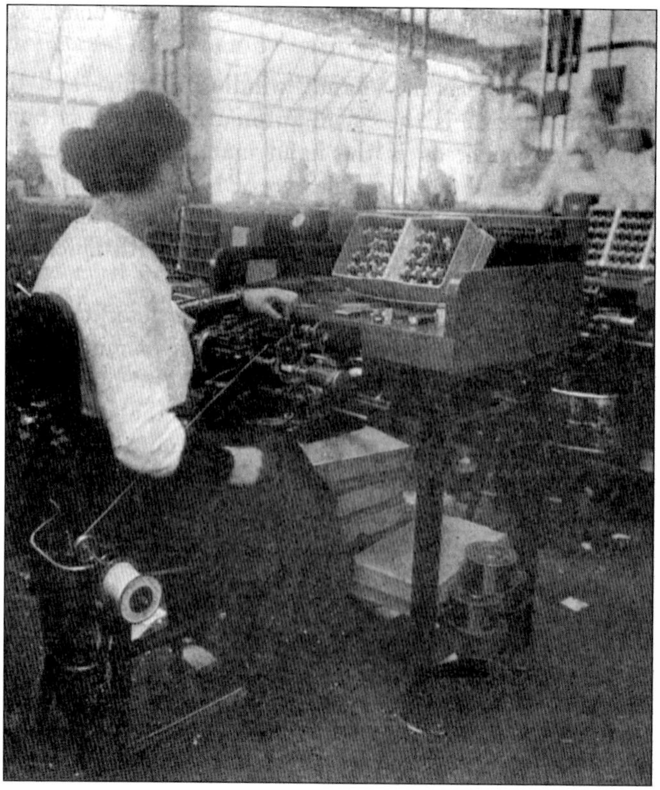

Not every Western Electric product transmitted the human voice. In the early days, Hawthorne's product line included vacuum cleaners, sewing machines, washing machines, and dishwashers, including the 1918 model seen here at the Hawthorne Works Museum. These modern conveniences promised the busy housewife more free time—maybe time to make a phone call? Western Electric sold its appliance business in the 1920s.

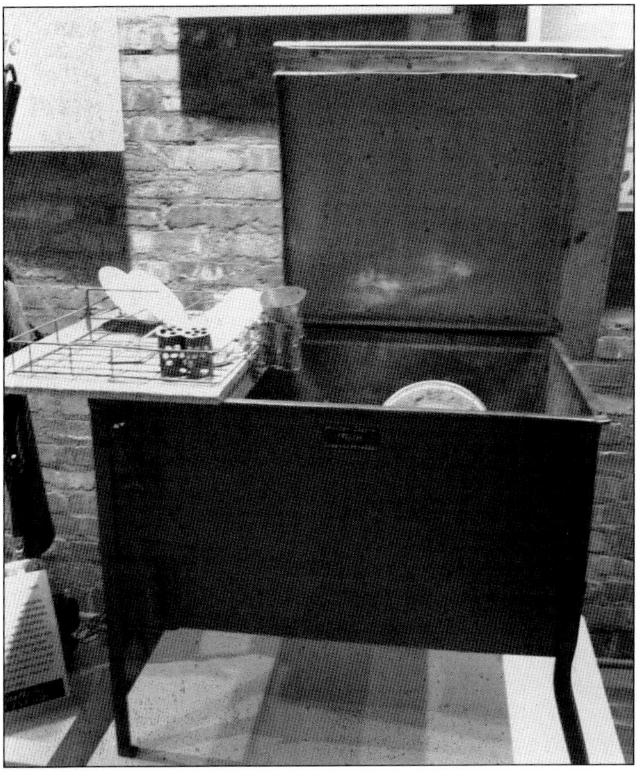

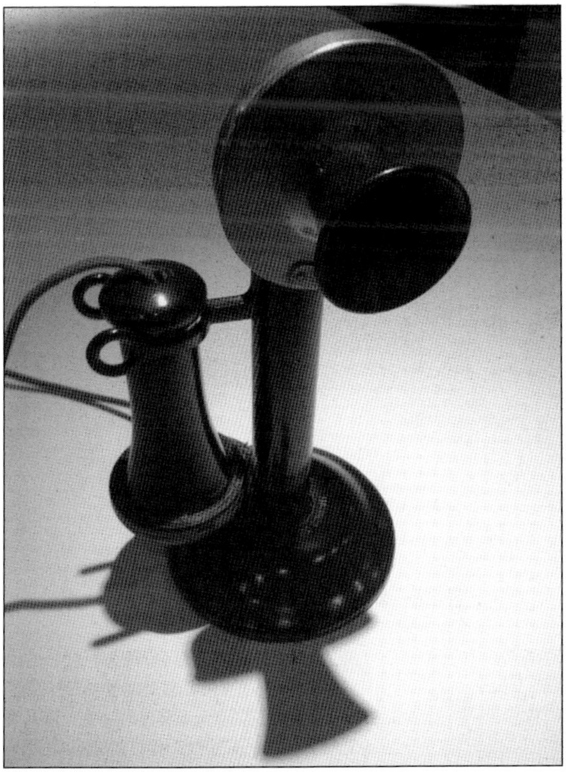

The Western Electric "candlestick" telephone went into production around 1900 and became the "Model T" of the industry: a standardized, instantly recognizable product. Operators completed calls made through the dial-less Model 20 series, seen here. The durable design remained popular for years despite its heavy metal construction and attachable "bell box."

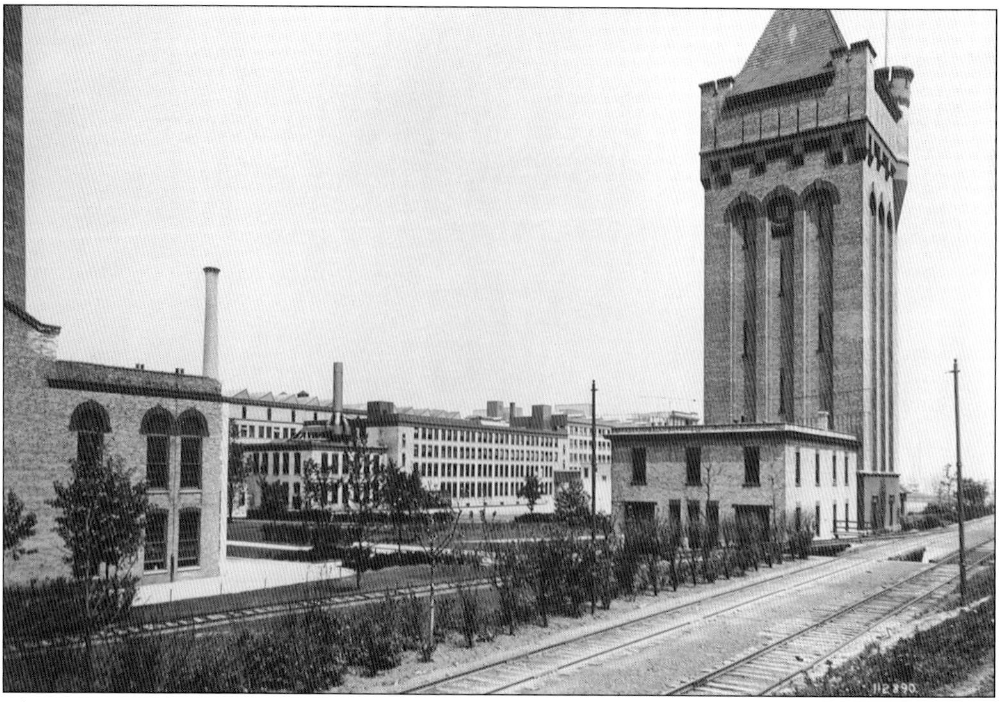

The Hawthorne Works dwarfed most large American factories. Western Electric's sole factory prospered and grew—and then grew some more. The original 2,000 workers in 1905 increased to 14,000 by 1914 and then doubled again in 10 more years. When Hawthorne opened, about 50 out of every 1,000 Americans leased a telephone. That amount doubled in a decade. Total workspace expanded from 600,000 square feet to over two million square feet by 1920, and then increased to four million square feet in 25 years. Over 100 janitors cleaned its shops and offices and shined its 6,500 windows. Each month, $1.5 million worth of raw materials came in and 190 tons of scrap went out. The Works was truly the Electrical Capital of America. (Above, courtesy of the Simak collection; below, courtesy of the *Western Electric News*.)

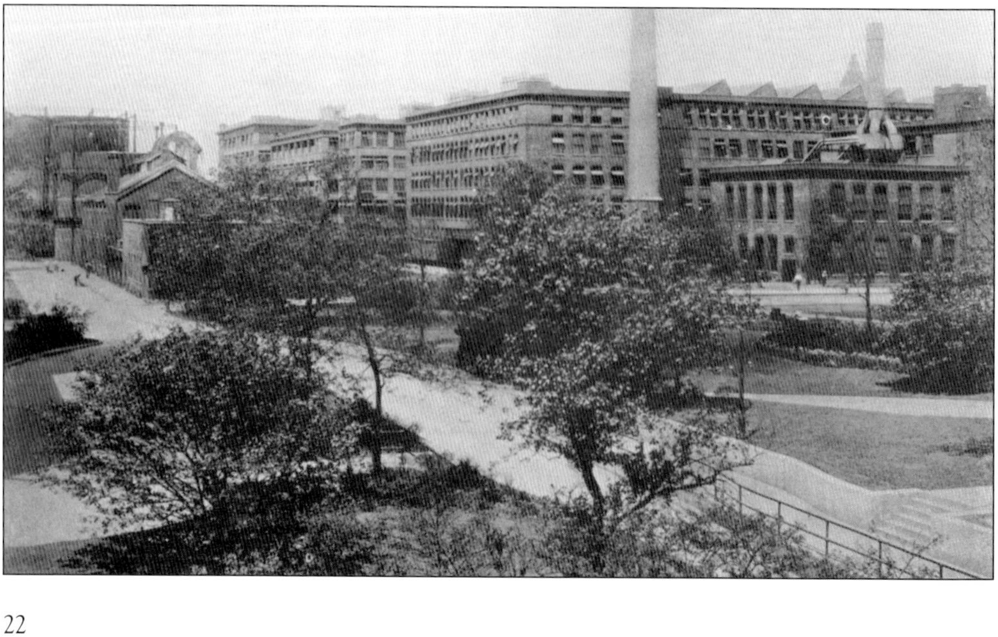

Two

World War I

Over There

When war broke out in Europe in 1914, Western Electric and the Hawthorne Works tried to adopt a neutral stance, as its workshops and offices in London, Paris, Antwerp, Vienna, and St. Petersburg all stood vulnerable to destruction by both the Allies and the Central Powers. Back home, the telephone business continued to grow, especially the Hawthorne Works, where Western Electric consolidated all of its manufacturing by the mid-1910s.

The United States entered the war in April 1917. More than any previous conflict, the "war to end all wars" was proving to be a contest of technologies. Since 1914, new lethal inventions—tanks, machine guns, poison gas, fighter aircraft, and Zeppelins—had raised the death toll. The armed forces also depended on new technology for transportation and communication. Hawthorne mobilized its resources to meet the demand, even as the draft depleted its workforce.

When the US Army Signal Corps brought Western Electric a request for aircraft communications equipment, its engineers devised the first successful air-to-air and air-to-ground radios within months. Navy vessels also installed Western Electric radios and telephones. Hawthorne's workers carried out the rigorous testing and mass production of these items for shipment to troops going "over there."

Western Electric and the Bell System contributed more than equipment. The Army also called on the skills and experience of their telecommunications workers. These soldier technicians created from scratch a battlefield phone network with thousands of miles of wire connecting 3,000 command posts and 100 central switchboards.

Over 700 Hawthorne employees served in the armed forces during World War I. Thirty gave their lives. For the first time, the US government called upon Hawthorne's human and industrial resources to provide for its defense needs, and the Works proved more than equal to the task. It would not be the last time. Through the wars and crises of the 1900s, Hawthorne would contribute its engineering and mass production capabilities to national defense. The minds and muscles in factories far from the battlefield gave American troops an edge, and the Hawthorne Works ranked as one of the nation's most innovative and reliable sources of supply.

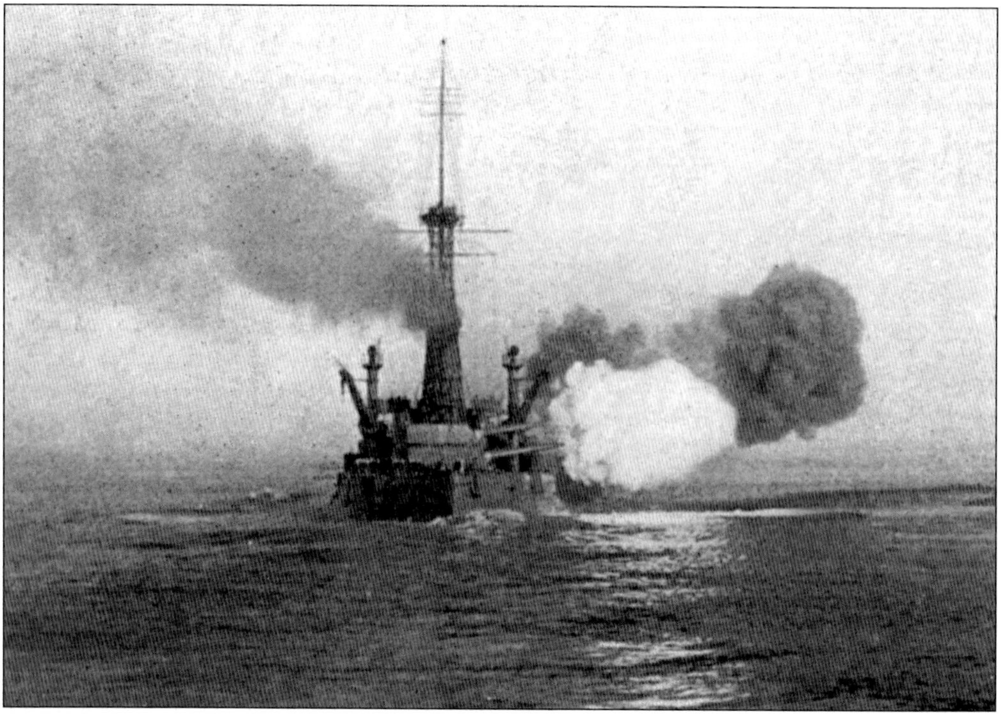

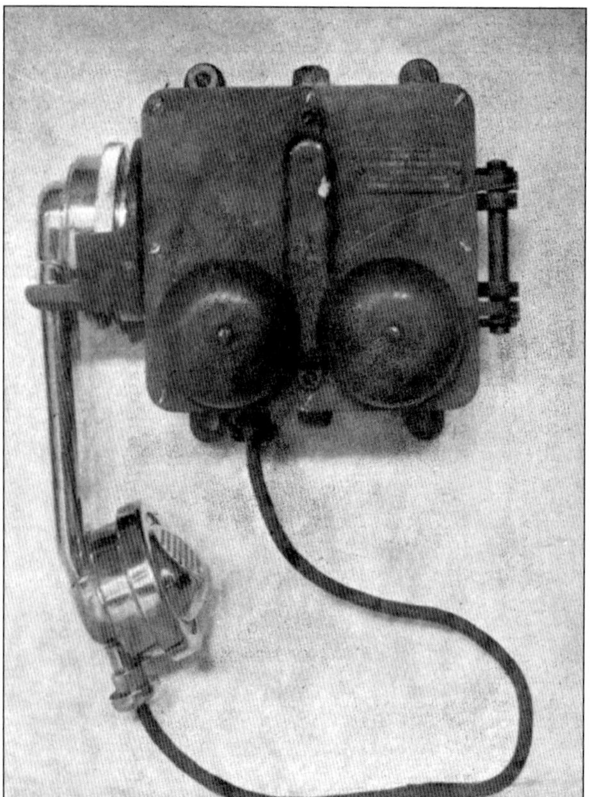

Western Electric worked with the Navy Department to devise shipboard radio and telephone systems. Above, the battleship USS *Utah* fires a broadside from its 14-inch guns during 1916 maneuvers. The towering radio masts became standard equipment on US warships as navy officials grasped the importance of telecommunications. At left, this Western Electric shipboard telephone connected officers and gun crews on the USS *Arizona*. Every warship was equipped with two separate telephone systems, one for communication throughout the ship and another to connect battle stations with command posts. Both of these ships were sunk during the Japanese attack on Pearl Harbor on December 7, 1941. (Both courtesy of the *Western Electric News*.)

The draft depleted Hawthorne's male workforce. Before the war, Western Electric preferred hiring single women over married women, assuming they were most likely to remain employed long-term. During wartime, the company opened more positions to married women, especially the wives of servicemen. Given the opportunity to operate complicated machinery, they proved to be efficient, capable workers. By 1918, over 6,000 of the Works' 19,000 employees were women. Thousands of women across the country took on positions previously reserved for men. The two young ladies seen here are clad in "Liberty Suits," which were specially designed for work on heavy machinery like the turret lathe, seen at right. (Right, courtesy of AT&T Archives; below, courtesy of the *Western Electric News*.)

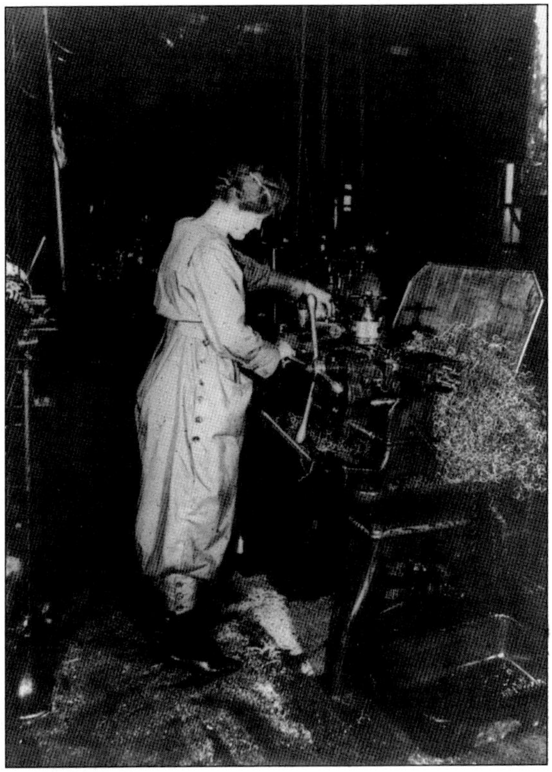

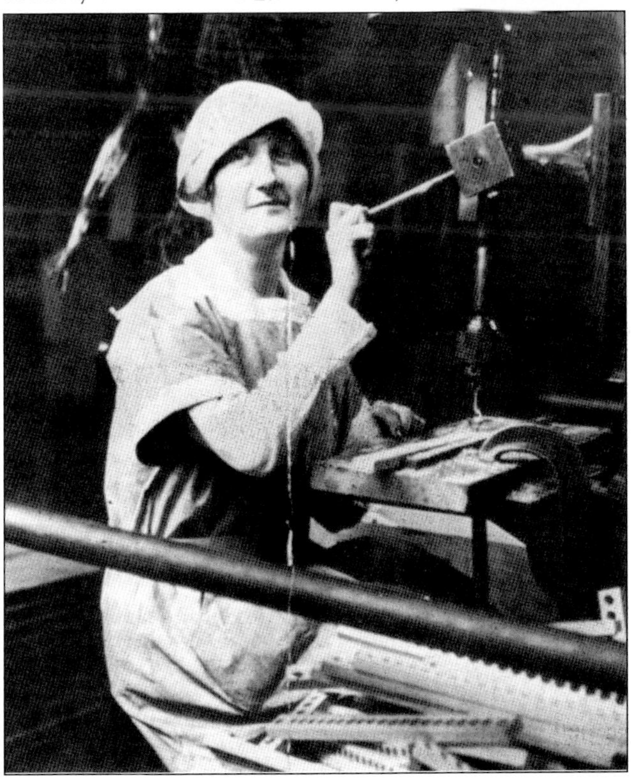

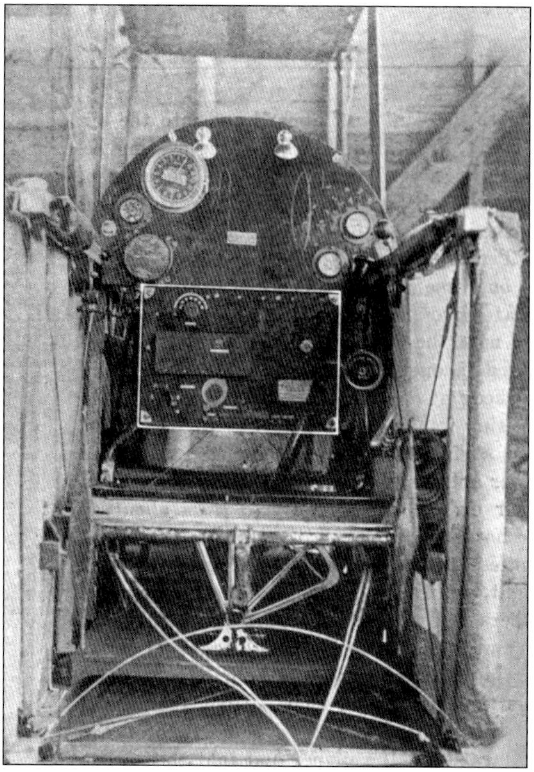

How does one make a radio audible above the din of an aircraft engine? How can it be made light enough for an airplane but durable enough to withstand rough landings? Western Electric engineers had to solve these riddles when designing a workable airborne communications system for the US Army Signal Corps. They fashioned a tight-fitting leather helmet (below) with embedded earphones and placed the radio inside a lightweight cockpit housing. As they perfected each part, the engineers shipped the prototypes to the Hawthorne Works, where toolmakers readied the parts for mass production. The radios began rolling off the assembly line in early 1918, another example of Western Electric's remarkable engineering, production, and delivery capabilities. (Both courtesy of the *Western Electric News*.)

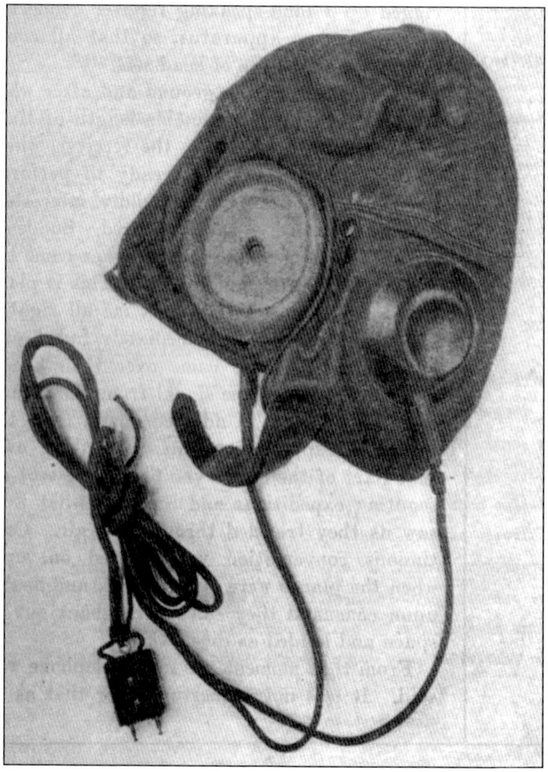

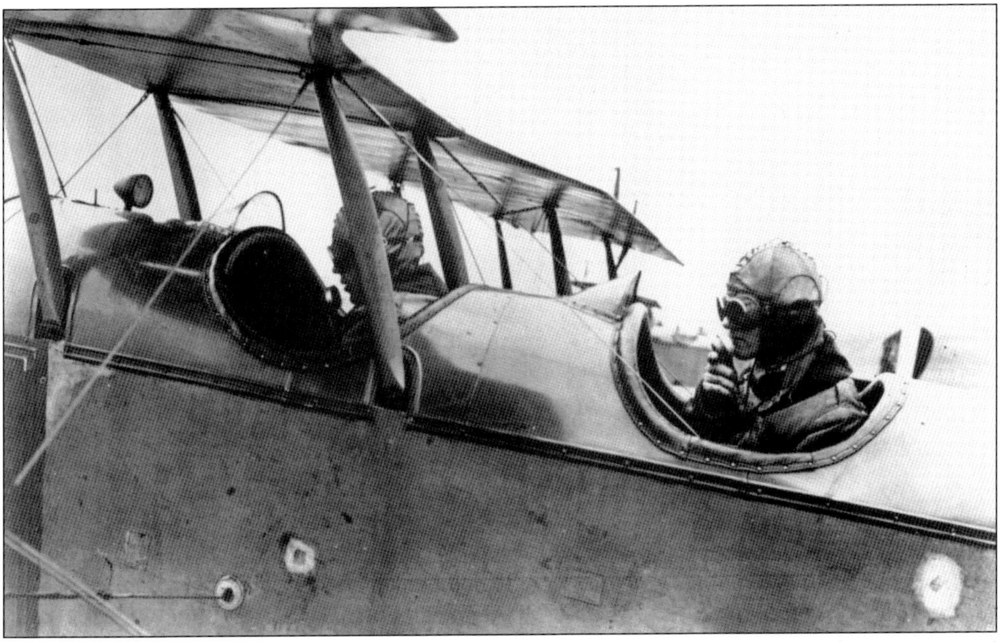

Above, American pilots test Western Electric cockpit radios. The US Army Signal Corps requested this equipment barely a month after the country entered the war, in April 1917. By August, Western Electric engineers had perfected an in-flight radio and an air-to-ground communication system. Below, Western Electric assistant chief engineer Edward B. Craft (far left) watches a demonstration of the new radio system. Ralph Bown (second from left) later became Western Electric's director of radio research. Maj. Nathan Levinson (second from right) became the director of the Warner Bros. Studios sound department. Lt. Col. Nugent H. Slaughter (right) won the Army Distinguished Service Medal for his radio development efforts.

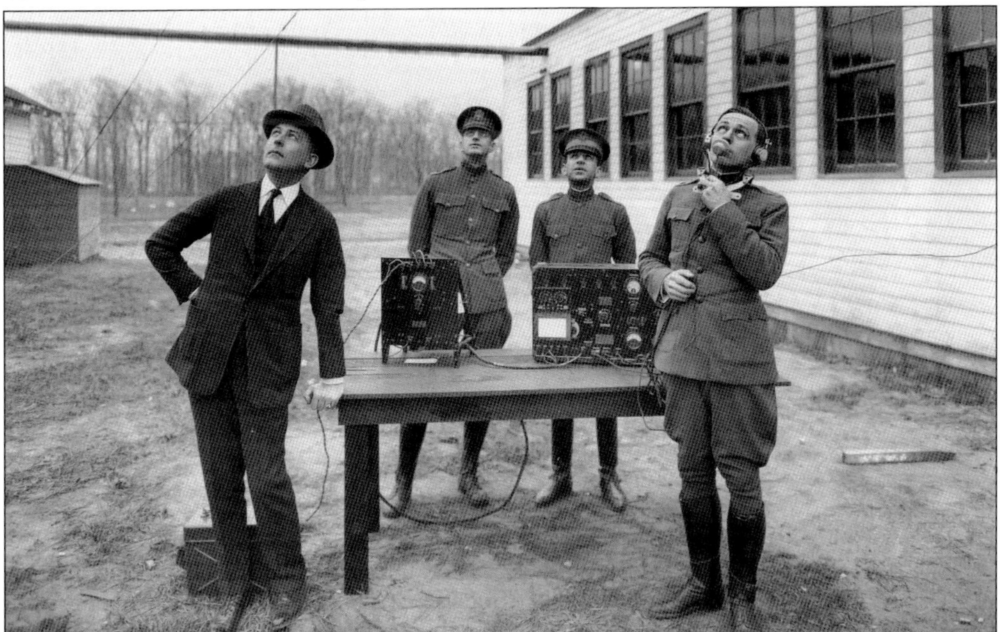

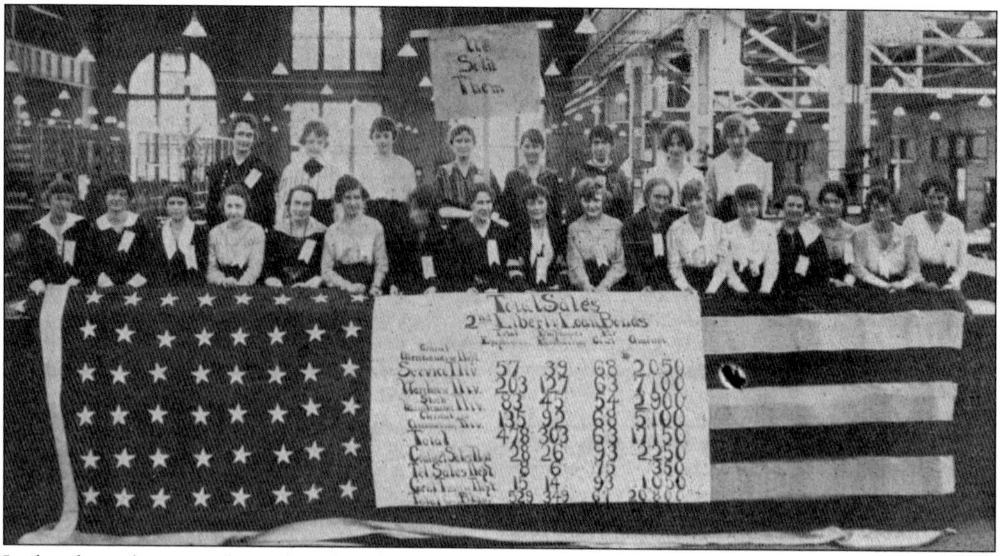

Ladies from the general merchandise department display their enthusiasm for the Liberty Loan drive in 1917. The government called on Americans to finance the war effort through the purchasing of savings bonds. Hawthorne employees contributed $1 per week from their paychecks, earning a $50 bond in a year. By the end of October 1917, Hawthorne employees had put in over $500,000. (Courtesy of the *Western Electric News*.)

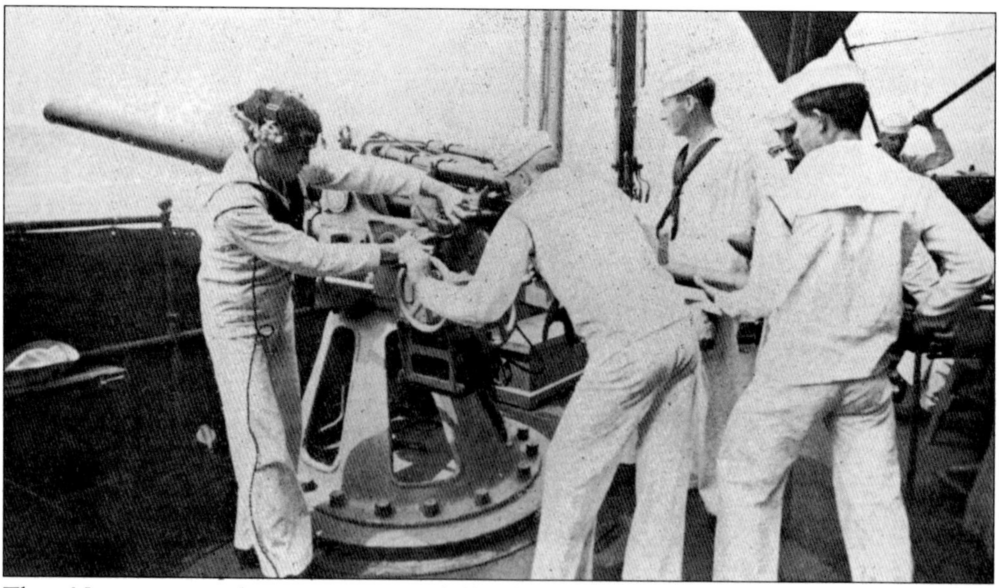

These Navy gunners taking part in a 1916 drill are testing the newest Western Electric shipboard communications system. The sailor on the far left is wearing a pair of headphones connected to the ship's fire control center, where gunnery officers relayed directions from range-finding observers stationed in the mast tops. During World War II, an improved Western Electric–designed and Hawthorne-built system automated this entire process. (Courtesy of the *Western Electric News*.)

Western Electric supplied radio and telephone equipment to the Navy. The shortwave radio telephone and telegraph console seen here was installed aboard the battleship USS *Wyoming* in 1917 and served as a central switchboard for ship-to-ship and ship-to-shore messaging. By the end of the war, over 2,000 similar sets were used by US Navy and British Royal Navy vessels.

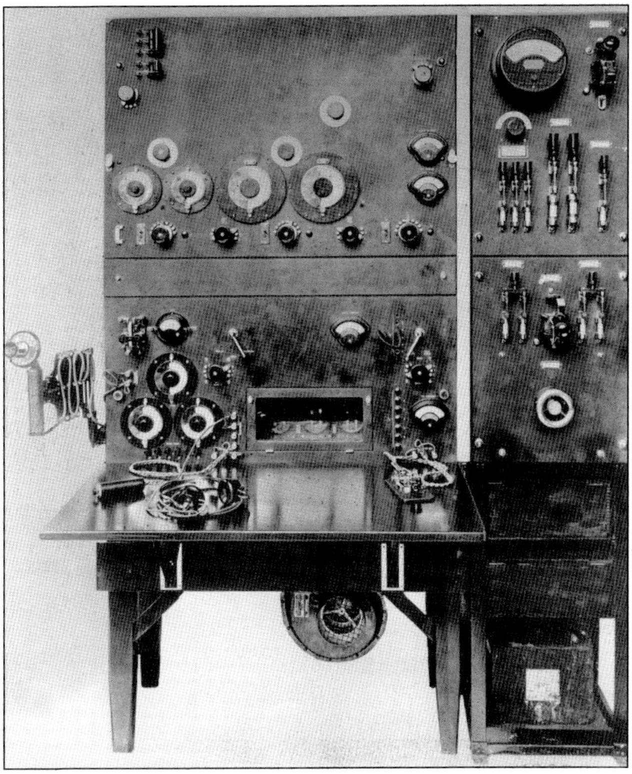

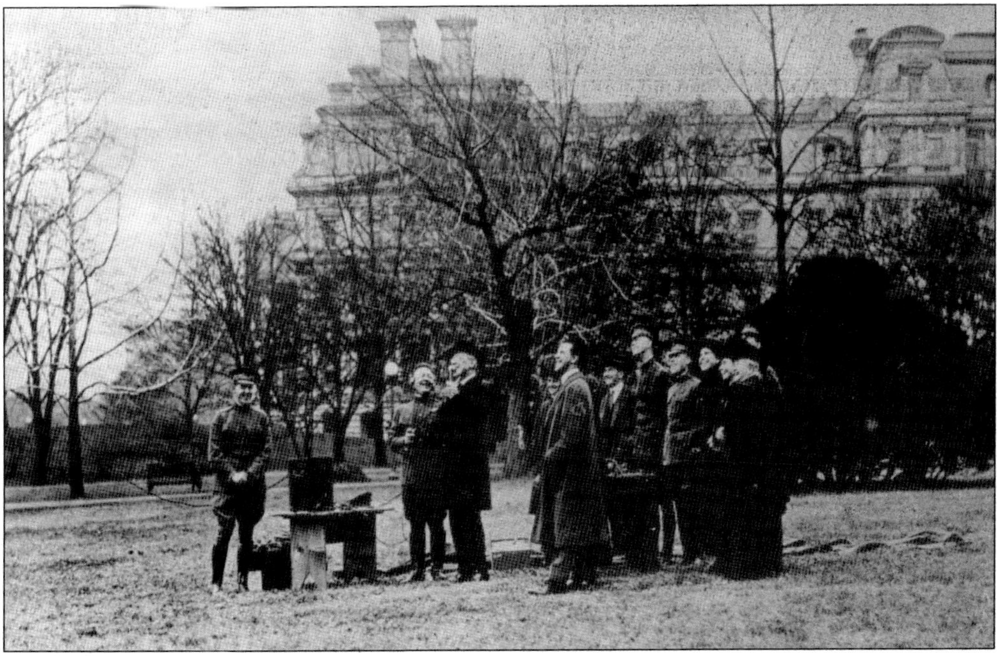

Pres. Woodrow Wilson directs Army planes over the White House using a Western Electric transmitter. The war turned Washington, DC, into the national nerve center. Telephone usage jumped eightfold in a year. The Bell System quadrupled the number of switchboards, added two million miles of wire, and reserved 15,000 miles of circuits for government use.

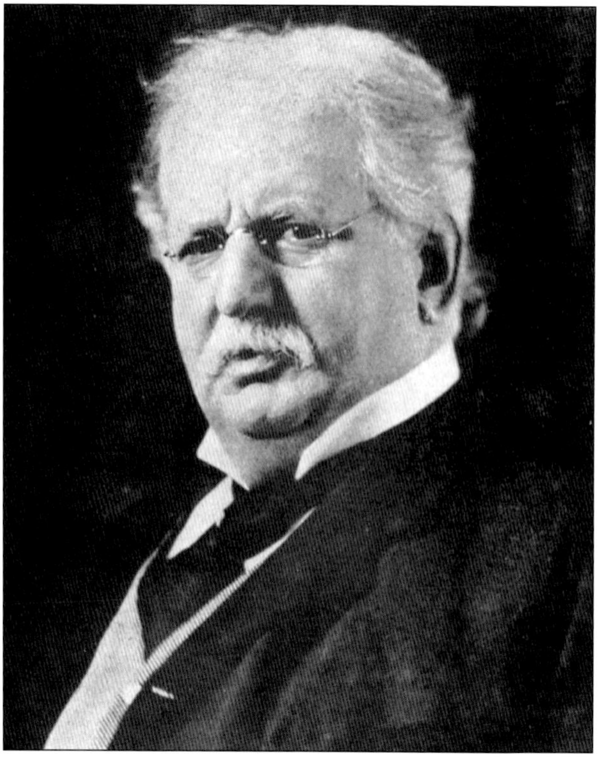

During the war, AT&T president Theodore Vail (left) feared that efforts to nationalize the Bell System would mean an end to its private ownership. Nevertheless, he agreed to the demand for the public good. In July 1918, the post office department assumed authority to ensure communications would be at the disposal of the war effort. The takeover actually changed little, but the government did hold final say over Bell System budgets. Seven months after the armistice ended the war, the telephone system returned to private ownership. Worn out by his tenure at AT&T, Vail retired in 1919 and died the following year. He was succeeded by Western Electric president Harry Thayer (below), the first of three WE chiefs who rose to lead its parent company. (Both courtesy of the *Western Electric News*.)

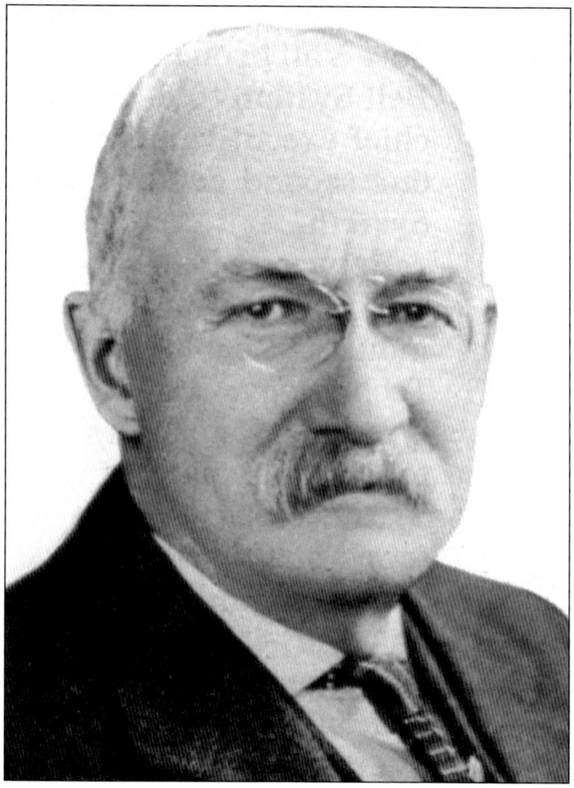

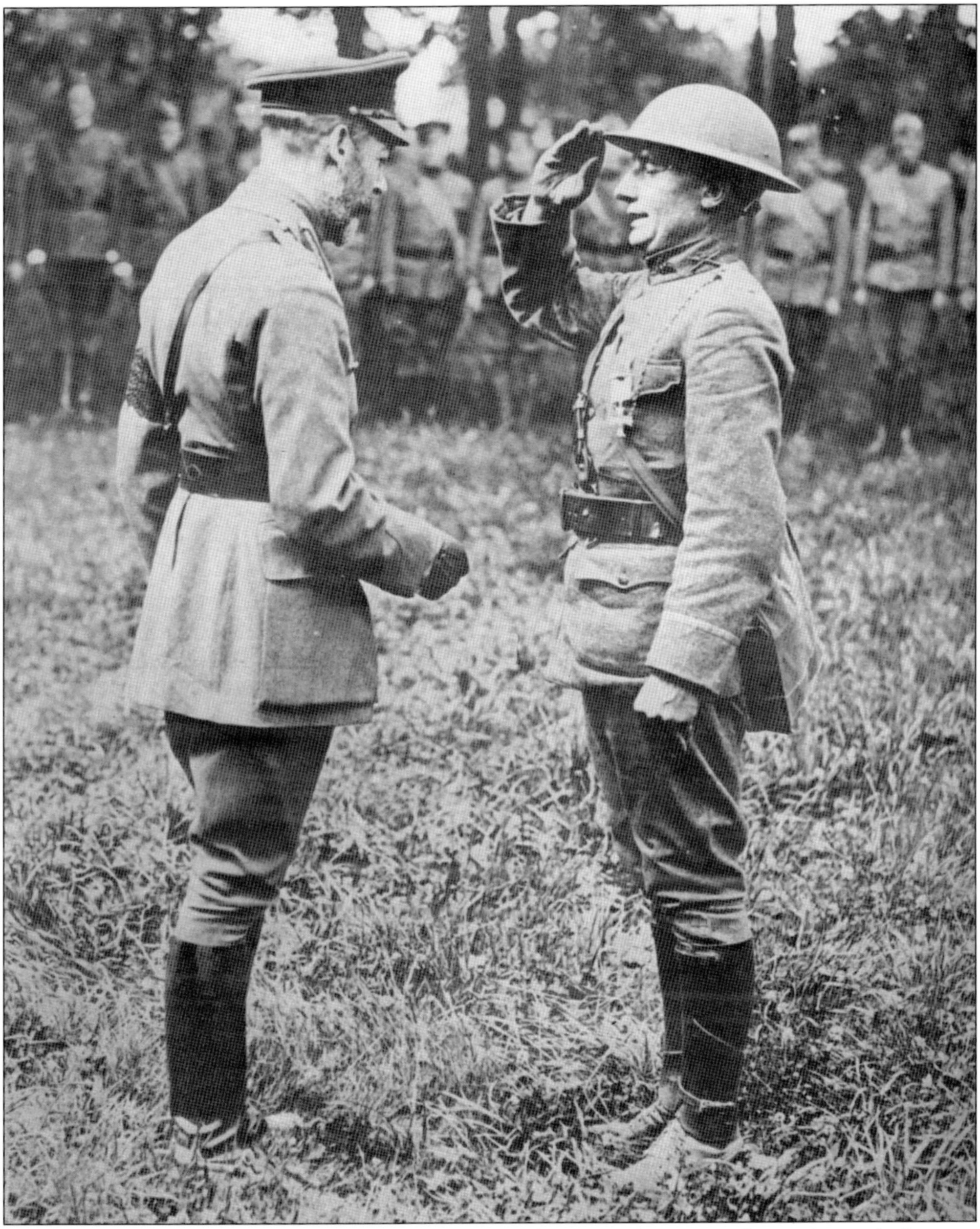

King George V (left) decorates Lt. Michael Komorowski, a Hawthorne Works employee, for bravery under fire on July 4, 1918. Already a veteran of two hitches in the Army (in the Philippines and on the Mexican border), Komorowski was told when the United States entered the war in 1917 that he could not serve overseas again because of his marital status. But, with his wife's permission, he took up arms one more time. Komorowski's service was but one example of Western Electric's Anglo-American connection. The company worked closely with the British, on the battlefield and in the research laboratory. Engineers at WE's London shops applied their expertise to their country's war effort by designing an early sonar system dubbed the "Nash Fish." This 15-foot-long torpedo-shaped device suspended under British warships helped detect German U-boats. (Courtesy of the *Western Electric News*.)

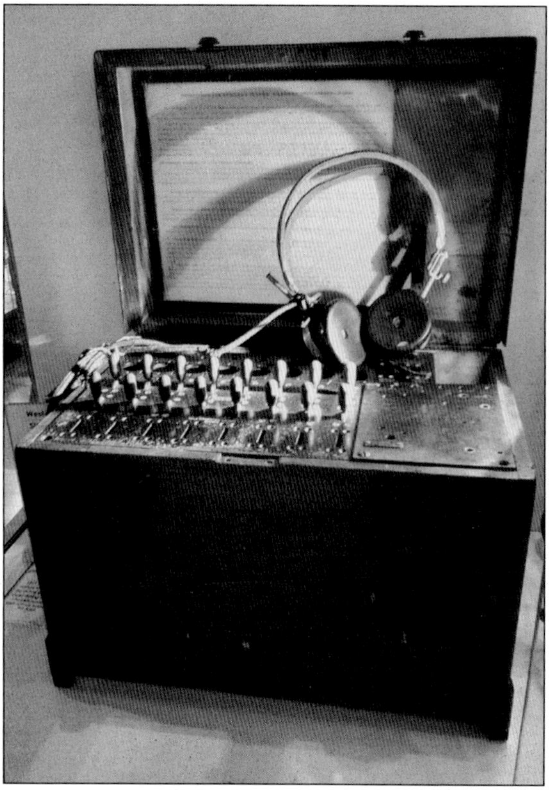

The vintage 1917 US Army field switchboard and headphones at left illustrate Western Electric's start-to-finish approach to manufacturing. First, the company's engineers in New York designed the items, and then passed the prototypes on to the Hawthorne Works for mass production. Hawthorne staff mapped out the assembly process and procured the necessary parts. Every element arrived at the Works as raw material: metals, wood, and fabric. Then, the cable plant drew out the copper wiring, the glass shop supplied illuminating bulbs, the foundry formed all the metal components, the carpentry shop shaped the wooden case, and, finally, assemblers pieced it all together for shipment overseas (below). The switchboard and headphones are on display at the Hawthorne Works Museum. (Below, courtesy of the *Western Electric News*.)

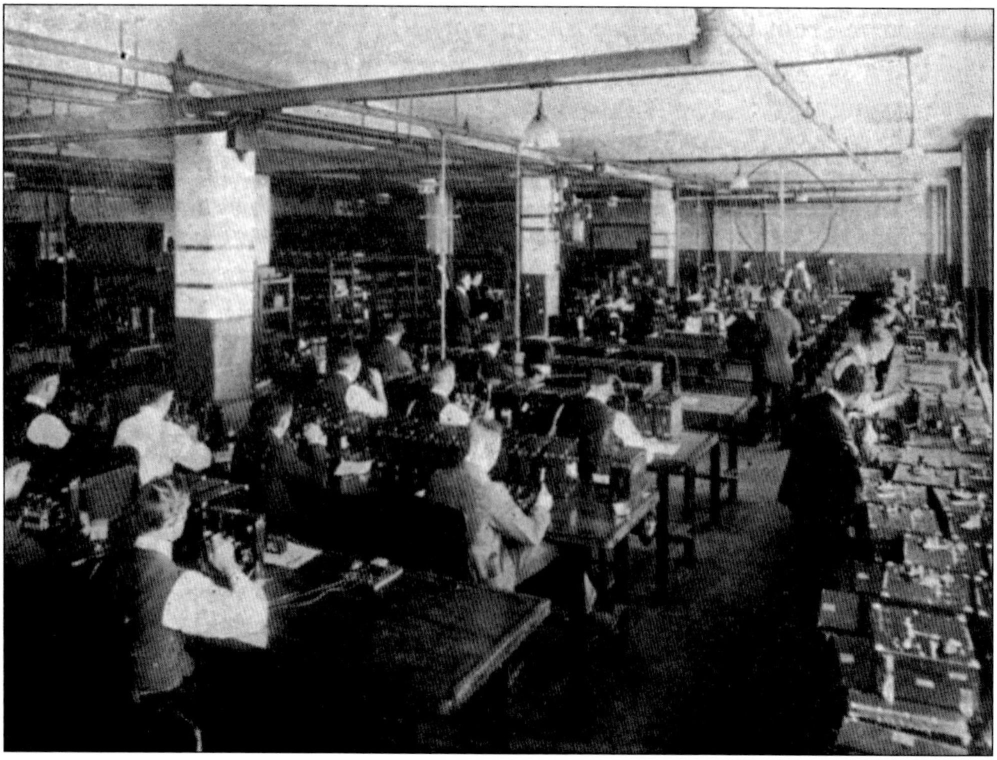

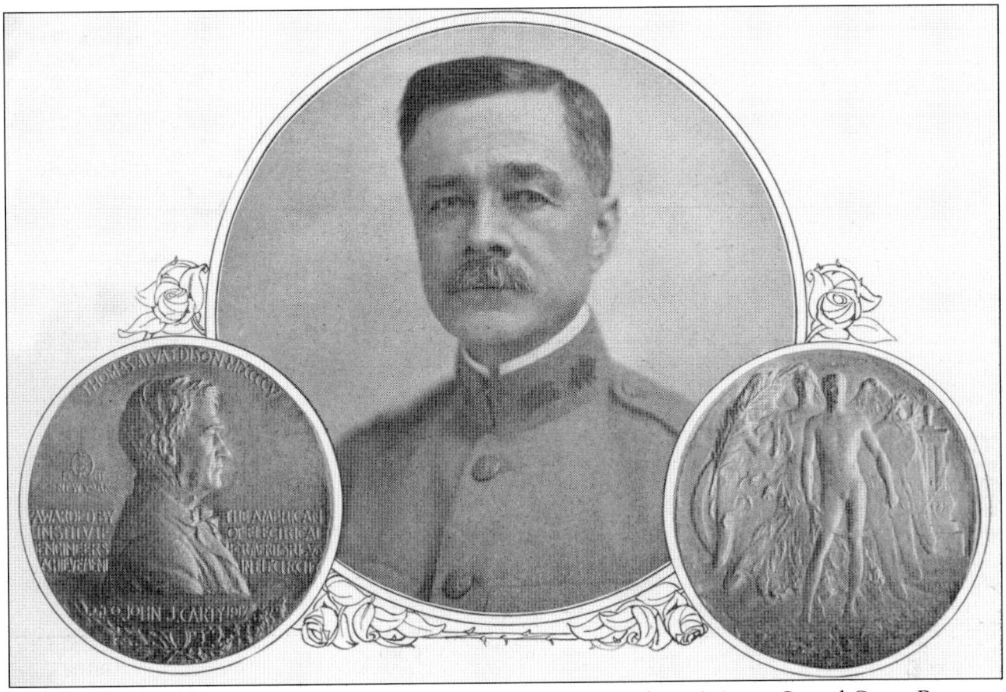

AT&T chief engineer John J. Carty, a major commissioned in the US Army Signal Corps Reserve, called for volunteers from among the Bell System's linemen, cable splicers, and radio operators. Western Electric contributed manpower for two units. One of them, Company A of the 314th Field Signal Battalion, known as the Hawthorne Radio Company, included 75 men from the Hawthorne Works. (Courtesy of the *Western Electric News*.)

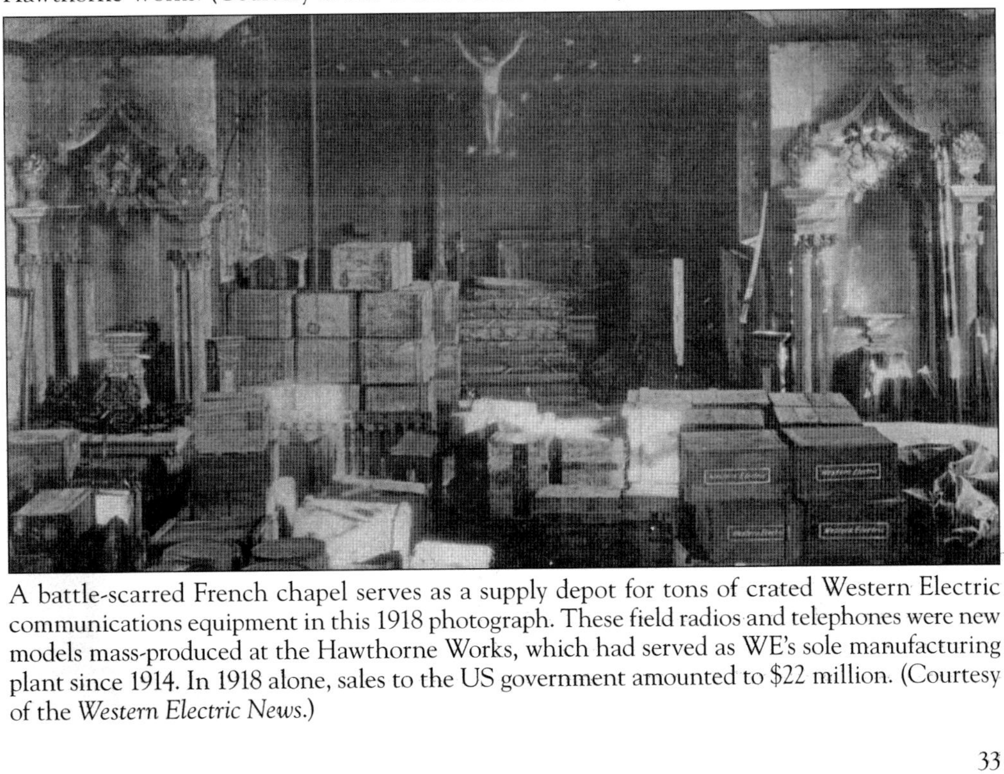

A battle-scarred French chapel serves as a supply depot for tons of crated Western Electric communications equipment in this 1918 photograph. These field radios and telephones were new models mass-produced at the Hawthorne Works, which had served as WE's sole manufacturing plant since 1914. In 1918 alone, sales to the US government amounted to $22 million. (Courtesy of the *Western Electric News*.)

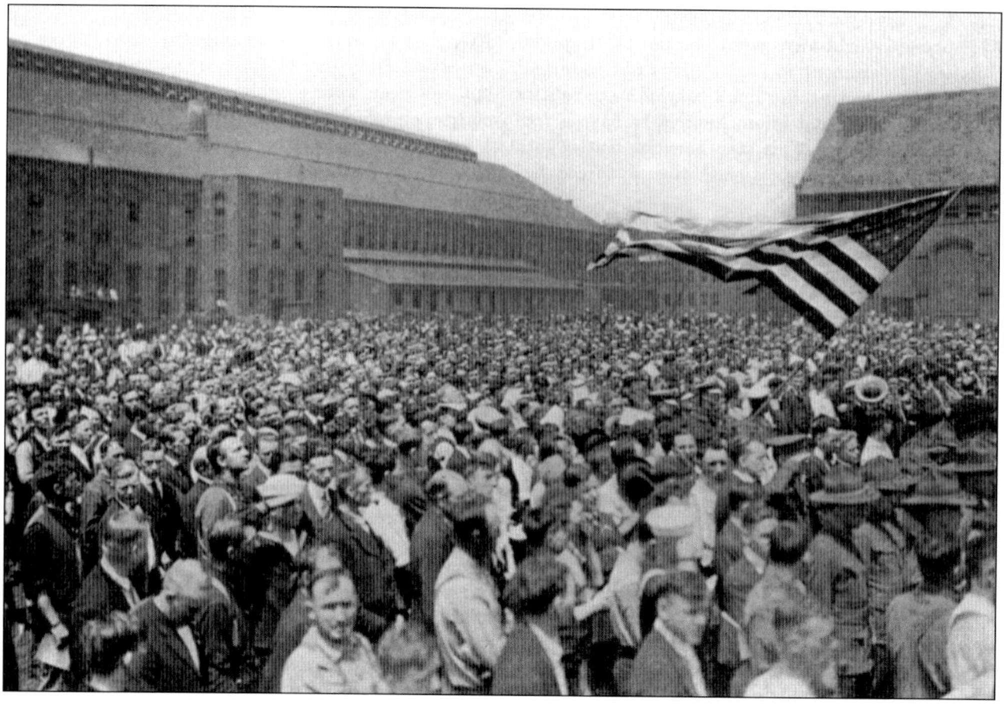

The Hawthorne Works turns out for a 1918 Flag Day rally. The Works employed 20,000 people by 1916, and the number of telephone customers nationwide approached 10 million. When the United States entered World War I, Western Electric workers joined the patriotic surge. Many at Hawthorne maintained strong connections to the warring European nations. Czechs, Slovaks, and Poles hoped the war would bring their homelands independence from crumbling empires. Those who did not enlist worked overtime, contributed money, sent care packages to the troops overseas (below), and lent their enthusiasm to the cause. The war in Europe also threatened Western Electric's overseas factories and warehouses. German forces occupied the Antwerp factory, and Bolsheviks seized the St. Petersburg plant in 1917. (Both courtesy of the *Western Electric News*.)

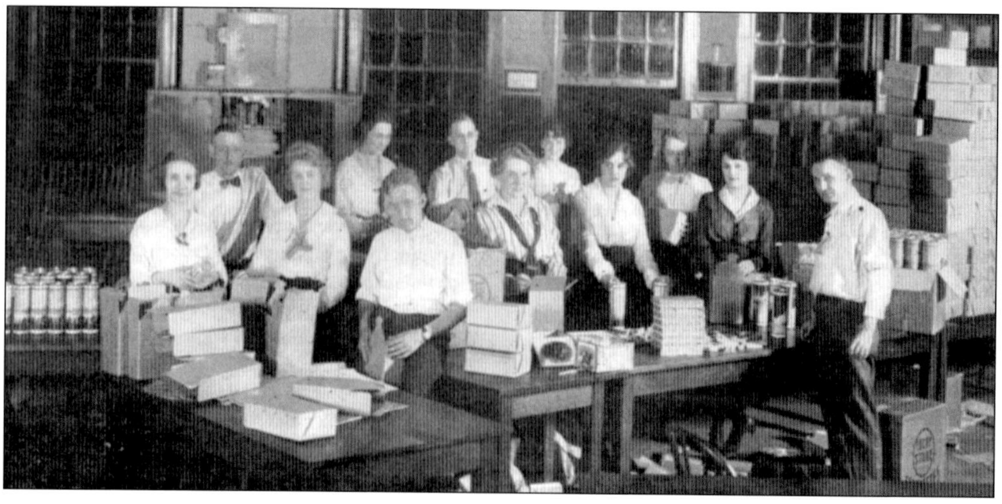

Three

The 1920s

Natural Monopoly

The Hawthorne Works' third decade proved to be its most challenging and most rewarding. The United States emerged from World War I transformed, with political and economic power to rival any European nation. Through postwar economic boom times, the Works grew stronger and larger than even the most optimistic booster could have imagined. By the end of the 1920s, the Hawthorne Works was the largest manufacturing plant for the biggest corporation in the world. New buildings filled the plant's confines, and a workforce that was doubled in size assembled products barely dreamed of a generation before. The corner of Twenty-second Street and Cicero Avenue would have been totally unrecognizable to those first workers who had entered the gates in 1905.

The Hawthorne Works turned Cicero, Berwyn, and the surrounding communities into boomtowns. Almost overnight, these prairie crossroads were transformed into busy, modern suburbs. Two-flats and bungalows replaced empty lots, new businesses welcomed steady streams of customers, faithful parishioners erected grand new churches, and children crowded new schoolhouses. The word was out that Hawthorne was the place to be, and, each day, more employees passed through its gates and manned its workstations.

American society was changing as well. The 1920 census showed a population that was for the first time more urban than rural, more ethnically diverse, and more likely to work in industry than agriculture. Women gained the vote, automobiles sped along paved city streets, and radios magically transmitted voices and jazz music from coast to coast. At the beginning of the decade, about one-third of American homes had telephones. Just 10 years later, nearly half did, and virtually all of them were manufactured by Western Electric and leased from the Bell System. Western Electric and the Hawthorne Works rode the wave of change and prosperity to emerge as one of the most profitable and innovative companies in the world. As the 1930s approached, the future looked bright for the Hawthorne Works family.

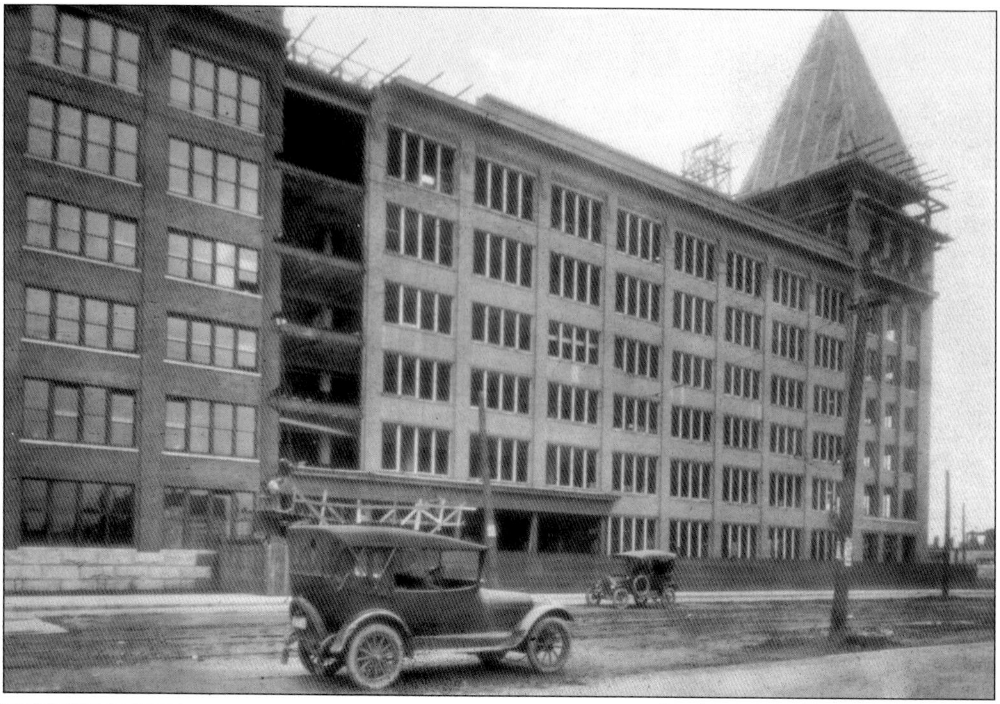

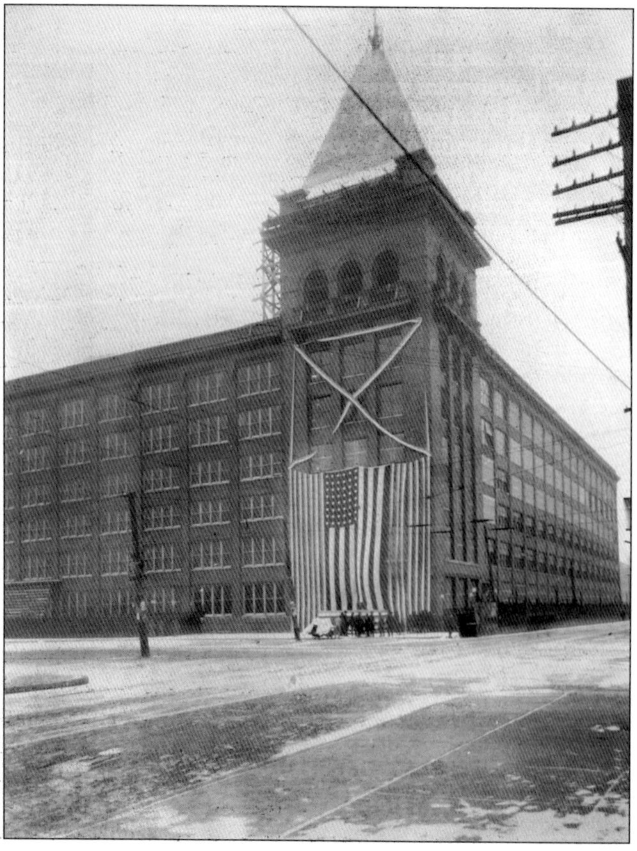

In the 1919 photograph above, Hawthorne's new executive tower nears completion. Designed by Works engineer Charles Prchal, the 183-foot-tall redbrick spire came to embody the strength and stability of Western Electric. Prchal later designed the Tivoli Theater in Downers Grove, Illinois, and the mausoleum at Chicago's Bohemian National Cemetery. At left, company officials dedicate the cornerstone of the flag-draped tower. The structure, said WE president Charles DuBois, symbolized the firm's past and future: "hard work of hand and brain, and square dealing with everyone." A time capsule placed in the cornerstone included corporate documents, vacuum tubes, and a new "candlestick" desk-stand telephone. (Both courtesy of the Simak collection.)

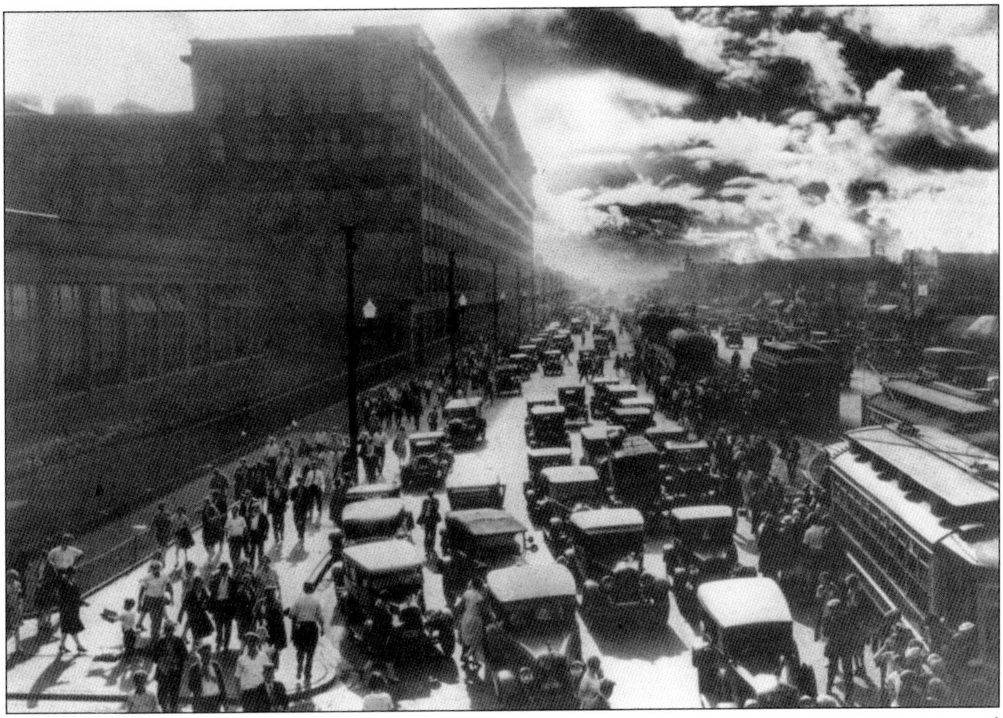

Quitting time turned Twenty-second Street into a carnival of street vendors, musicians, and hurrying commuters. The Hawthorne Works employed 40,000 people in 1929, but it still barely kept pace. The number of local calls a year would soon reach 28 million, and telephones in service rose to 20 million. In 1925, Bell Laboratories became a separate unit and a new Western Electric plant opened in New Jersey, followed by another in Baltimore in 1929. Many Hawthorne employees transferred to the new locations, but, within a few years, the number of staff in Cicero climbed back to nearly 38,000. Hawthorne was by far the largest single factory in Illinois, with an annual payroll of $58 million. (Above, courtesy of AT&T Archives; below, courtesy of the *Western Electric News.*)

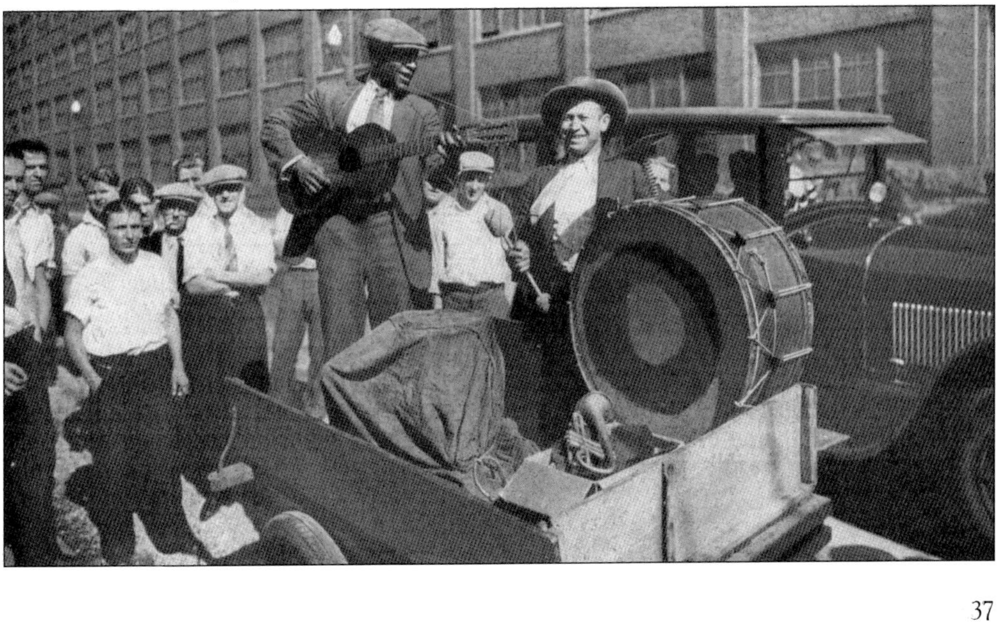

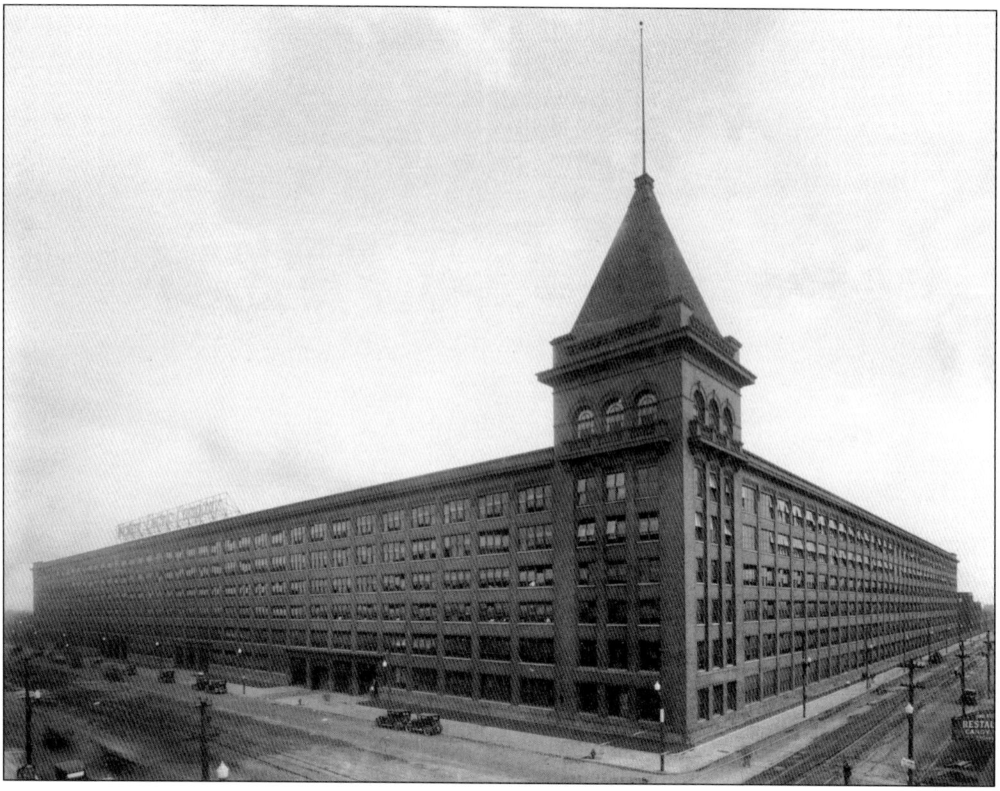

The Hawthorne Works' grand facade and expanding footprint illustrate its prominence in the booming 1920s. The Bell System grew rapidly after the passage of the Willis-Graham Act in 1921. AT&T had argued that they had not simply entered the telephone market as a competitor; they had designed, built, installed, and maintained the nationwide network. With Willis-Graham, the government concurred. The statute granted AT&T and its Bell System companies "natural monopoly" status, exempting them from antitrust penalties. Western Electric's sales grew to $210 million by 1922, and the Hawthorne Works invested $3 million in new facilities. AT&T set about buying up smaller local telephone companies, and, by decade's end, it stood as the world's largest corporation. (Above, courtesy of the Jezek collection; below, courtesy of the *Western Electric News*.)

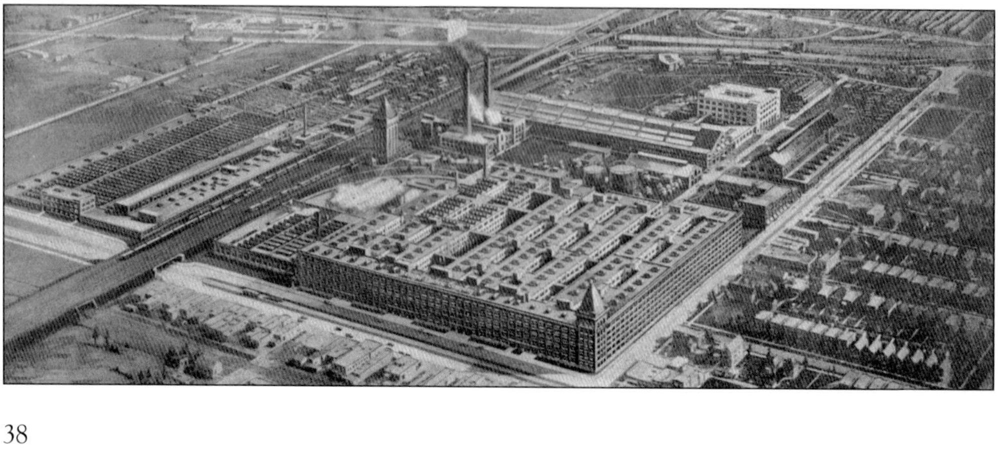

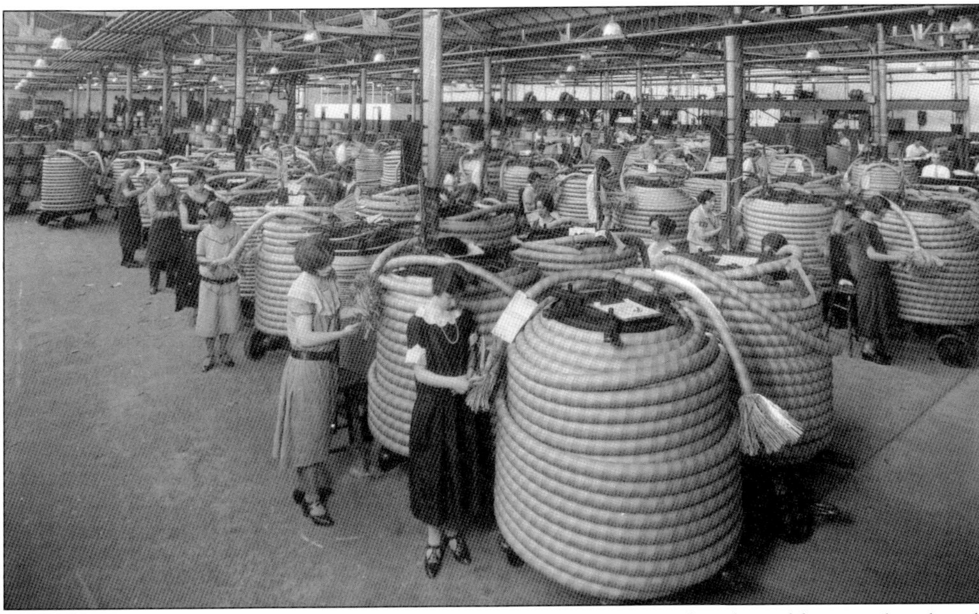

Hawthorne Works employees inspect cable in this 1925 photograph. The cables, insulated with paper wrapped around lead sheathing, were needed to keep up with growing demand for long-distance calls. By the late 1920s, AT&T was spending $42 million annually on cable production. The Hawthorne Works turned 45,000 tons of copper into wire each year, accounting for 80 percent of all the lead cable manufactured in the United States. (Courtesy of the Jezek collection.)

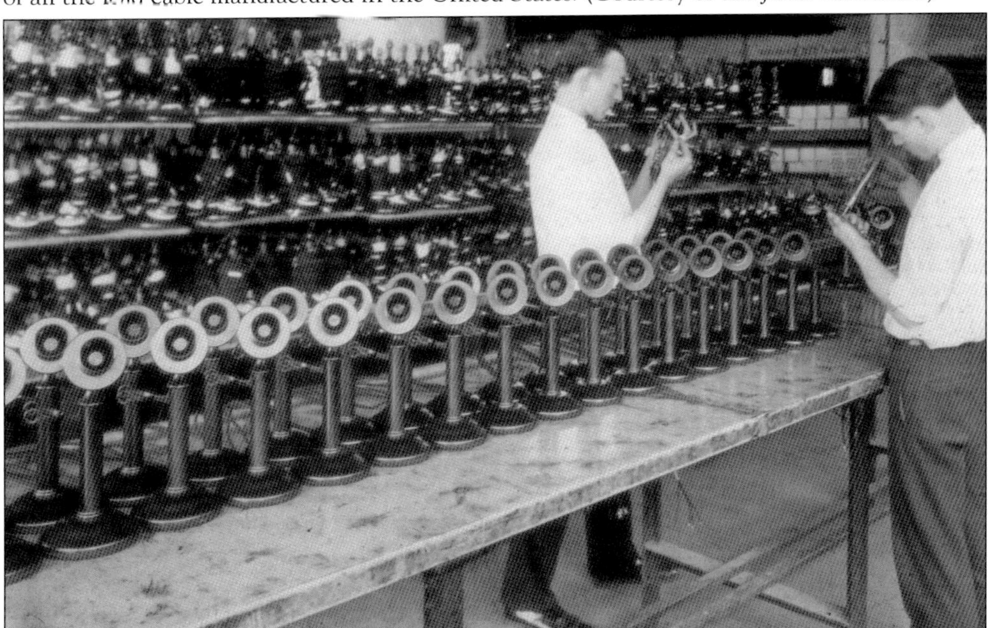

A new regiment of candlestick telephones awaits inspection by Hawthorne technicians. Western Electric began producing rotary dial telephones and Step-by-Step automatic switching equipment in the early 1920s. By 1930, when the Hawthorne Works marked its 25th anniversary, the plant had assembled over 22 million telephones. The Works also kept the Bell System stocked with 9,000 varieties of telephone apparatus.

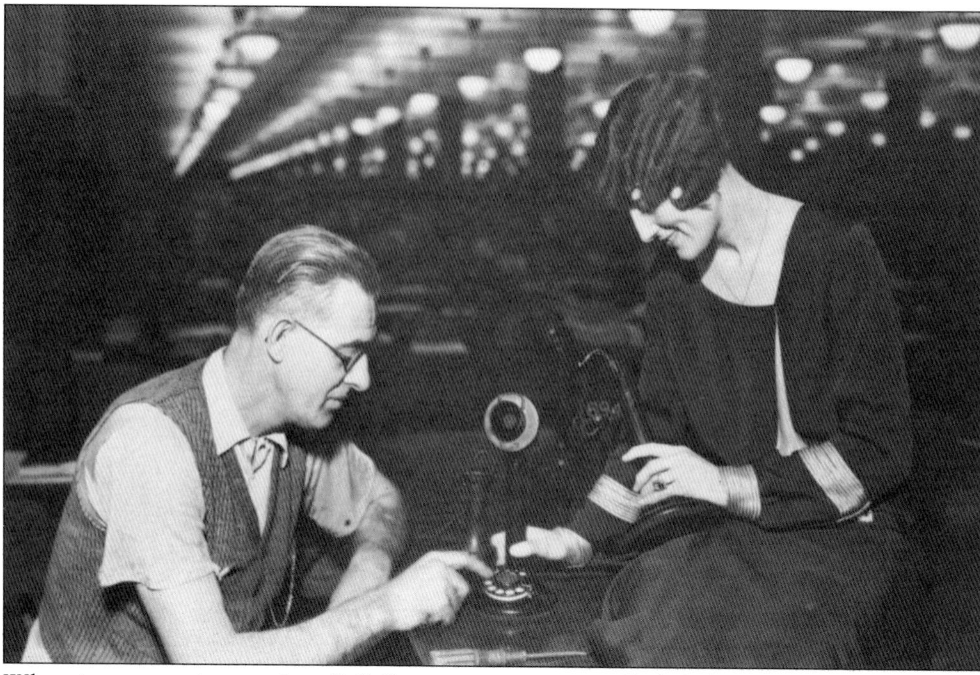

When it came to innovation, Bell System engineers usually led the way. However, the dial telephone switching system was introduced in the 1890s by Almon Strowger and made by the Automatic Electric Company (later GTE). Bell did not adopt the rotary dial until 1919. These two Hawthorne employees are learning the skill of dialing a phone number.

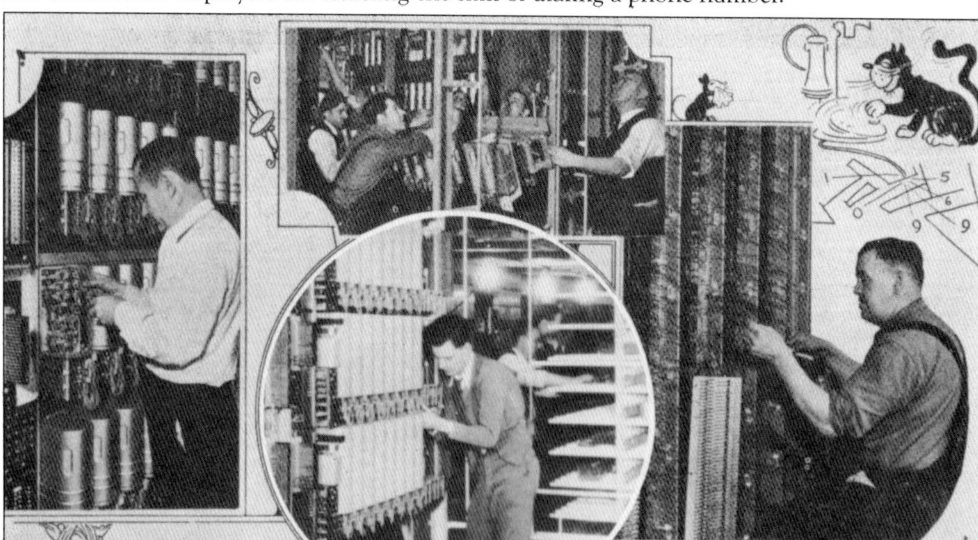

Step-by-Step switching allowed subscribers to directly connect to an individual telephone line with their rotary dial telephone. Hawthorne filled several of its new buildings with Step-by-Step production lines beginning in 1926. This durable system replaced many office switchboards and remained in widespread use for decades. Succeeding years saw the introduction of Crossbar switching and Electronic Switching Systems (ESS).

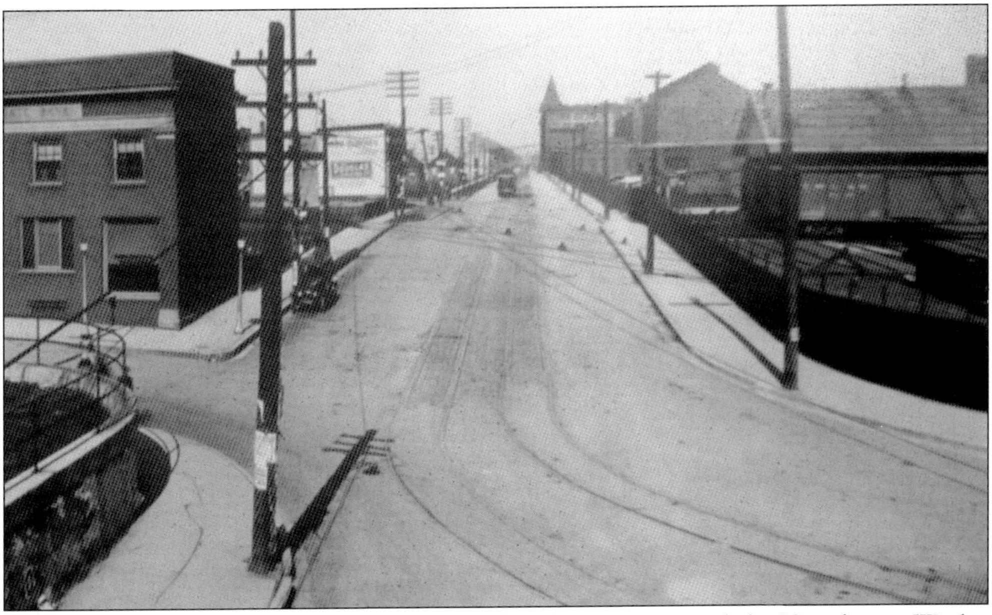

In less than two decades, bustling suburbs replaced prairies around the Hawthorne Works. This view shows homes and businesses lining Cicero Avenue opposite the Works. The town's population grew from 4,500 in 1900 to 45,000 by 1920. The boomtown atmosphere attracted the bad along with the good. It was on this street that Al Capone's brother Frank died in a hail of police gunfire in 1924.

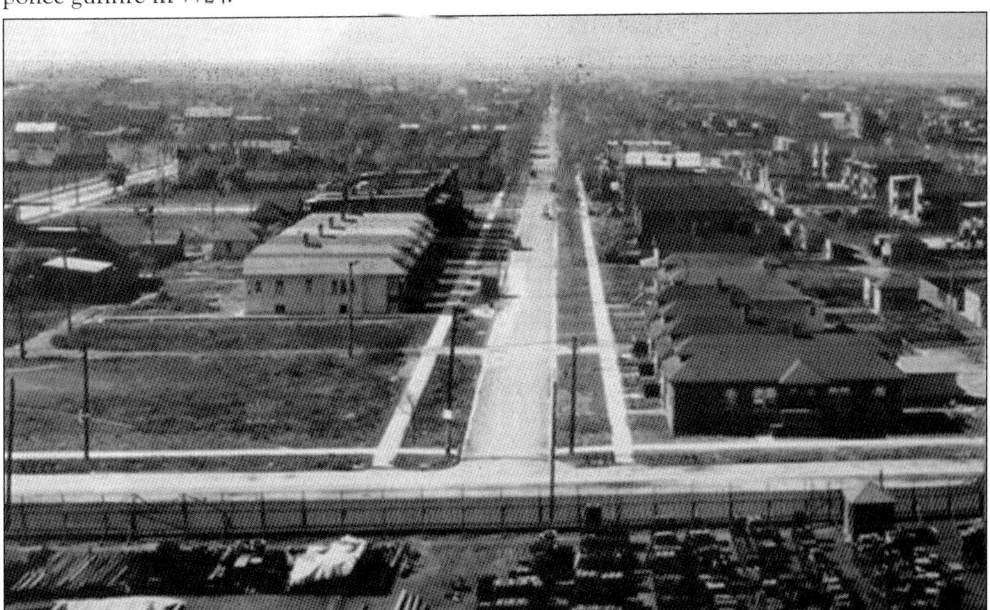

This look west in the early 1920s shows new homes rising where, just 20 years before, Hawthorne workers lunched in shady groves. By decade's end, local lots were selling for $15,000. The Hawthorne Club Building & Loan Association funded nearly $5 million worth of home loans, and the town of Cicero claimed the highest percentage of homeowners anywhere in Illinois. (Courtesy of the Simak collection.)

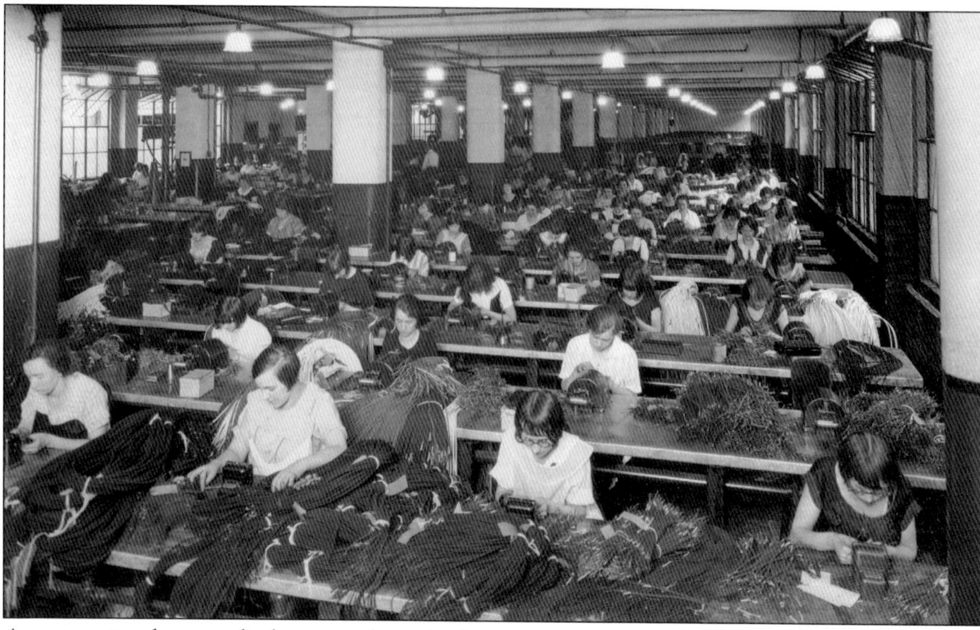

A part as simple as a telephone cord required copper wiring, wood pulp insulation, and a woven silk covering. In this 1925 photograph, row after row of young women in the cord finishing department inspect, trim, and bundle their work. By that time, Hawthorne employed nearly 8,000 women out of a total crew of 25,000. (Courtesy of the Jezek collection.)

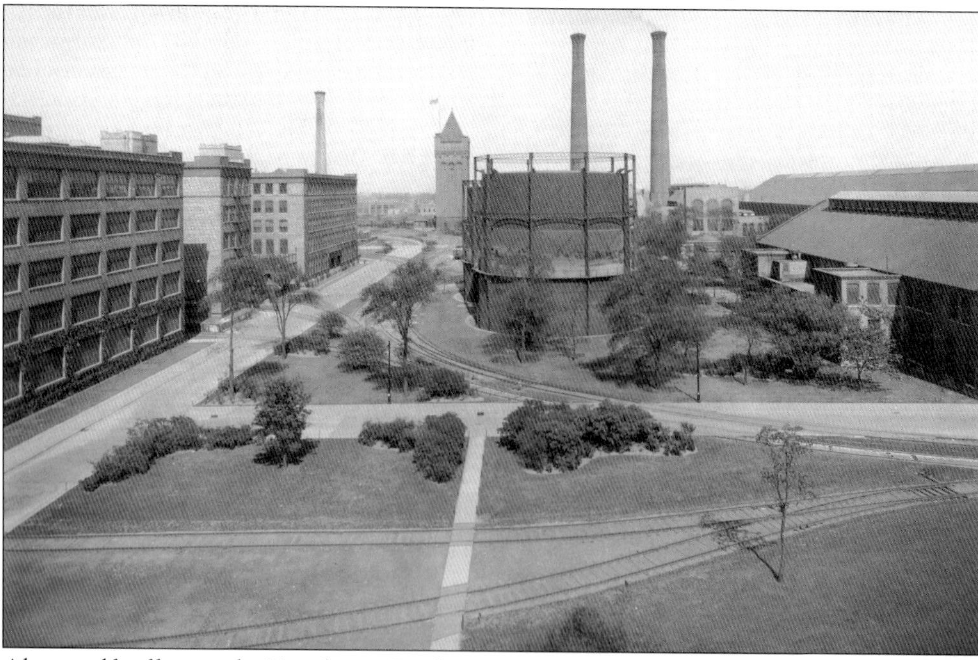

Always self-sufficient, the Hawthorne Works operated its own gas plant. The Works' foundry and laboratories functioned on homemade fuel. Blast furnace–heated coke and steam conjured up more than 100,000 square feet of gas every hour. Centrifugal boosters sent the gas to far corners of the Works. The circular steel tanks seen here stored the gas in expandable rubber balloons. (Courtesy of the Jezek collection.)

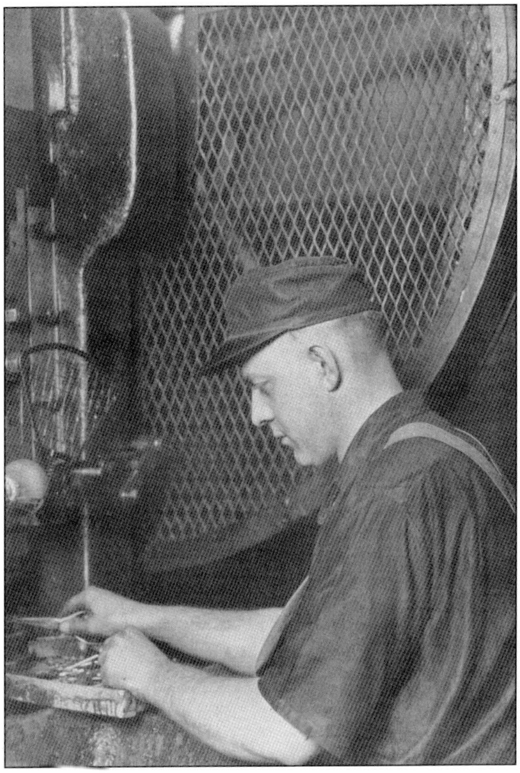

Photographer Lewis W. Hine snapped some of the most memorable images of the early 1900s, especially those exposing the abusive child labor system. In 1922, the *Western Electric News* hired Hine to photograph WE employees across the country, including these simple, dignified portraits of machinists at Hawthorne. Later, in 1931, Hine's final assignment tested his aging body and creative skills. He hauled his camera up the rising Empire State Building to photograph ironworkers riveting girders 1,000 feet above the Manhattan pavement. (Both courtesy of the *Western Electric News*.)

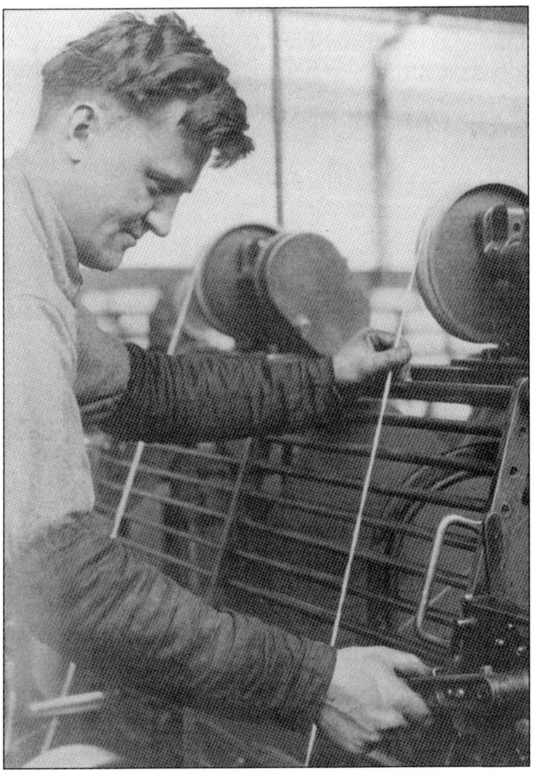

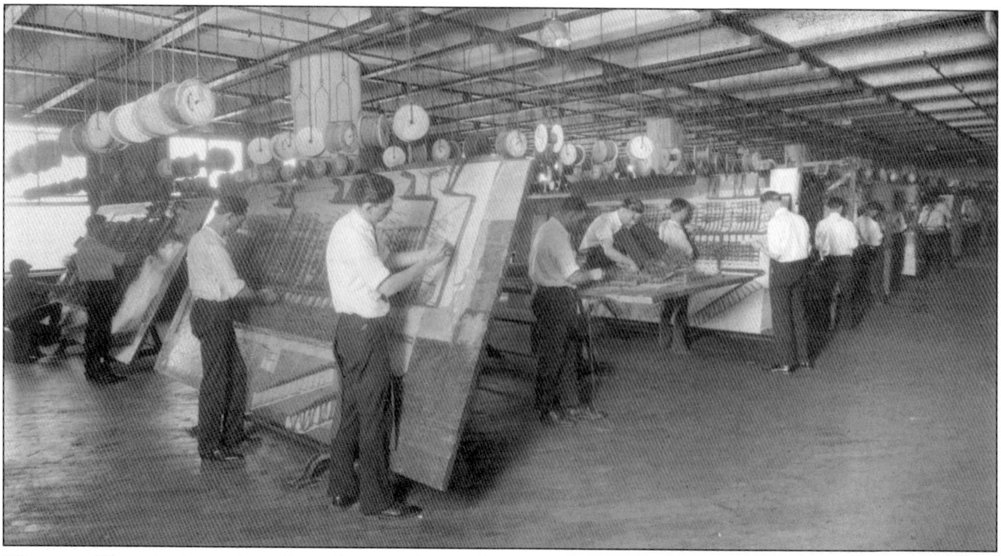

Western Electric introduced mechanized switching in the mid-1920s. Hawthorne crews patiently threaded yards of cable through layout patterns to wire every switchboard. The new equipment enabled the Bell System to handle increasing volume. In 1920, Americans made 33 million calls on just over eight million telephones. Just five years later, the number of calls had risen to 50 million, with 12 million telephones in service. (Courtesy of the Jezek collection.)

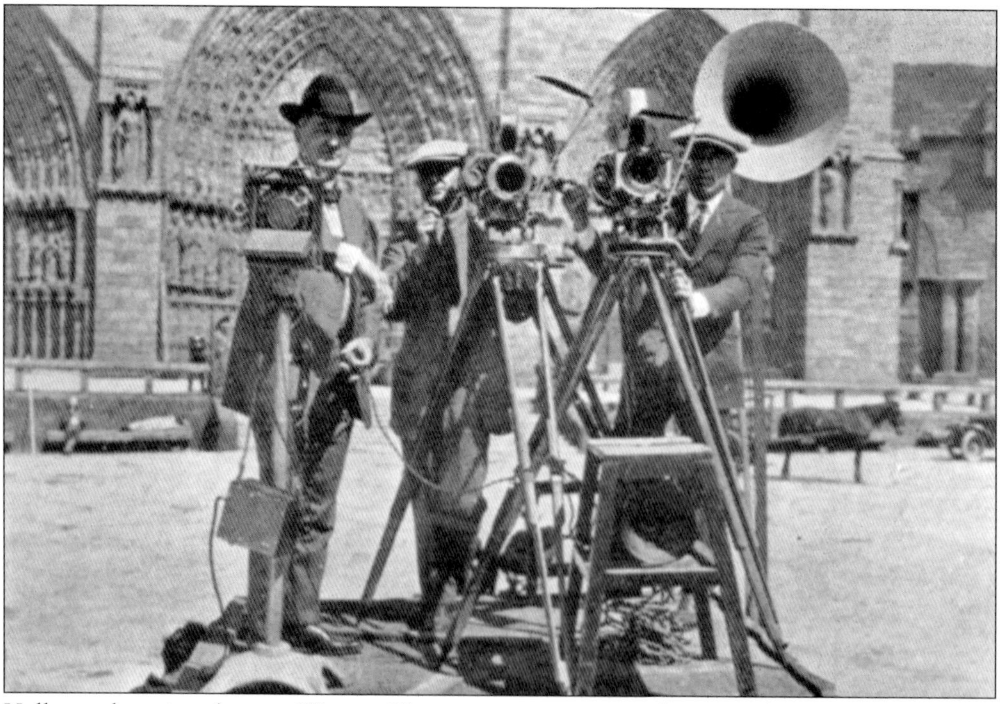

Hollywood moviemakers put Western Electric inventions to good use even before motion pictures talked. Here, Wallace Woolsey (left), the director of the 1923 silent version of *The Hunchback of Notre Dame*, learns how to use a Western Electric public address system to command a horde of costumed extras filming a crowd scene. The director's amplified voice coordinated the performers' movements. (Courtesy of the *Western Electric News*.)

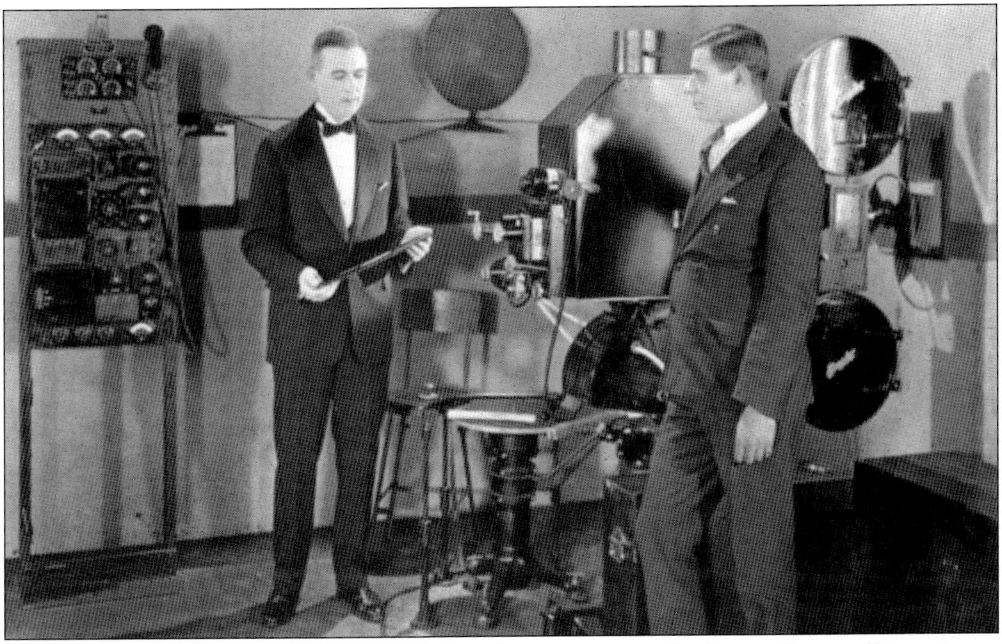

In the early 1920s, Western Electric and several competitors rushed to perfect a talking picture system. Hollywood studios backed RCA's Photophone sound-on-film technique, while researcher Theodore Case created Movietone, combining soundtrack and image. But not until Warner Bros. used Western Electric's Vitaphone system in 1927 to record *The Jazz Singer* did moviegoers see a full-length feature film with recorded dialogue. Vitaphone recorded the soundtrack on a 16-inch disc. In these photographs, Western Electric's E.B. Craft (in tuxedo) demonstrates the projector and observes filming with studio boss Sam Warner. By 1931, sound-on-film rendered Vitaphone obsolete, but Western Electric manufactured Movietone projectors, loudspeakers, and recording equipment at the Hawthorne Works. (Both courtesy of the *Western Electric News*.)

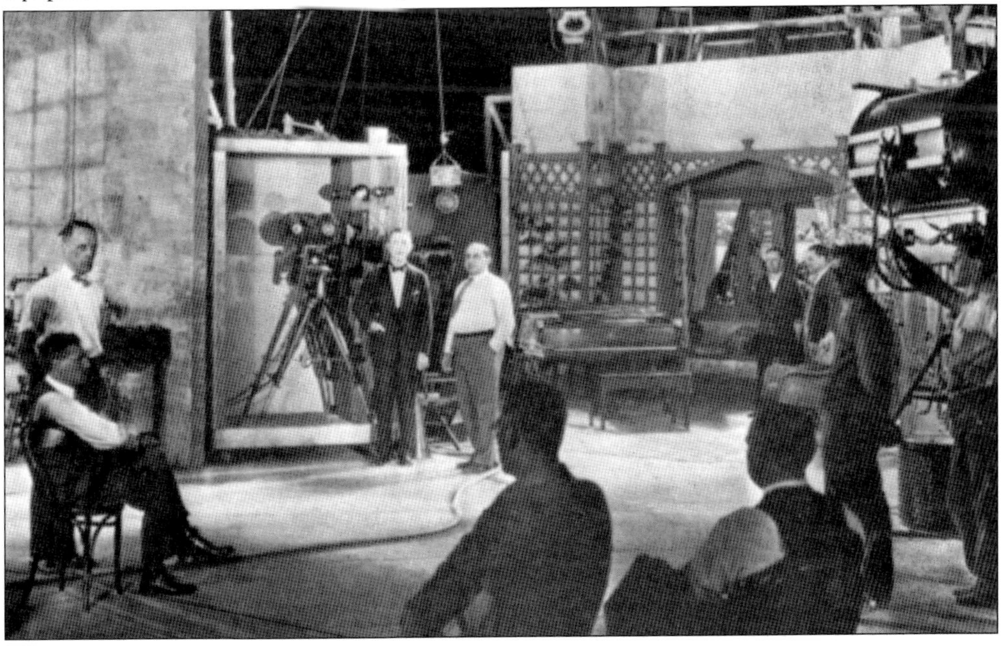

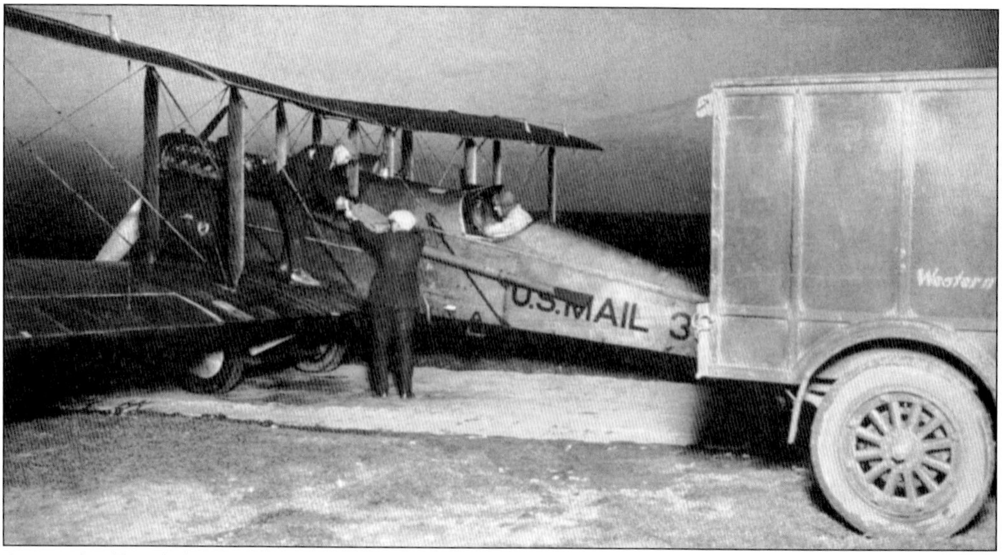

Airmail offered the fastest and most reliable means of overnight delivery in 1925. Hawthorne assigned one of its trucks to daily courier service, driving mail pouches to an airstrip in Maywood, seven miles away. Each afternoon at 2:40 sharp, the messenger left the Works loaded with urgent communications. Two US mail Curtiss biplanes departed each day for points east and west. (Courtesy of the *Western Electric News.*)

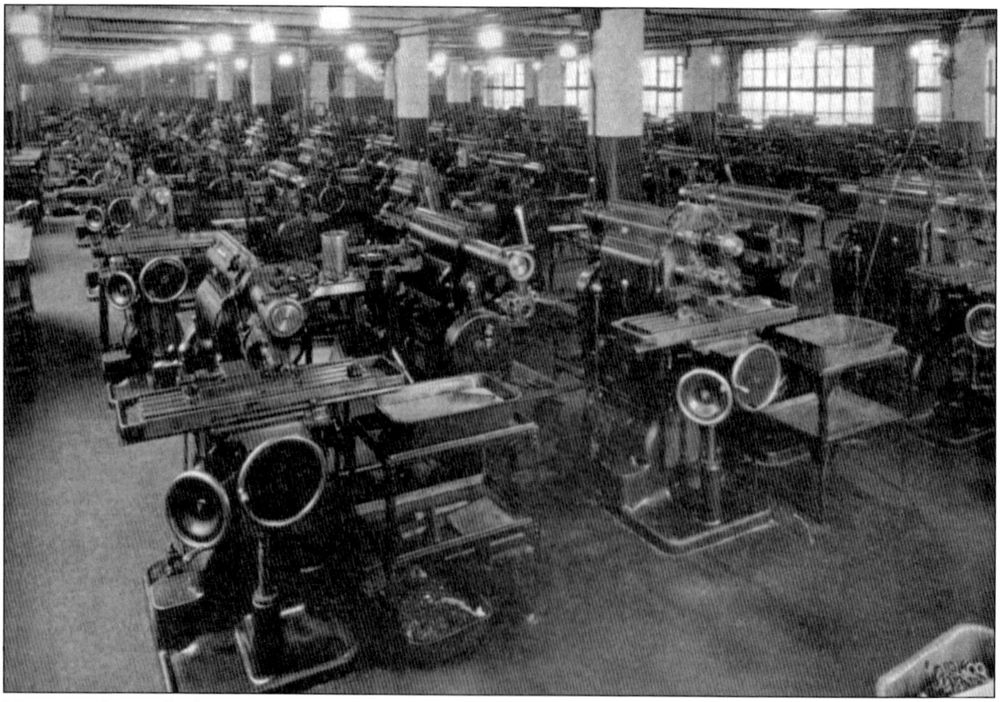

Nearing the end of a 10-year-long upgrade program in 1925, the Works could show off a shop full of motor-driven machines, like the ones seen here in the metal milling department. The new equipment replaced belt-driven units connected to overhead drive shafts running the length of the room. The improved apparatus could be switched on and off individually, creating a more efficient, less noisy workplace. (Courtesy of the *Western Electric News.*)

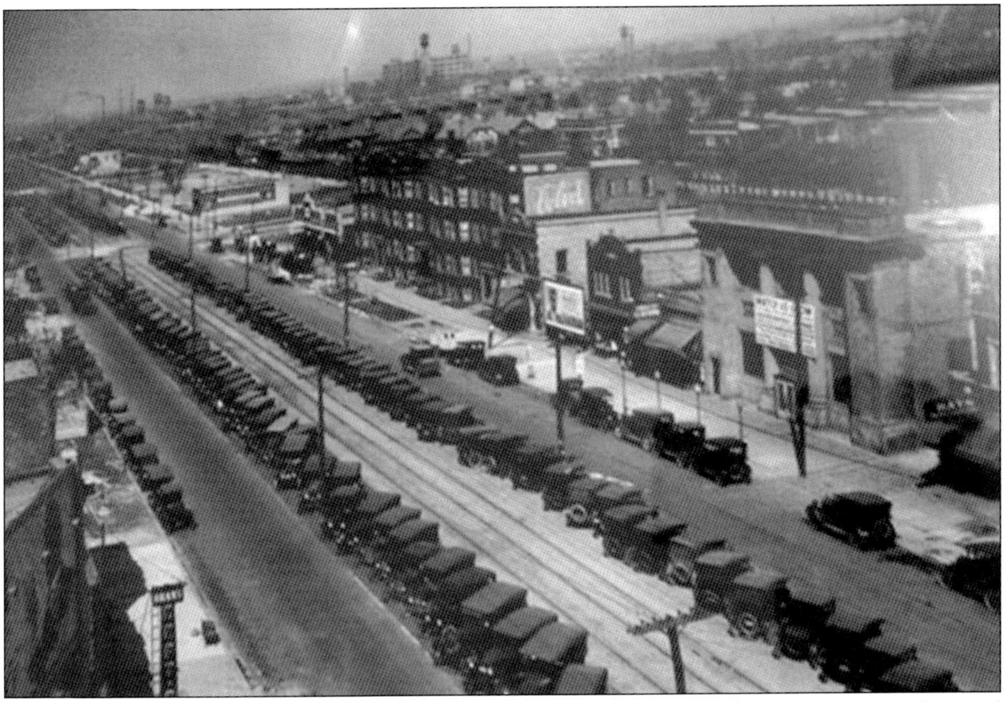

Prohibition left its mark on the decade. Hawthorne workers were as thirsty as anyone else, and they did not have to go far to find a drink. Thriving speakeasies operated within walking distance. When Al Capone elbowed his way into Cicero in 1924, he set up headquarters in the Hawthorne Inn (far left), just west of the Works. (Courtesy of the Simak collection.)

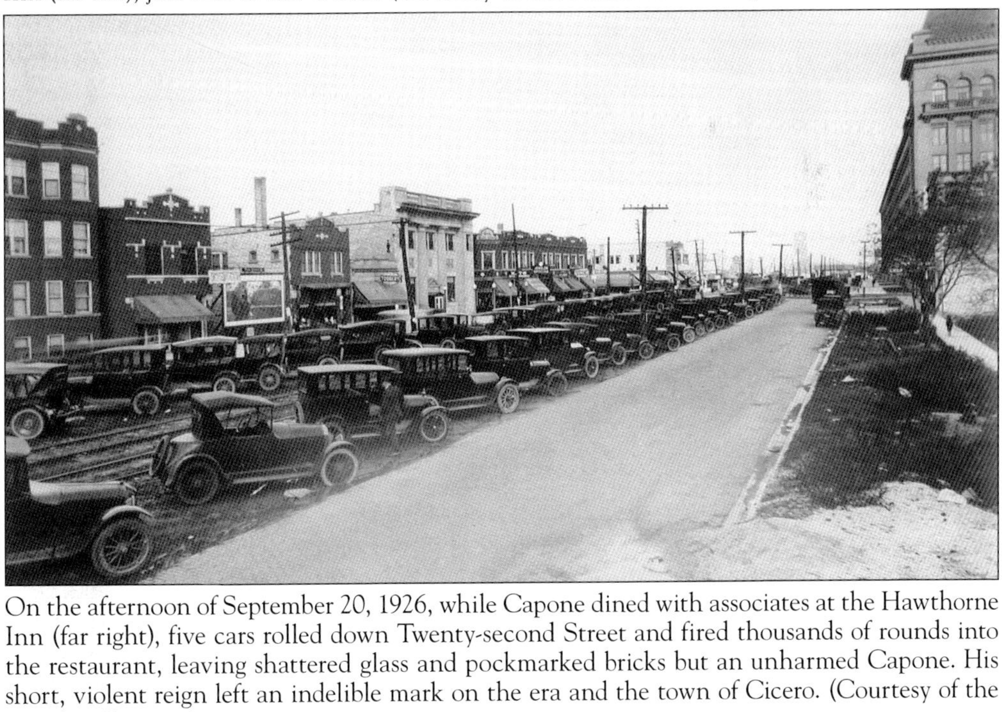

On the afternoon of September 20, 1926, while Capone dined with associates at the Hawthorne Inn (far right), five cars rolled down Twenty-second Street and fired thousands of rounds into the restaurant, leaving shattered glass and pockmarked bricks but an unharmed Capone. His short, violent reign left an indelible mark on the era and the town of Cicero. (Courtesy of the Simak collection.)

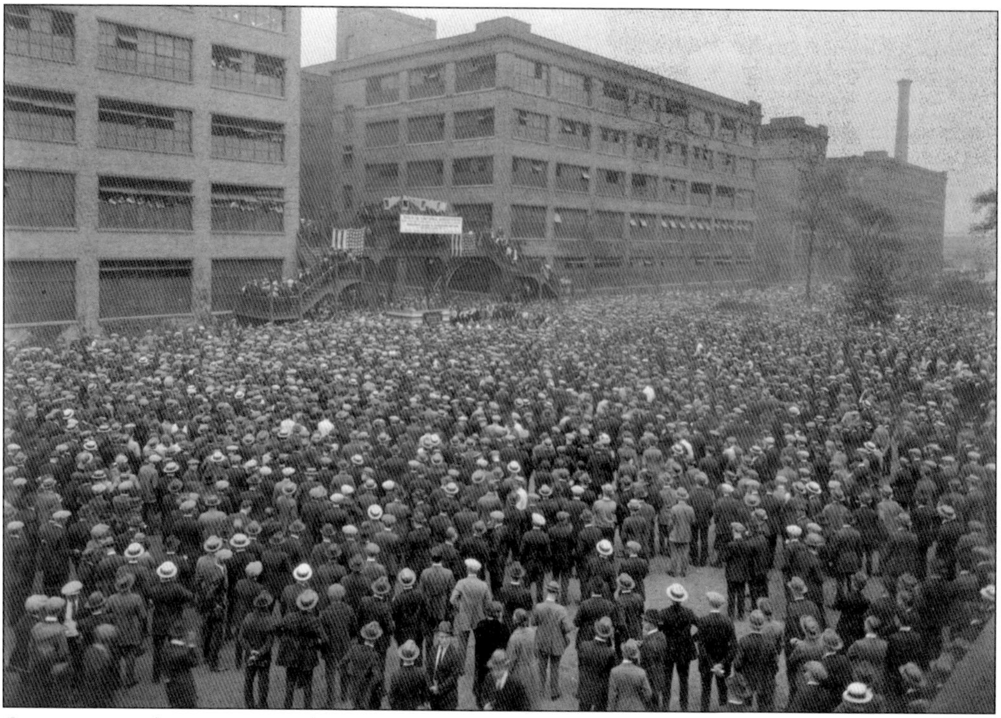

One man in a distant city speaks into a microphone, and a crowd 1,000 miles away hears his words almost instantly—the very idea of this amazed everyone. In this 1924 photograph, the Hawthorne staff gathers to hear Western Electric president Charles DuBois over the first permanent public address system. Western Electric engineers perfected long-distance speech transmission. (Courtesy of the Jezek collection.)

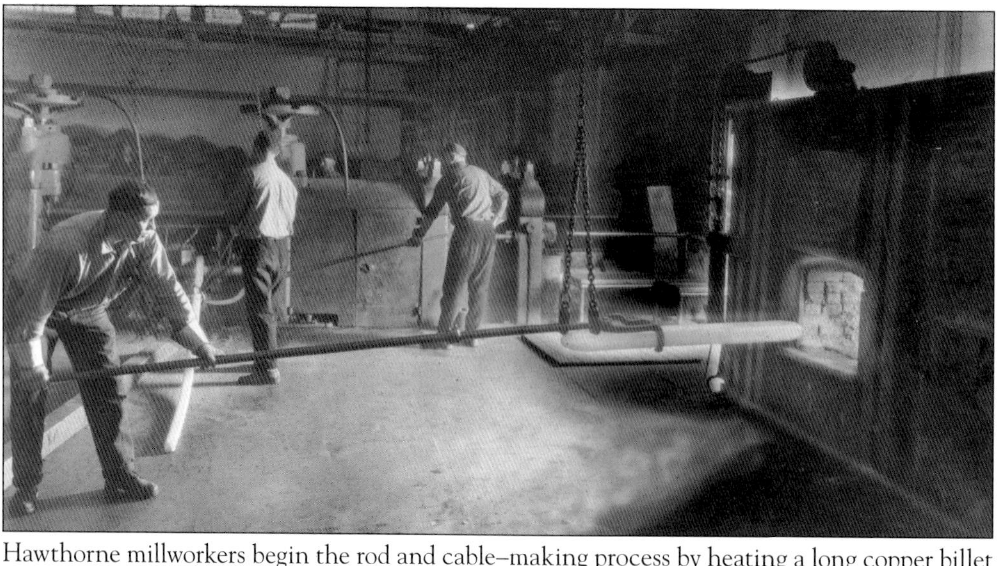

Hawthorne millworkers begin the rod and cable–making process by heating a long copper billet in a furnace. Heavy-metal raw materials like copper rolled into the plant on freight cars from the Manufacturers' Junction Railroad. Hawthorne did much of the heavy lifting for the Bell System, supplying the hardware that connected and switched millions of calls each day. (Courtesy of AT&T Archives.)

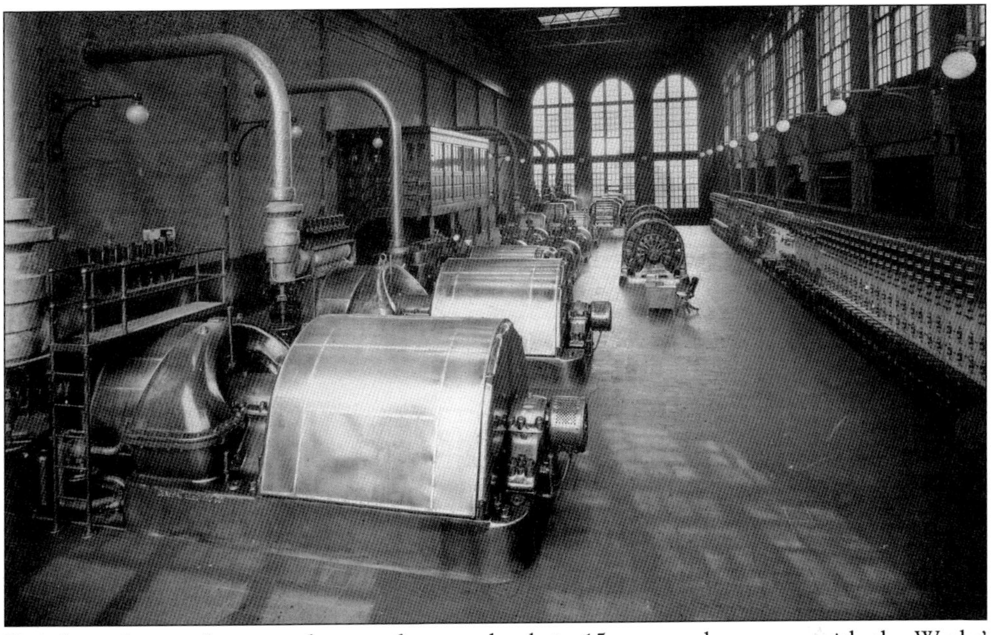

Hawthorne's powerhouse underwent four overhauls in 15 years to keep pace with the Works' electricity demands. This 1923 photograph shows the newest turbines, which increased capacity to 20,000 kilowatts. Each upgrade added more muscle, so these machines delivered seven times the power generated in 1905. Even as these machines revved up, engineers were already planning further improvements. (Courtesy of AT&T Archives.)

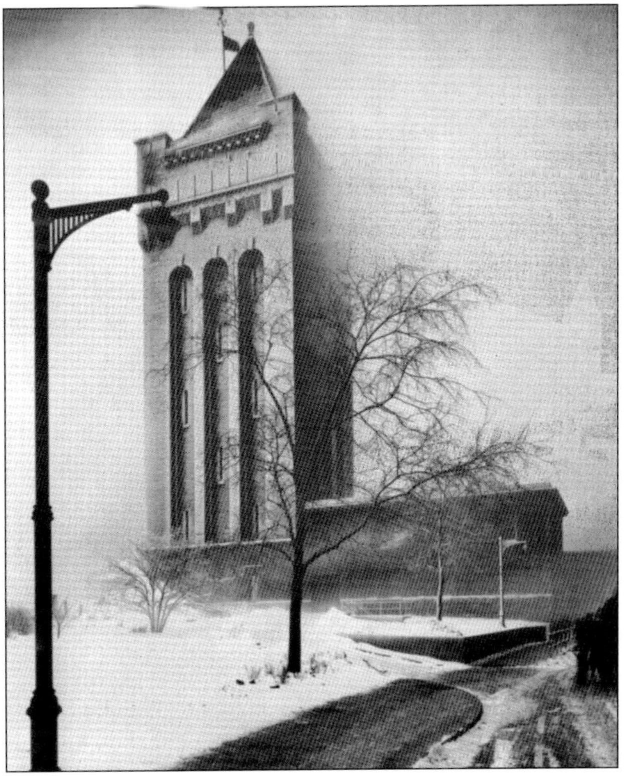

A frigid Chicago winter day in 1929 reveals the stately elegance of the Hawthorne Works water tower. More than just a decorative showpiece, the tower performed a number of important functions. Besides serving as the headquarters of the security force and the fire brigade, it also housed six steel tanks with a capacity of 213,000 gallons that were connected to the fire hydrants and sprinkler system.

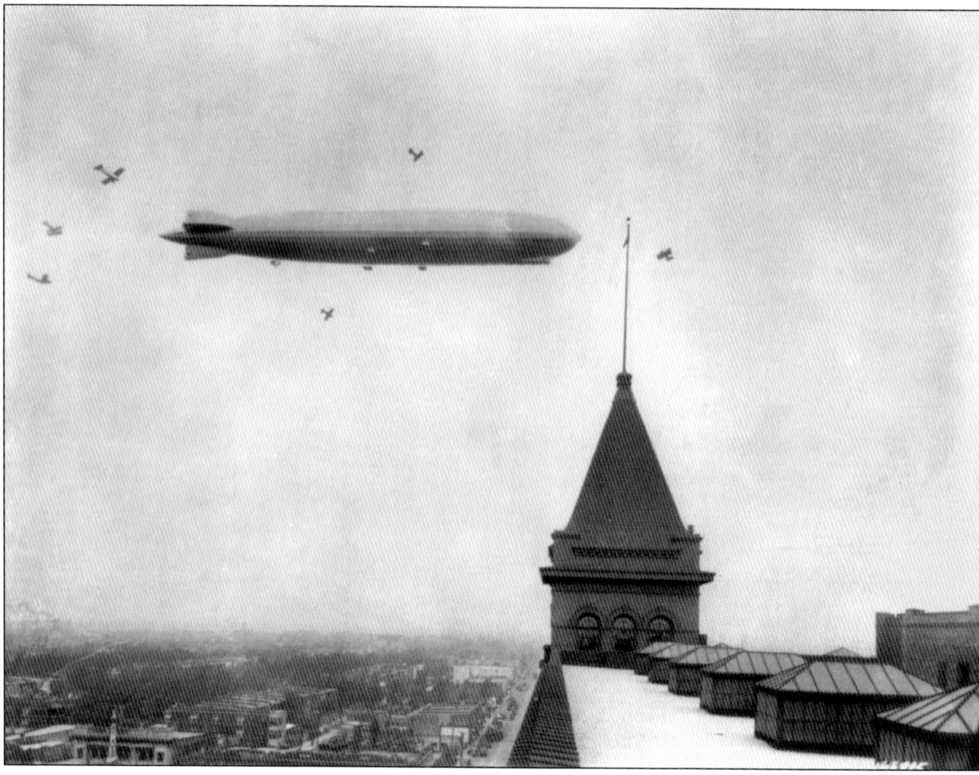

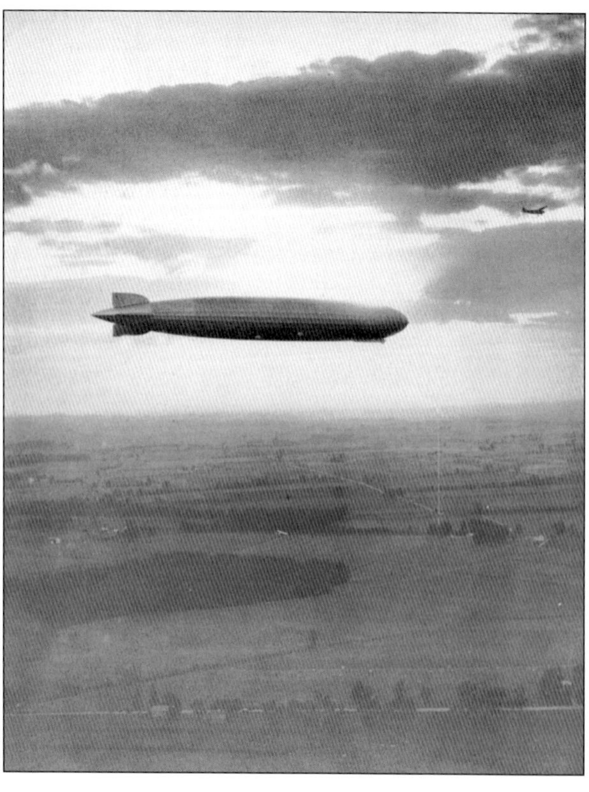

Above, the German airship *Graf Zeppelin* floats majestically over the Hawthorne Works on August 28, 1929, during its around-the-world flight. With a top speed of 80 miles per hour, airships were the era's fastest means of international travel. At left, the *Graf Zeppelin* concludes its journey in New Jersey, escorted by an airplane equipped with a radio telephone designed by nearby Bell Laboratories. The world seemed full of technological marvels in 1929, and the future looked bright for both air transport and telecommunications. But just two months after these events, the stock market crash triggered a worldwide depression. Within three years, Hawthorne had laid off four-fifths of its employees, and the age of airships ended in 1937 when the *Graf Zeppelin*'s sister *Hindenburg* exploded. *Graf Zeppelin* was grounded and scrapped. (Both courtesy of AT&T Archives.)

Four

The 1930s

Products of Craftsmen

In 1930, the Hawthorne Works celebrated its 25th anniversary, displaying justifiable pride in its many accomplishments. In just two and a half decades, the plant had grown into a world-renowned center of ingenuity and the embodiment of America's industrial might. In the 1920s, the plant and Western Electric had earned record profits, and had nearly doubled in size and number of employees. The *Western Electric News* had good reason to be optimistic about the future, crowing in the anniversary issue, "With all this accomplished in 25 years, the news of the year 2005 won't have enough room to tell all about Hawthorne's centennial."

The crash did not slow Hawthorne immediately. Expansion continued, taking advantage of lower construction costs. Western Electric, and the nation as a whole, had seen hard times come and go. Pres. Herbert Hoover was inclined to allow market forces to resolve the crisis naturally. However, steadily growing unemployment alarmed the public, and Hoover agreed to limited federal efforts to address the worsening situation. He created the President's Organization on Unemployment Relief (POUR) in 1931, appointing AT&T president Walter Gifford as its director. POUR had a negligible effect on the worsening economy. Gifford, like President Hoover, was unwilling to distribute direct relief funds. He told a Senate committee that he still believed state and local governments could handle the emergency. When a senator observed, "You are always hopeful," Gifford responded, "I find it pleasant, Senator, to be hopeful."

But "pleasant" did not describe what was happening in Gifford's own domain. Revenue plummeted as customers gave up home telephones they could no longer afford. Western Electric, with negative demand for its products, bore the brunt of the Bell System's crisis. Its sales fell by half in three short years, and 80 percent of its workforce found themselves out of a job. The Hawthorne Works laid off a similar percentage, and the bustling Cicero workshops that had crafted the finest electronics were reduced to cobbling together household items.

The Hawthorne Works survived the traumatic decade, and only found a renewed sense of purpose and vigor when called to aid in the next national crisis.

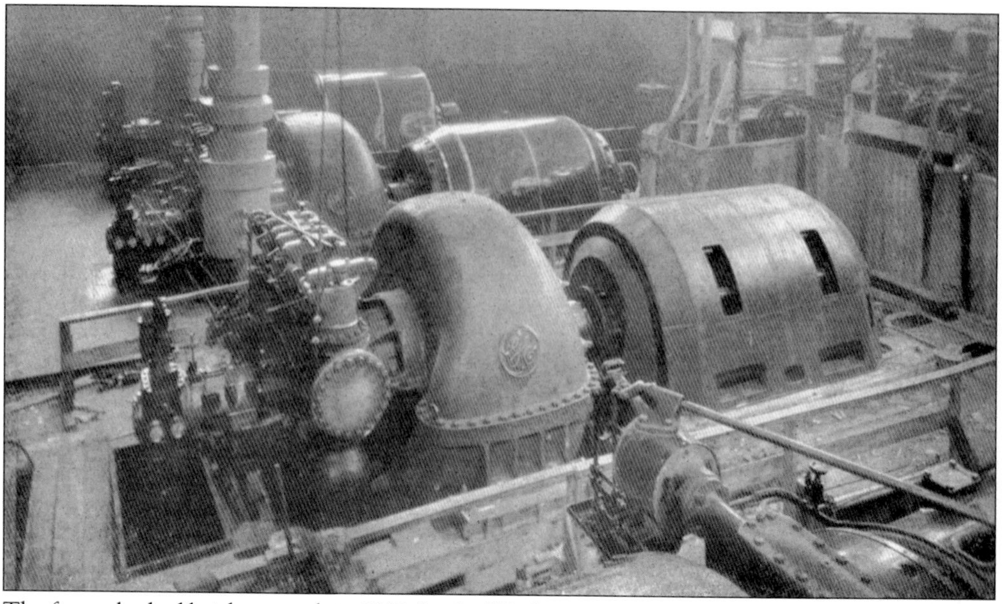

The future looked bright enough in 1930 for the Works to again revamp the power plant. Seen here are two 12,000-volt turbo generators that boosted the plant's output to nearly 35,000 kilowatts. The General Electric logo is prominent on the generator in the foreground. Western Electric had exited the power apparatus business 30 years before, and so purchased the equipment from its rival. (Courtesy of the *Western Electric News*.)

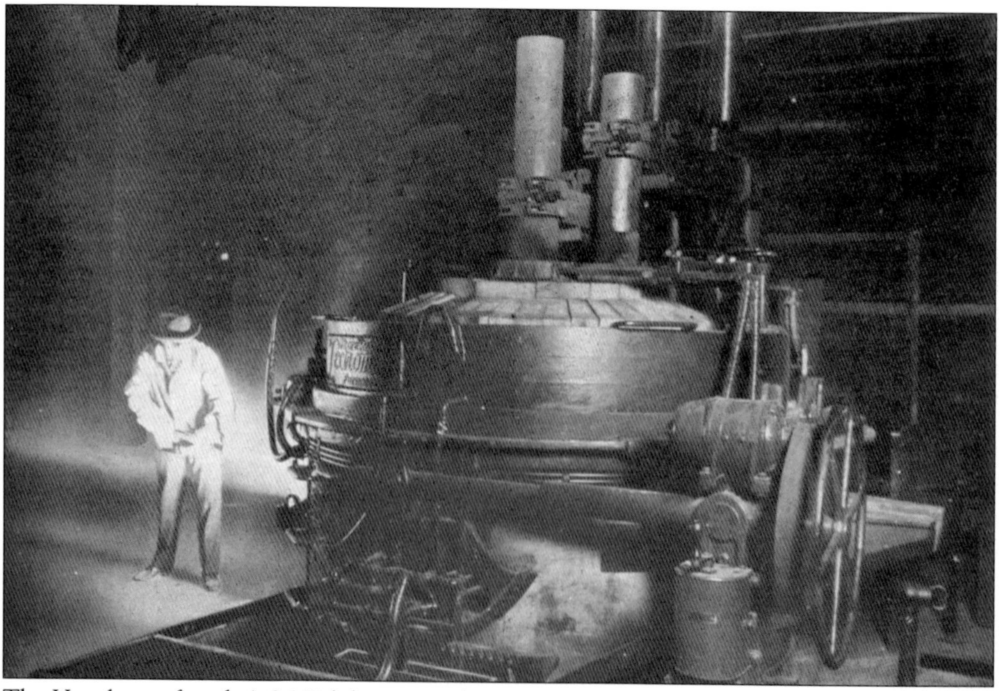

The Hawthorne foundry's 2,000-kilowatt arc furnace still burned brightly in the early 1930s. Used only at night to avoid taxing the power supply, the metal melter raised alloys to a temperature of 4,500 degrees Fahrenheit, purifying 6,000 pounds of iron ore and nickel per hour. The three graphite electrodes protruding from its top arced high current to the furnace. (Courtesy of the *Western Electric News*.)

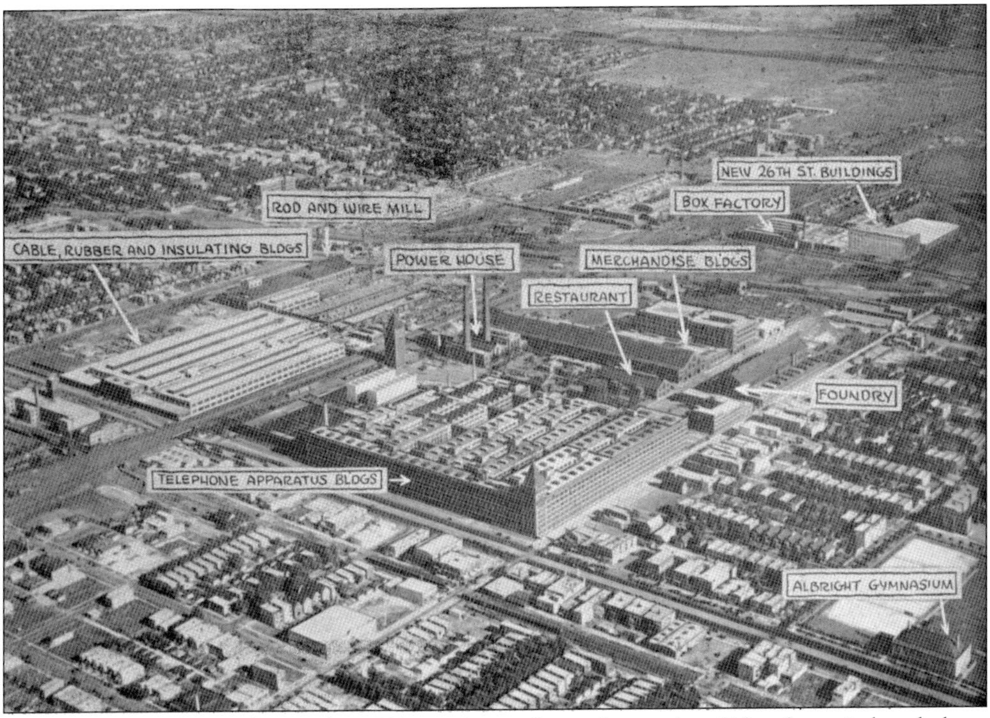

Looking toward the southeast, this 1931 aerial view shows the results of Hawthorne's decade-long building program. In the 1920s, the Works added the executive tower, Albright Gymnasium, the rod and wire mill, and the Twenty-sixth Street buildings. The cable plant expanded and the powerhouse added new cooling towers. Within two years, much of the complex seen here sat idle and empty. (Courtesy of the *Western Electric News*.)

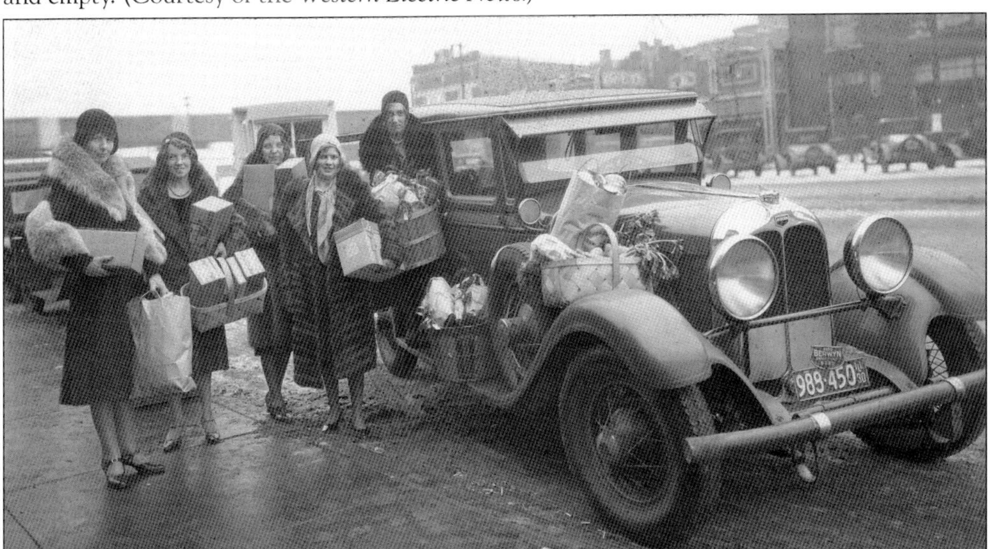

In 1930, as the economy worsened, a Hawthorne workers' committee extended a charitable hand by adopting a needy family of seven and pooling resources to keep them fed through the year. Here, members of the committee prepare to deliver Christmas baskets. Soon, many former Hawthorne employees would require similar assistance.

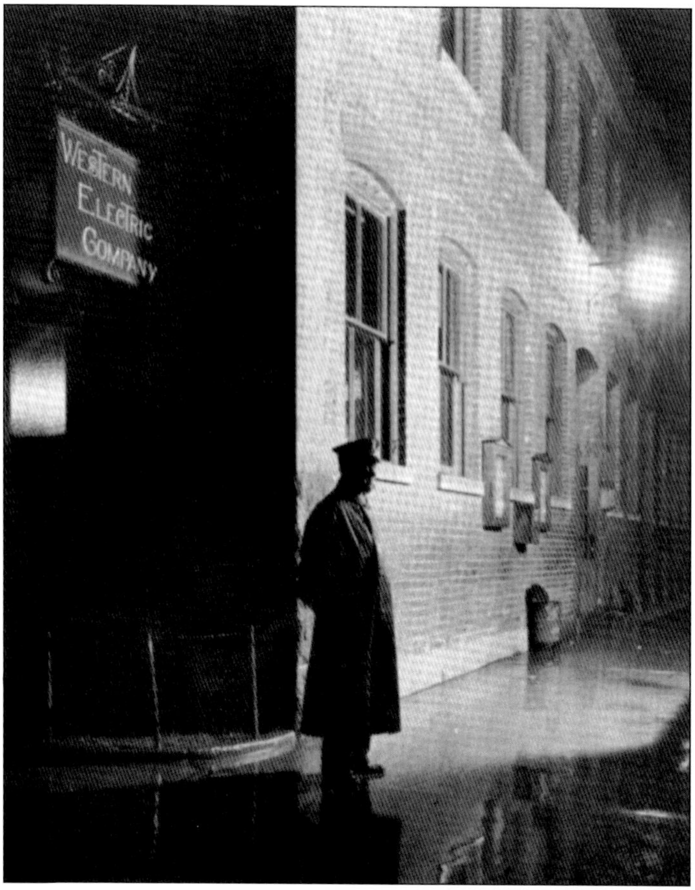

At left, a member of the security staff stands a lonely vigil on a rainy night in May 1931. The Depression had begun to have an impact on the Hawthorne Works by this time. It was clear this was not another short-term slowdown. Western Electric set sales records nearly every year in the 1920s, peaking at $411 million in 1929. Sales dropped to $229 million in 1931. That same year, the number of Bell telephones in service declined by 300,000, the first such reversal in history. Western Electric's fortunes were tightly bound to the Bell System, and when the Bell Telephone Companies stopped expanding, so did Western Electric. Crowds no longer pushed through Entrance No. 1 (below) as they had in 1924.

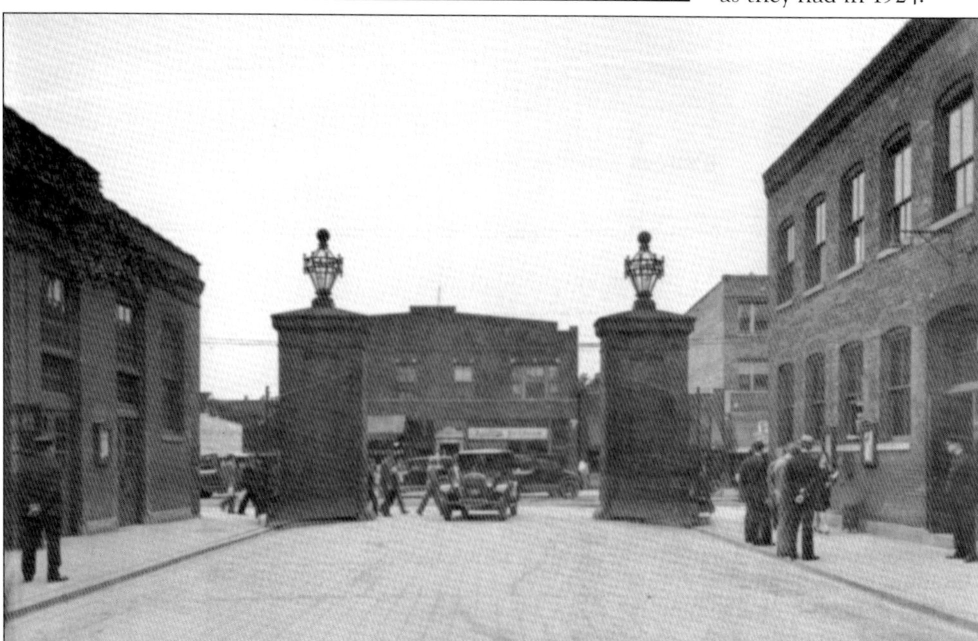

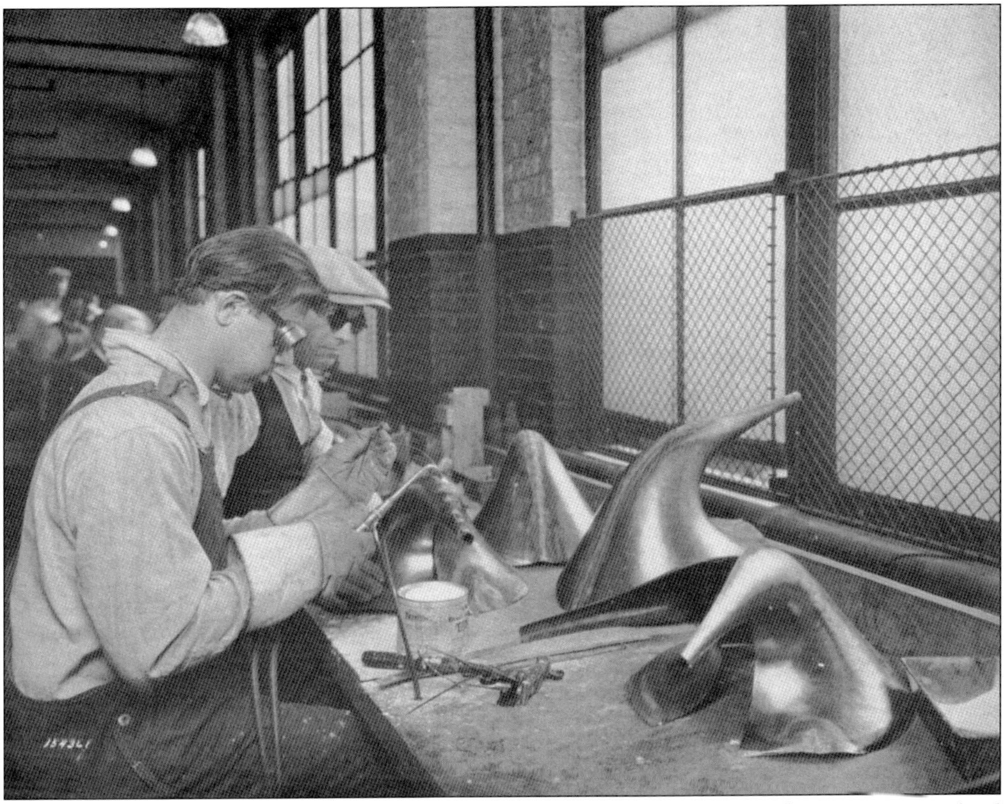

Welders shape Western Electric–brand public address speaker horns. Hawthorne units involved in the new and growing motion picture sound business stayed relatively busy during the early Depression years. As "talkies" took hold, older theaters added speakers and projectors built by Western Electric, while new theaters incorporated the new equipment into their design. (Courtesy of the *Western Electric News*.)

Western Electric
THE VOICE OF ACTION
SOUND SYSTEM
MADE BY THE MAKERS OF YOUR TELEPHONE

Moviegoers in the 1930s—and there were millions each week—grew familiar with "the Voice of Action" logo. Theaters equipped with Western Electric speakers proudly advertised the fact. The making of sound movie apparatus involved 10 percent of the Hawthorne staff early in the decade. (Courtesy of the *Western Electric News*.)

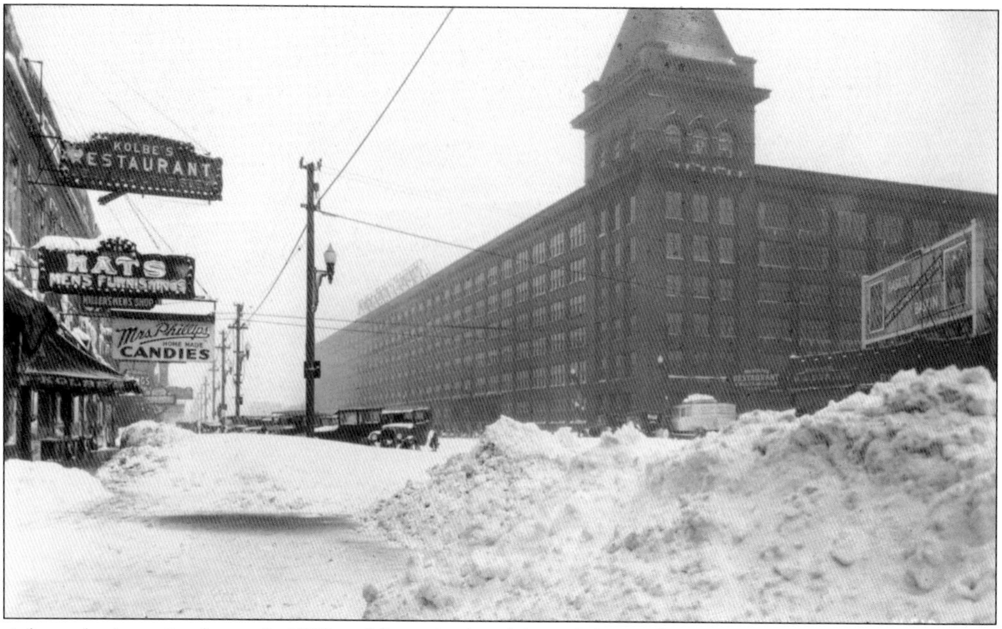

A brutal winter in the early 1930s adds to the hardship. After reducing hours and pay, Hawthorne executives resorted to layoffs as a "temporary expedient." By 1933, over 30,000 workers, some with decades of experience, found themselves out on the streets. That same bleak year, *Western Electric News* ceased publication, and Hawthorne's magazine, the *Hawthorne Microphone*, closed for three years.

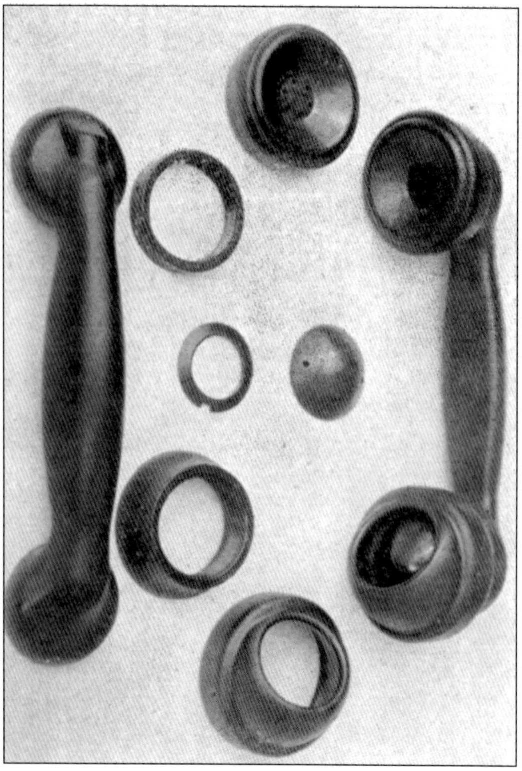

The new cradle handset phones introduced in 1930 contained molded plastic parts fashioned at Hawthorne. Western Electric chemical engineers formulated a material lighter, cheaper, and simpler to make than the hardened rubber and metal parts found in candlestick phones. However, the Works still stocked replacement parts for the popular old models into the 1940s. (Courtesy of the *Western Electric News*.)

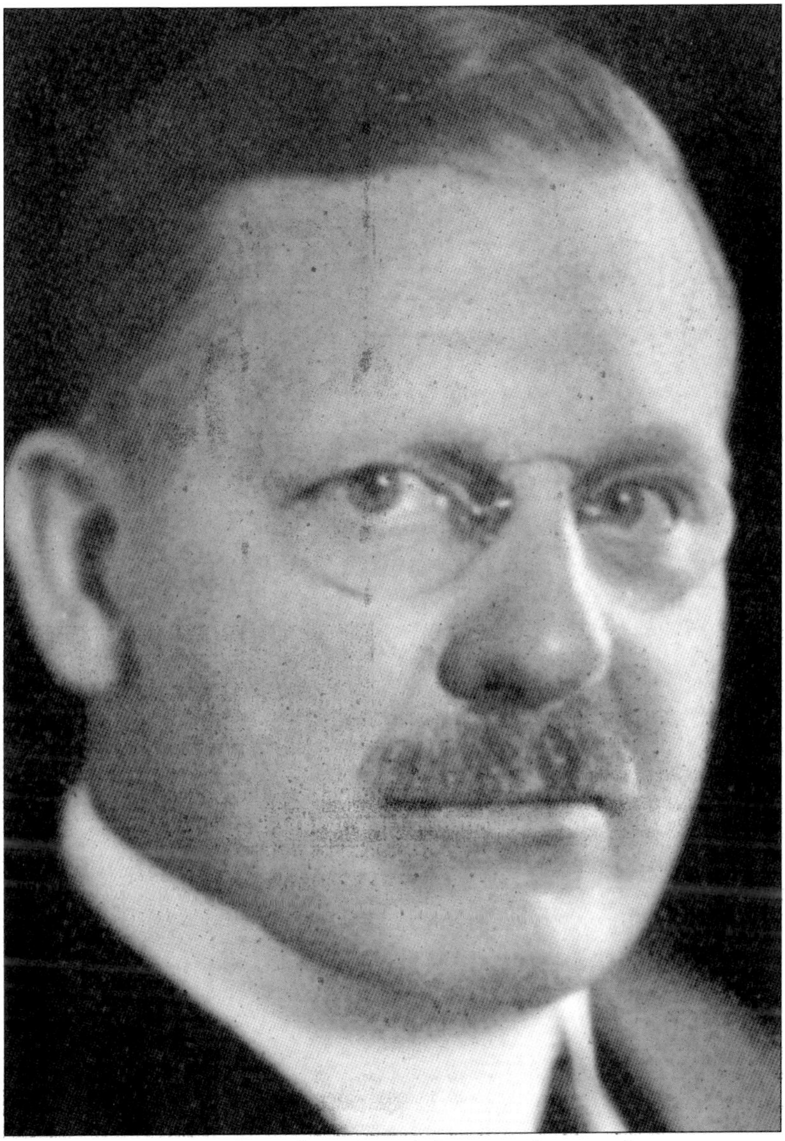

Commerce continued to wither through 1932 until the nation's unemployment rate peaked at an estimated 25 percent. The coming year promised more of the same. Western Electric president Edgar S. Bloom, seen here, addressed these harsh realities in a message to employees in the January 1933 issue of the *Hawthorne Microphone*: "This situation has produced the most difficult problems which the Company . . . has ever had to face. We cannot predict when our business will commence to improve." The chief also reminded the Hawthorne family that their "obligations as neighbors in our communities have grown as the numbers without employment have become greater." WE personnel responded admirably, contributing a combined $65,000 to the Cook County Emergency Welfare Fund, in addition to the company's own $50,000 donation. "You have no idea," wrote fund chairman Robert Gardner, "how much the cooperation and support of the employees of the Western Electric Company means at this time." Despite this generosity, the fund still operated with a $1 million deficit. Unemployment remained in double digits through the decade and Hawthorne's employment did not rise back above 10,000 until 1936. (Courtesy of the *Hawthorne Microphone*.)

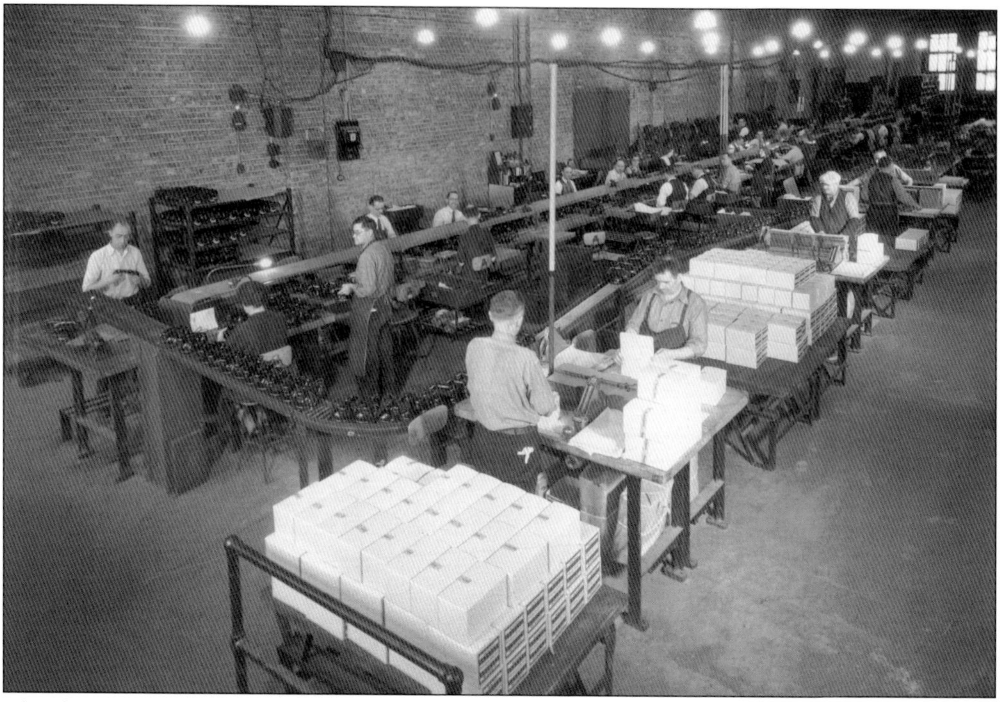

The shipping department packaged a dwindling number of cradle-style desk-set phones in 1932. That year, telephones in use fell by another 1.6 million, and Western Electric posted a loss of $12.6 million, the first of three consecutive red-ink years. By 1933, about 15 percent of Bell Telephone customers across the nation had disconnected.

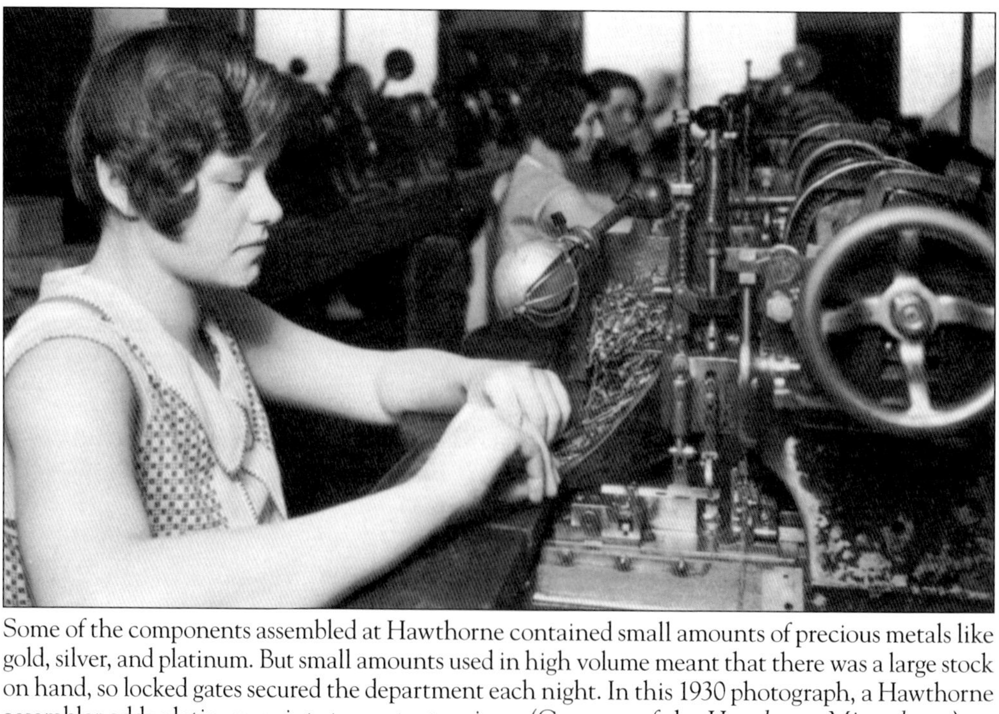

Some of the components assembled at Hawthorne contained small amounts of precious metals like gold, silver, and platinum. But small amounts used in high volume meant that there was a large stock on hand, so locked gates secured the department each night. In this 1930 photograph, a Hawthorne assembler adds platinum points to contact springs. (Courtesy of the *Hawthorne Microphone*.)

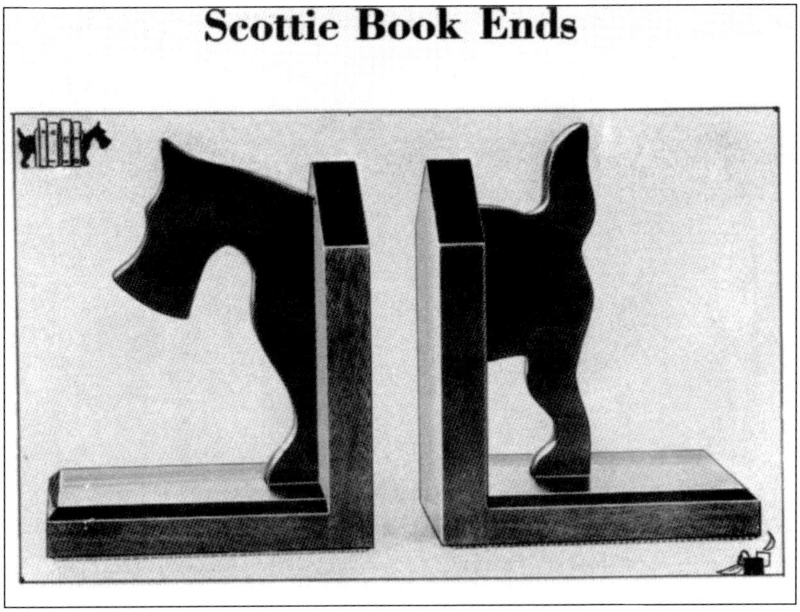

By 1933, the Depression-ravaged Hawthorne Works resorted to desperate measures to keep its few remaining employees in paying jobs. The Hawthorne Club, along with clubs in other WE factories across the country, opened in-house stores where employees could purchase an assortment of household items made by their metal and woodworking shops. The clubs' *Products of Craftsmen* catalog included the solid walnut "Scottie" bookends above and the hammered-copper ashtray below. According to the catalog, they were produced "with the same pride . . . demonstrated as makers of telephones." The goods were sold at cost to coworkers. Hawthorne also arranged for its skilled workmen to perform handyman tasks. For a reasonable fee, an underemployed Hawthorne craftsman—some were reduced to one or two days' work a week—would tend to your painting, plumbing, carpentry, or gardening needs.

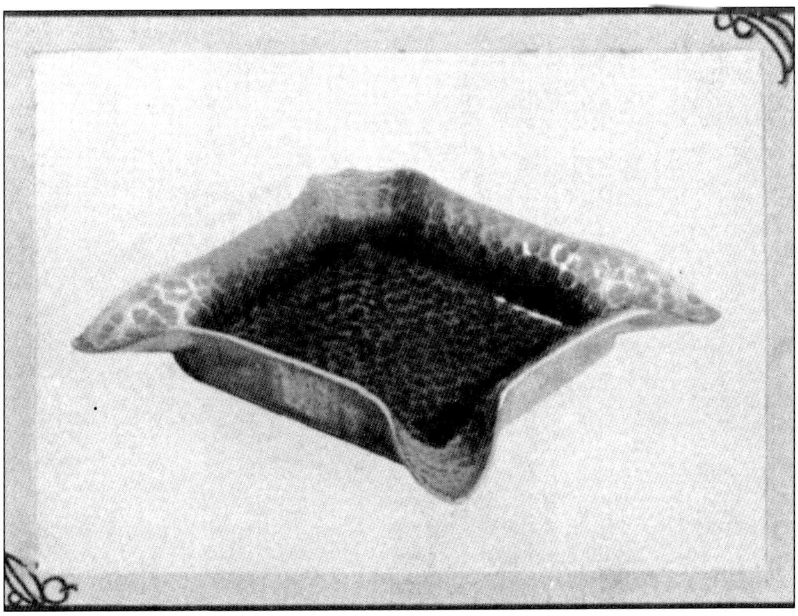

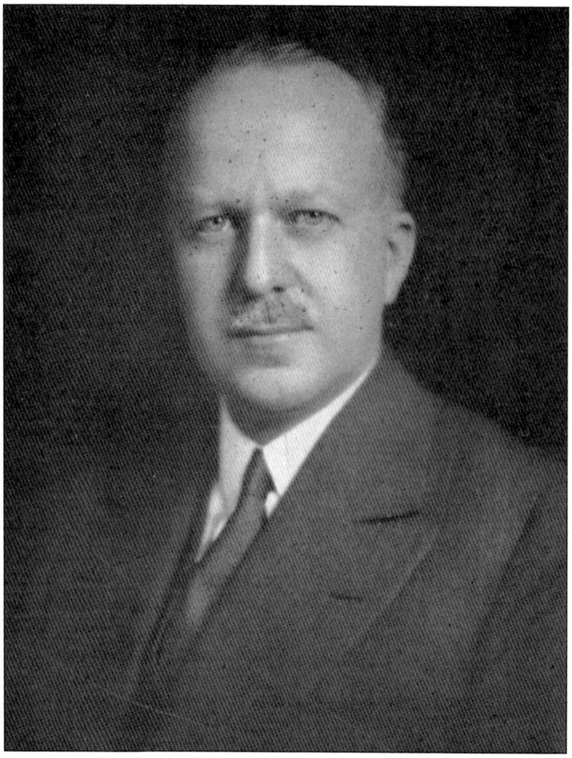

Walter S. Gifford, the president of Bell System parent company AT&T, faced widespread criticism for continuing to pay stockholders dividends during the Depression years while reducing payroll by 20 percent. Gifford believed this commitment to investors would build loyalty and attract greater investment when good times returned. Furthermore, he argued, there simply was not enough work to maintain full staffing. But Gifford's stance changed after the National Labor Relations Act of 1935. The statute guaranteed workers' rights to bargain through union representatives of their own choice. Many corporate executives tried to disregard the law, but Gifford decided to comply. He did not grant a system-wide contract, but the telephone industry avoided labor violence. Below, Gifford enjoys a Utah vacation with his sons. (Both courtesy of the *Western Electric News*.)

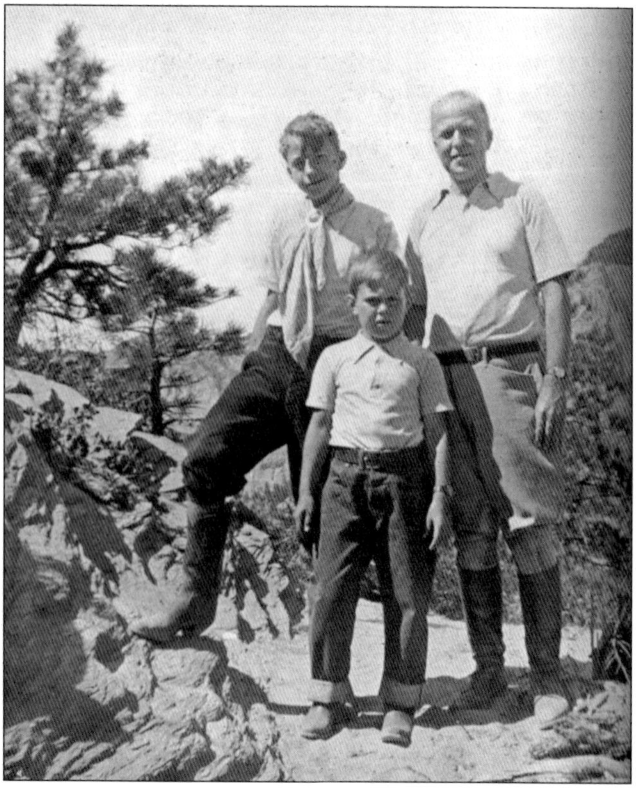

The Model 300 series of telephones debuted in 1936. More than 25 million of them poured out of Hawthorne and other Western Electric factories over the next 18 years. The square base held all the circuitry, so, unlike candlestick models, the 300s did not need the separate ringer unit. However, the consumer's choice of color was still limited to black.

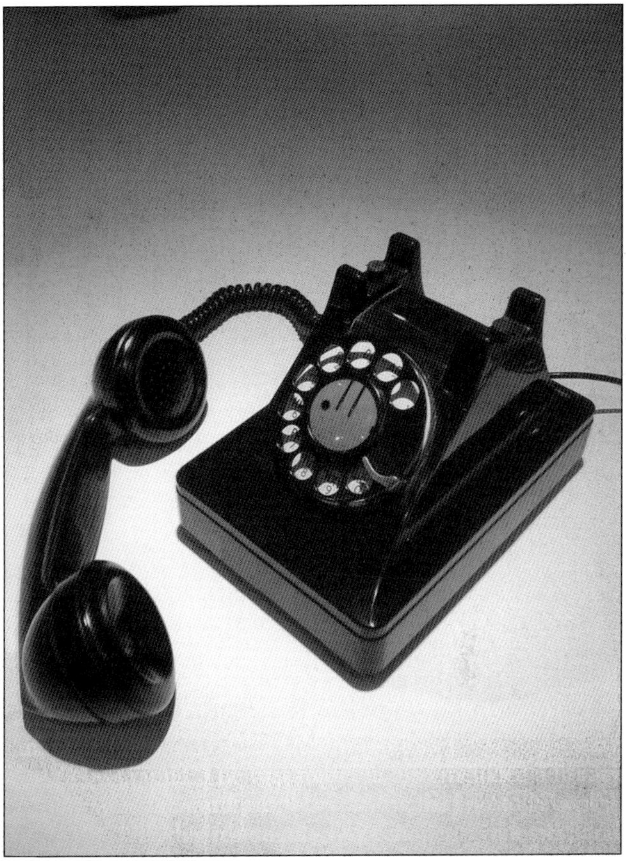

The transition to the Crossbar switching system, introduced in 1938 and seen below, helped revive Hawthorne during lean times. Crossbar's grid matrix configuration multiplied the number of possible connections to speed service. First patented by a Western Electric engineer in 1915 and then improved by Bell Labs, Crossbar units rolled out of Hawthorne's shops until their production was moved to Omaha in the 1950s.

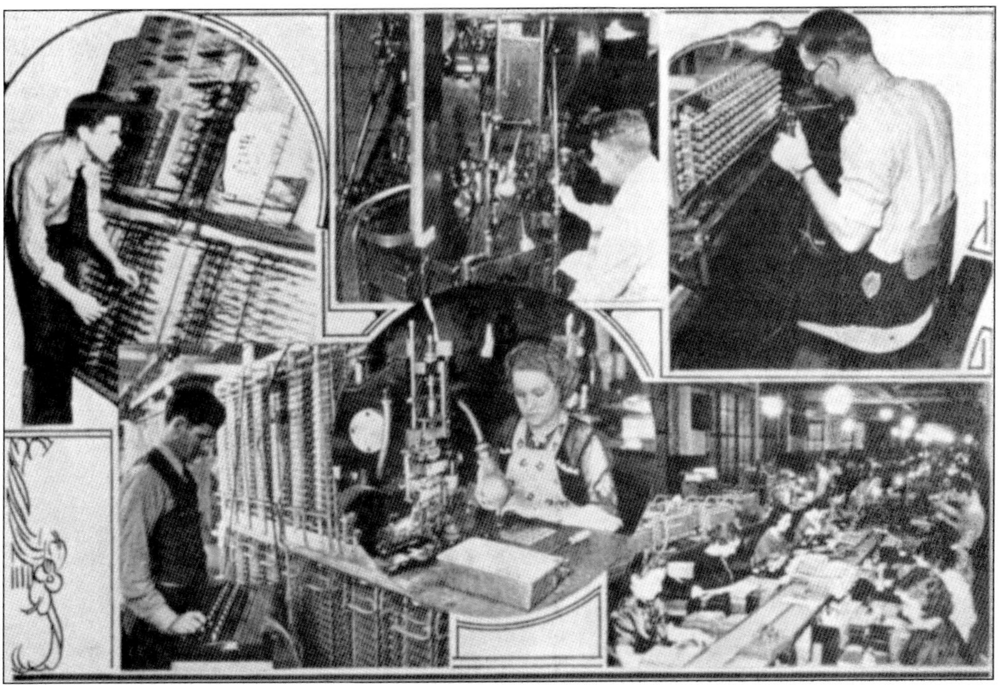

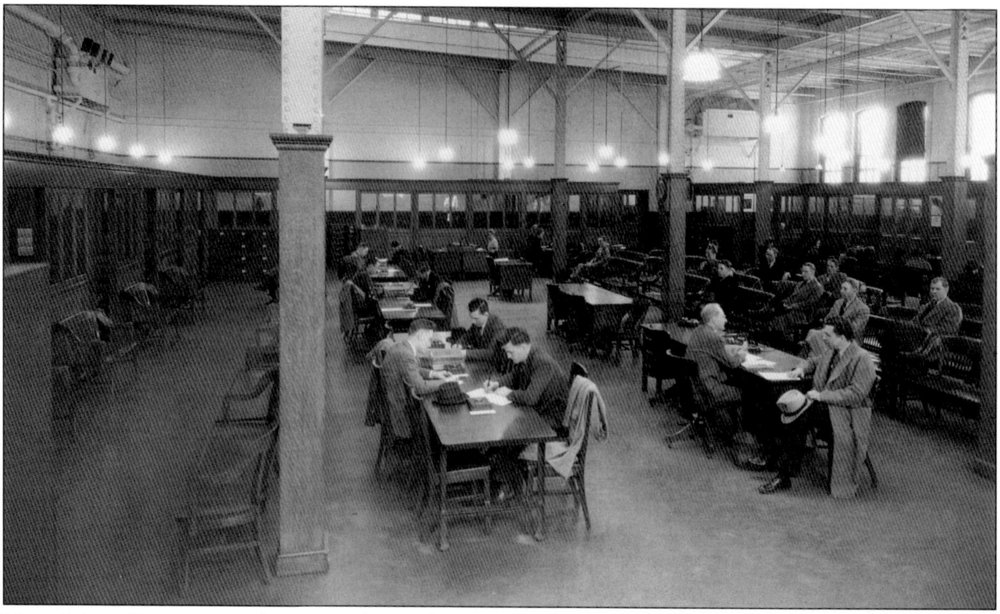

Hopeful applicants wait their turn for a job interview at Hawthorne's employment office in 1938. By then, the turnaround was well underway. Western Electric's sales had risen 39 percent in 1937, and the number of telephones in use rose by close to one million each year in the late 1930s. Employment at Hawthorne rebounded to over 12,000.

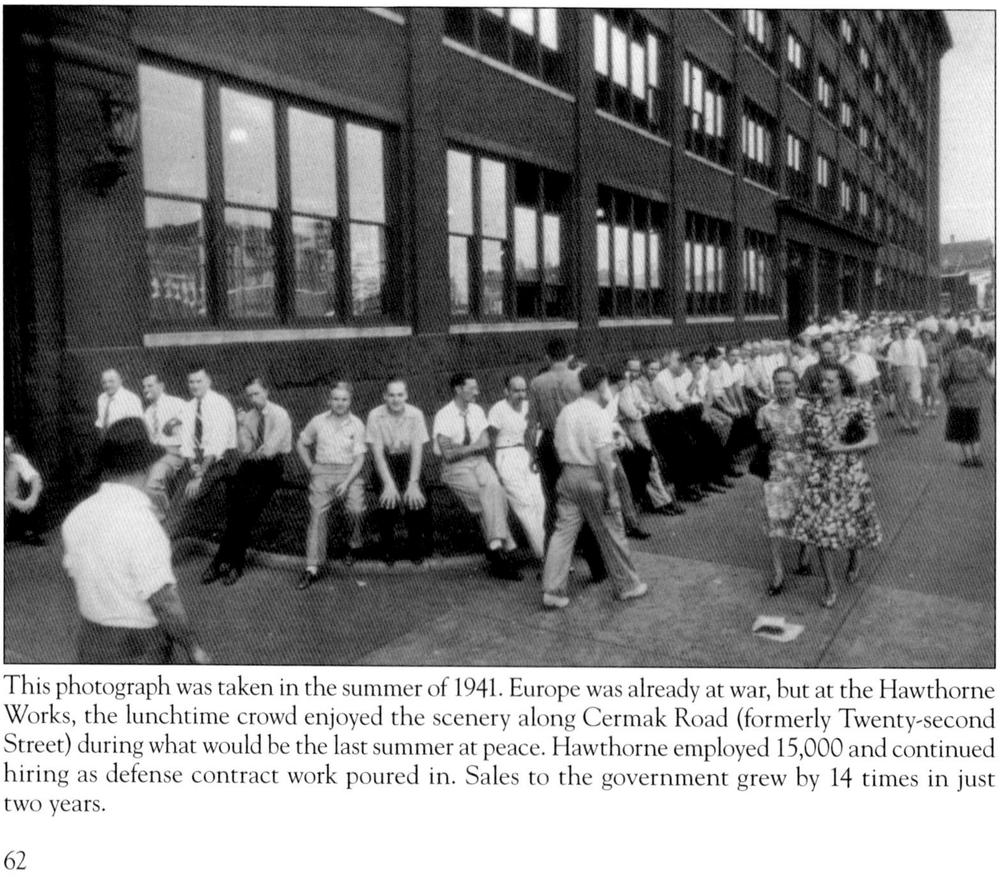

This photograph was taken in the summer of 1941. Europe was already at war, but at the Hawthorne Works, the lunchtime crowd enjoyed the scenery along Cermak Road (formerly Twenty-second Street) during what would be the last summer at peace. Hawthorne employed 15,000 and continued hiring as defense contract work poured in. Sales to the government grew by 14 times in just two years.

Five

THE STUDIES

HUMAN RELATIONS

After World War I, researchers reviewed business practices and procedures with the same scientific approach that had been used to examine soldier fatigue and warfare efficiency. Recognizing the high cost of training new employees, manufacturers like Western Electric were curious about employee motivation and incentive. In the late 1920s and early 1930s, Hawthorne Works was the site of a landmark series of workplace experiments exploring working conditions and productivity. The initial Illumination Studies and the later Hawthorne Studies were born out of management's desire to understand the sociological and psychological factors at work in the workplace.

With Elton Mayo and other Harvard scientists, plant management administered experiments from 1924 to 1933. These were later dubbed the Hawthorne Studies. In five separate experiments, scientists tested worker productivity against a series of factors, including pay, nonfinancial incentives, break periods, workplace conditions, and social environments. Their goal was to determine what physical and psychological factors were most important to workers.

The dominant interpretation of the studies at the time, published in Fritz Roethlisberger's and W.J. Dickson's 1939 publication *Management and the Worker*, was that the increases in productivity noted throughout the experiments were not related to financial incentives but to the environment of the workplace, specifically to increased supervision. The Hawthorne Effect describes the change in a test subject's behavior simply because they are being observed. Managers and social scientists continue to debate the findings and interpretations of the studies today. Criticized both for their lack of control groups and for disregarding political factors, the studies nevertheless instigated the development of human relations both at Hawthorne and in companies worldwide, and dramatically changed the methodology of future sociological research. The Hawthorne Studies also led to further experiments conducted on-site, including a pioneering, multi-decade study of the causes of coronary heart disease.

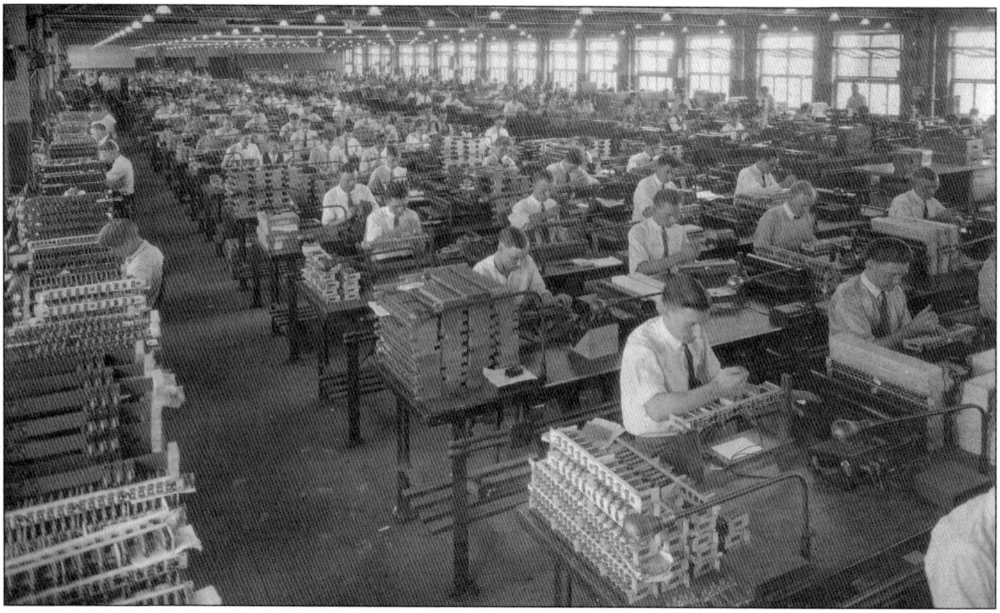

General Electric and the National Research Council funded the first studies at Hawthorne in 1924. Looking at the effects of illumination on worker productivity, operators in several departments, such as the coil-winding department (below), were observed at different levels of lighting. The hypothesis was that greater light would increase productivity. However, workers' output increased as the lights were both turned up and dimmed. Some workers were able to meet shift goals while working in near darkness. Hawthorne management decided that other factors must be at work and that further study was needed. Elton Mayo of Harvard was called in to form a formal study on factors affecting productivity. The Hawthorne Studies, conducted over the next nine years, involved hundreds of workers from several departments and would have dramatic effects on business and the study of sociology for decades. (Both courtesy of the Jezek collection.)

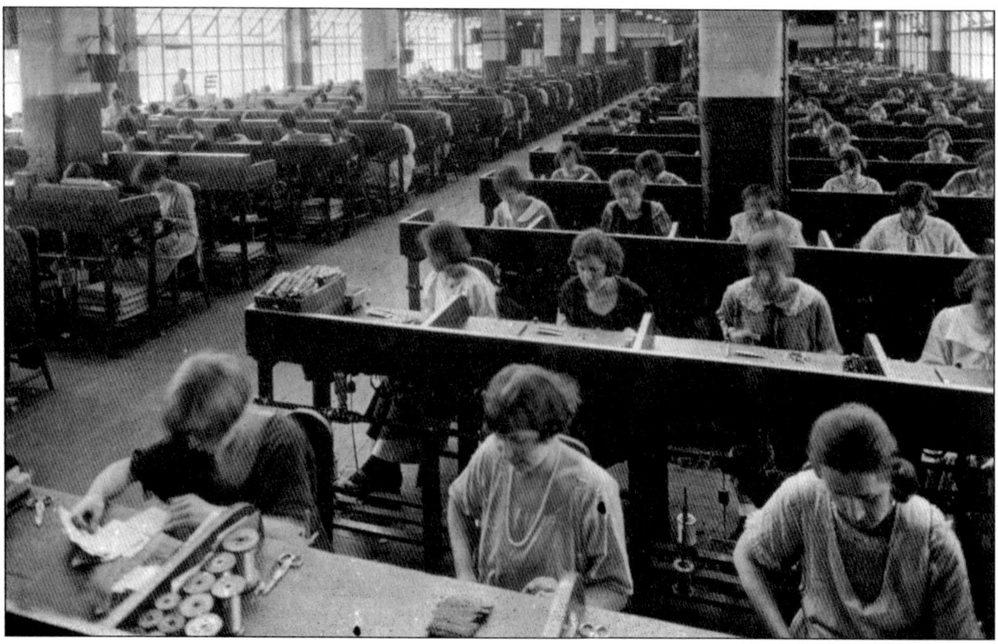

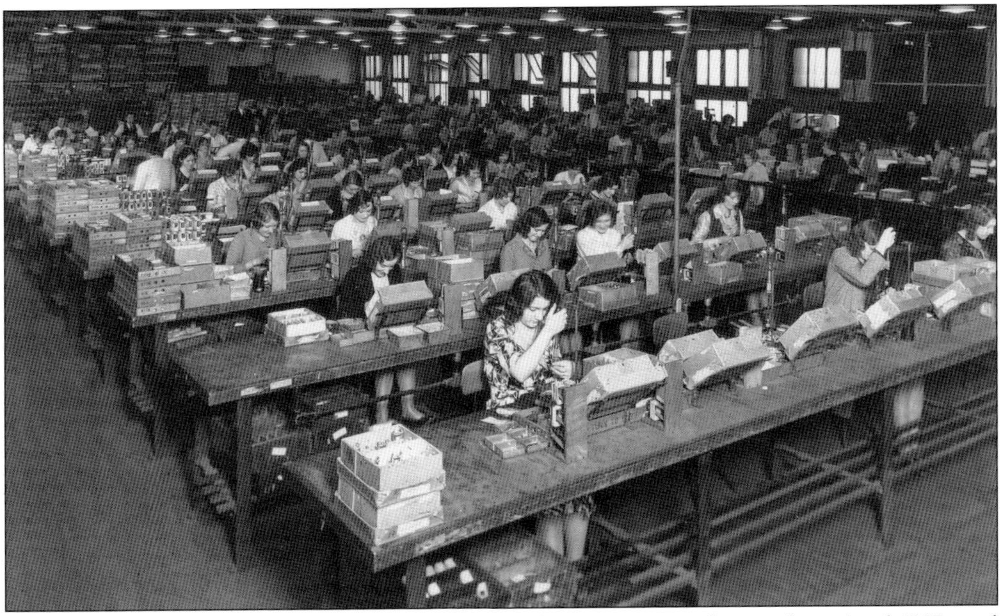

The relay room was the first and longest running of the experiments, lasting from April 1927 until June 1932. The experiment tested workers' response to financial incentives, the changing of hours in the workday and the workweek, varying break times, and shifts in environmental conditions. In all, the relay room operators experienced 23 changes in their work environment.

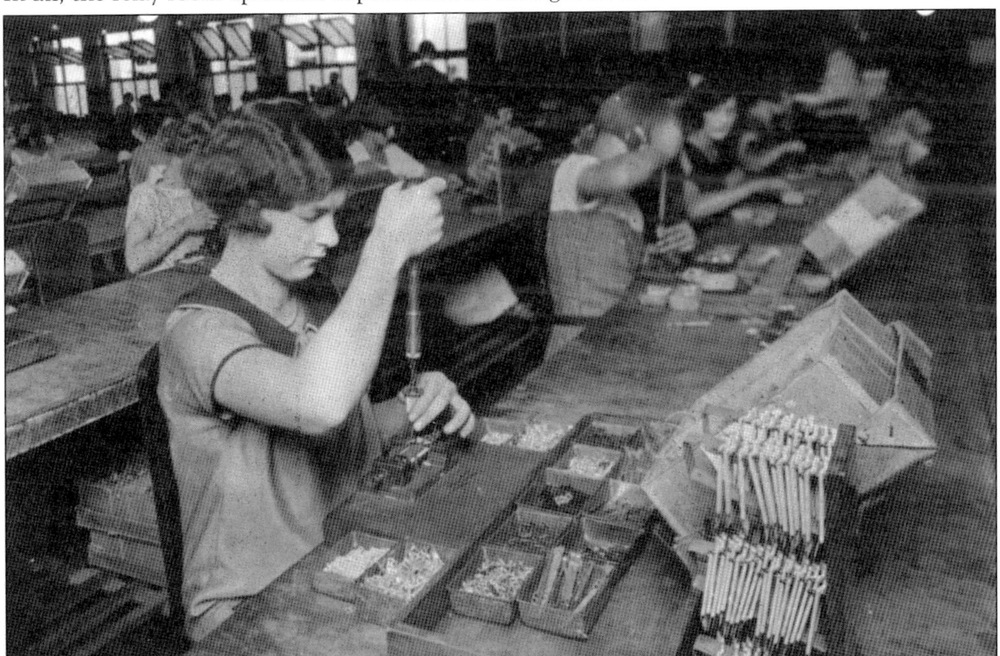

A relay, like the one being assembled here, is an electromagnetic switch used to amplify a signal. Various types of relays were constructed from 35 or so smaller parts. Each one took about one minute to assemble. This task was done 50 times an hour, nine hours a day, five days a week. The relay room was chosen for the study because no machines were involved and because of the highly repetitive nature of the job.

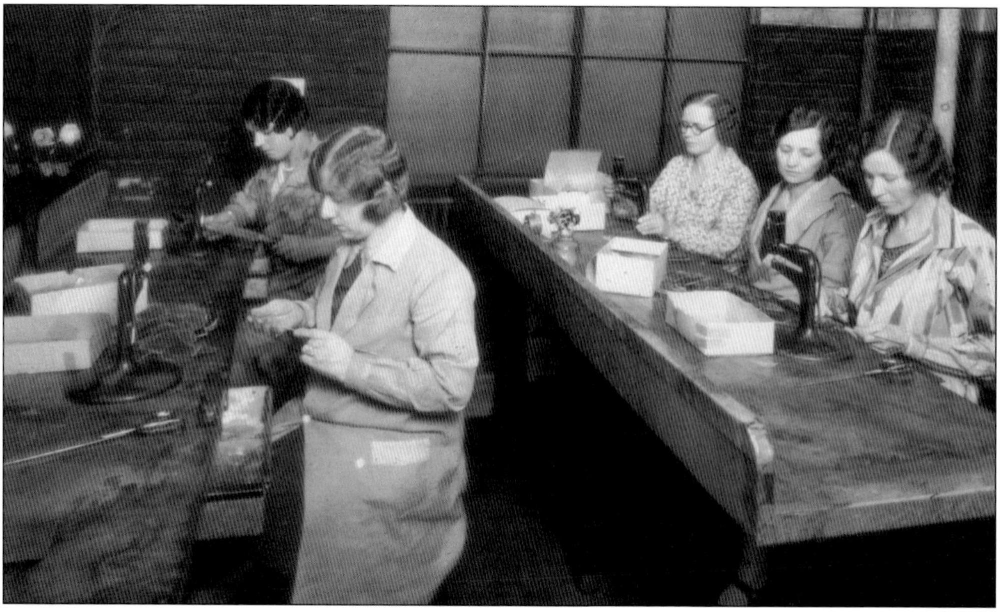

The operators in the relay room study were isolated from the regular department to avoid competition. Separated from the larger group and from floor bosses, the women found they had a lot to talk about. All of the women participating in the experiment were between the ages of 18 and 30 and from Chicago's ethnic communities. A key finding of the study was that group dynamics play an important role in production.

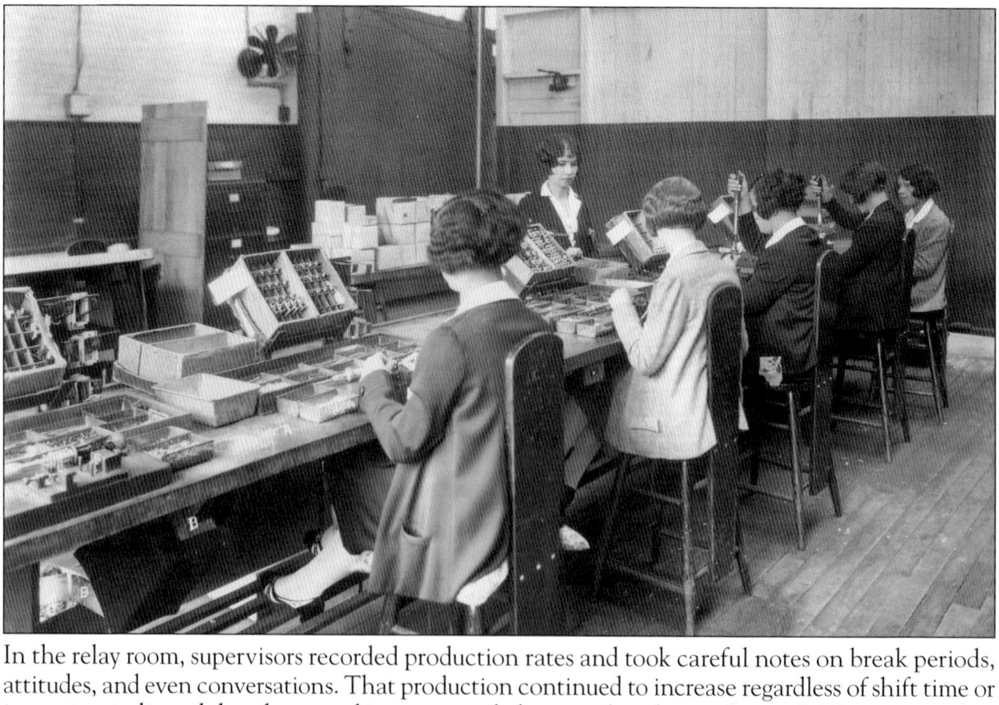

In the relay room, supervisors recorded production rates and took careful notes on break periods, attitudes, and even conversations. That production continued to increase regardless of shift time or incentives indicated that the test subjects responded positively to being observed. That a researcher could affect an experiment simply by their physical presence came to be known as the Hawthorne Effect. The accuracy and interpretation of these findings continues to be debated today.

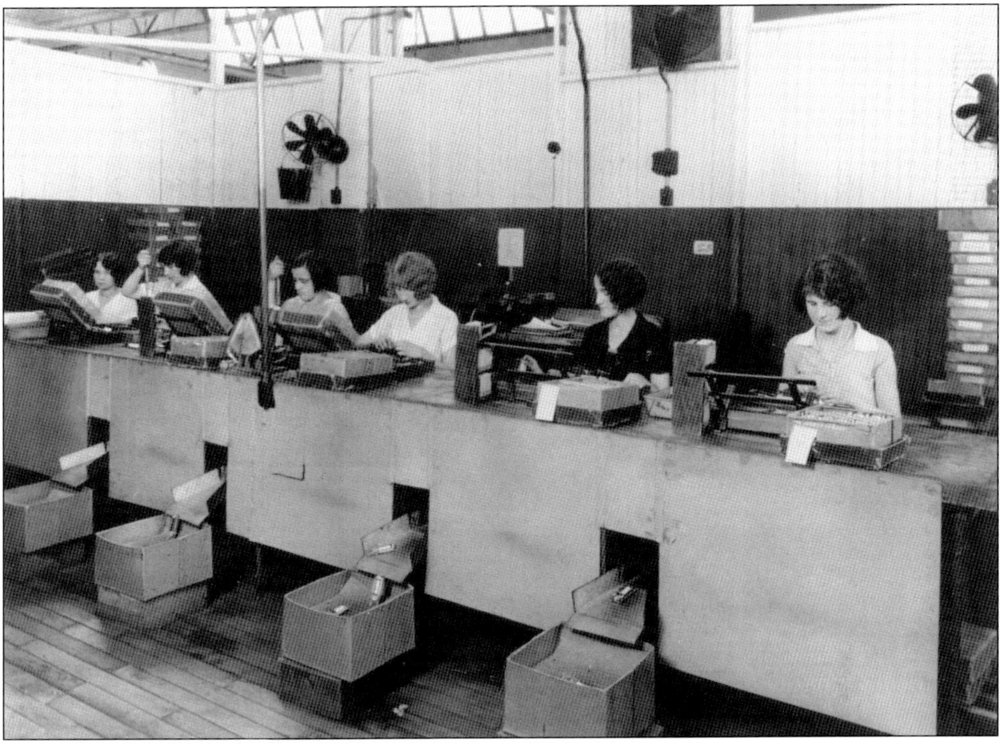

Theresa Layman (above, third from right) participated in the relay room experiment. She is seen at right recounting her experience over 50 years later with other veterans of the study. Outside researchers visited the plant periodically to interview workers and add their own interpretations to the growing body of literature concerning the studies. Don Chipman, a study supervisor, recounted in 1985 that "none of us knew at that time that the Studies were anything special, certainly not that they would become world famous and the basis of a revolution in management/worker relationships. To us, it was just a local experiment, interesting to be a part of but nothing extraordinary." He believes the studies had a dramatic effect on the Hawthorne plant, saying, "They made supervisors more sensitive to people problems and that led to better relationships between supervisors and workers." (Both courtesy of the *Hawthorne Microphone*.)

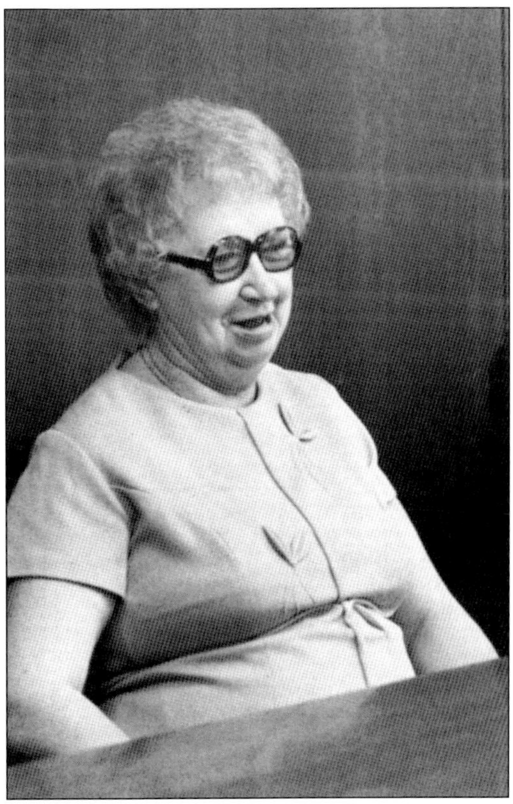

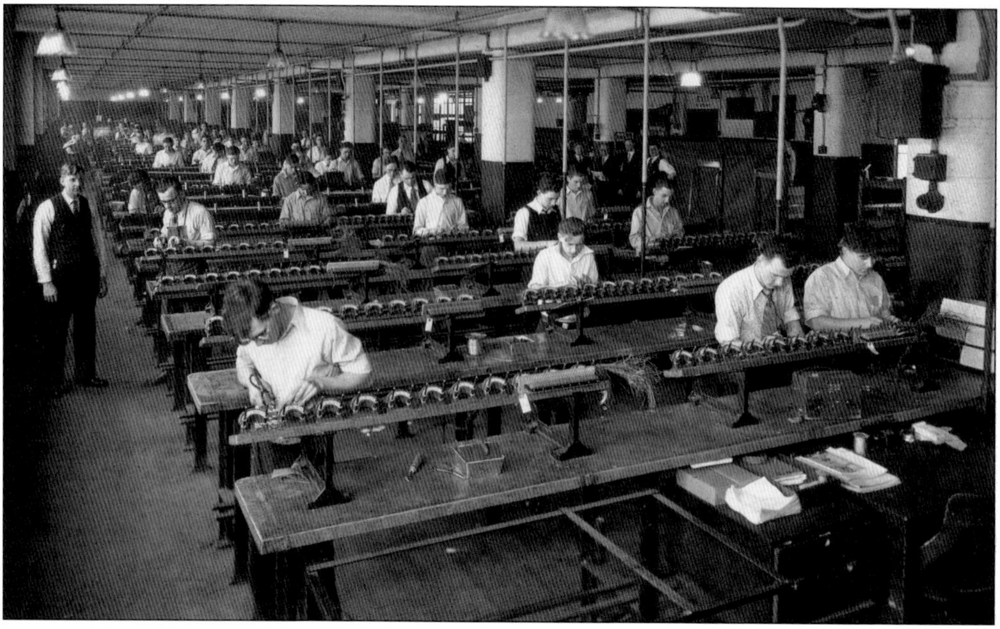

One of the final experiments looked at group dynamics and motivation in the bank wiring room, seen above. Observing the effect of incentive pay on the productivity of 14 workers, researchers found that workers responded more to the production norms established by the group than to outside factors. As a separate part of the study, management instituted a plant-wide interview program, asking employees how they felt about their jobs, their supervisors, and what was on their minds in general. Over 21,000 employees were interviewed between 1928 and 1931. Below, an operator takes a psychological test in 1926 that may have been part of an interview or placement review. Before the studies, employees were often hired and trained by the floor department supervisors. The studies altered the way management and supervisors interacted with and trained employees and led to the development of specialized on-site personnel departments.

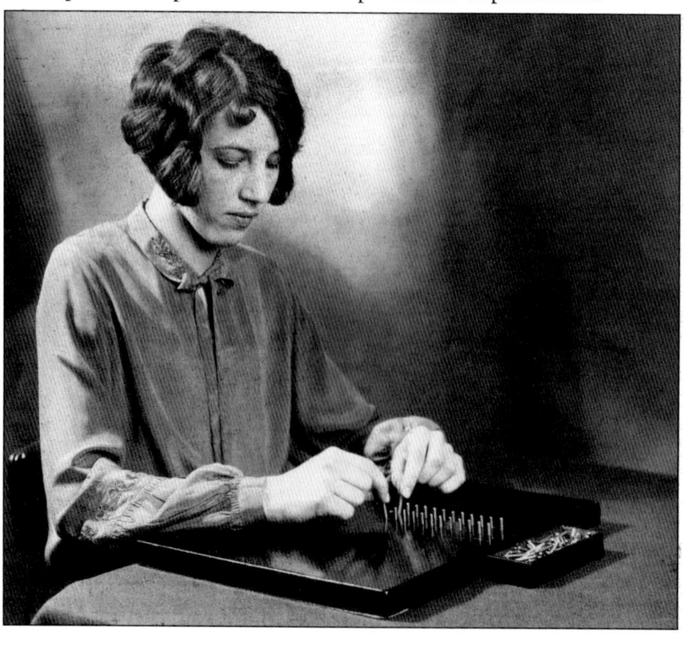

Six

Life

Join the Club!

"I like my job. And I'm very fond of my boss and co-workers . . . if that were not the case, I'd be out of here in a flash."

"There are good conditions, good bosses; nobody bothers you as long as you do your job."

"We have our gripes, but somebody has to do this work . . . You get benefits. They don't bother you. The bosses are real human beings."

"All those years were not merely preparing for life, they were life itself . . . it was a very good way to live."

"Loyalty had a lot of meaning when you were employed by Western Electric. If you were fortunate to have landed any kind of job there you were pretty much set for life . . . Loyalty was a fact of life at Western Electric."

"The employees were treated as though they were part of the family."

"This plant kept my family standing through hard times. It supported us. It was a monument in the town."

These are not the words of "yes men" spouting company slogans. They are the words of everyday people who found a road to a better life at the Hawthorne Works. For the hundreds of thousands who worked at "the Western" over the years, Hawthorne offered stable employment and a caring, friendly community. Even if one's job was not the most stimulating or challenging, one did it right, and the effort paid off. Likewise, the employer realized that the lives of employees did not begin and end with the daily shift. Responsibilities and rewards, mutually understood, created a profitable and humane workplace.

Of course, Western Electric desired production and profits above all. Their generosity was rooted in pragmatism. Better to invest in your employees' well-being than contend with their frustration. The Hawthorne life included benefits like a night school, a hospital, a credit union, and bowling leagues. A Hawthorne executive knew his workers were secure but not complacent, and an employee knew the boss was demanding but not oppressive. The outcome: the Hawthorne Works likely came closer to building the "virtuous circle" than most American workplaces.

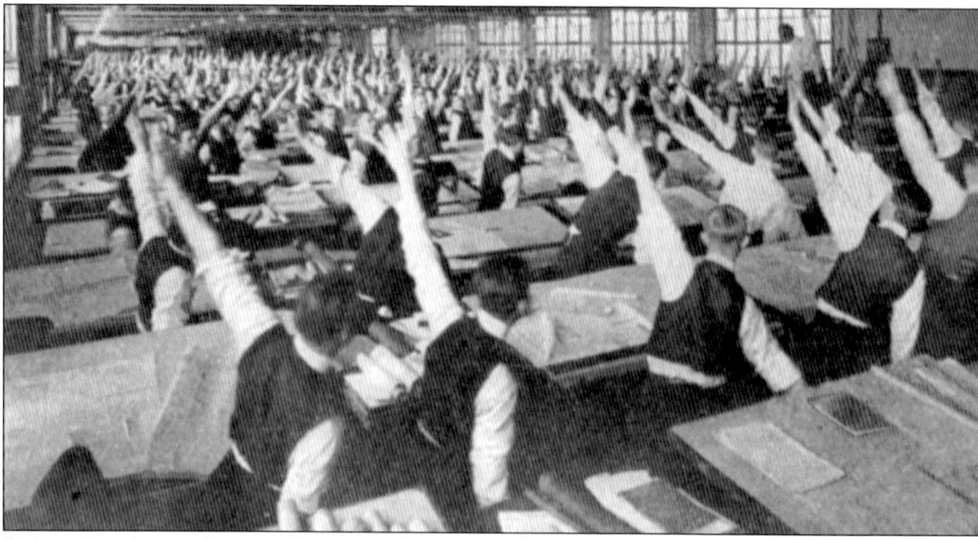

Before the advent of air conditioning, the company granted "fresh air breaks" every morning and afternoon. The windows were thrown open and the rank-and-file desk jockeys stretched their limbs. Even before the Hawthorne Studies examined how environment affected production, the company knew monotony was the enemy of efficiency. Many Hawthorne offices retained their row-upon-row configuration all through the decades before cubicles, and the rest periods remained a fixture of the daily routine. A whistle signaled the start of the break, and carts rolled down the aisles selling coffee, sweet rolls, and milk. (Both courtesy of the *Western Electric News*.)

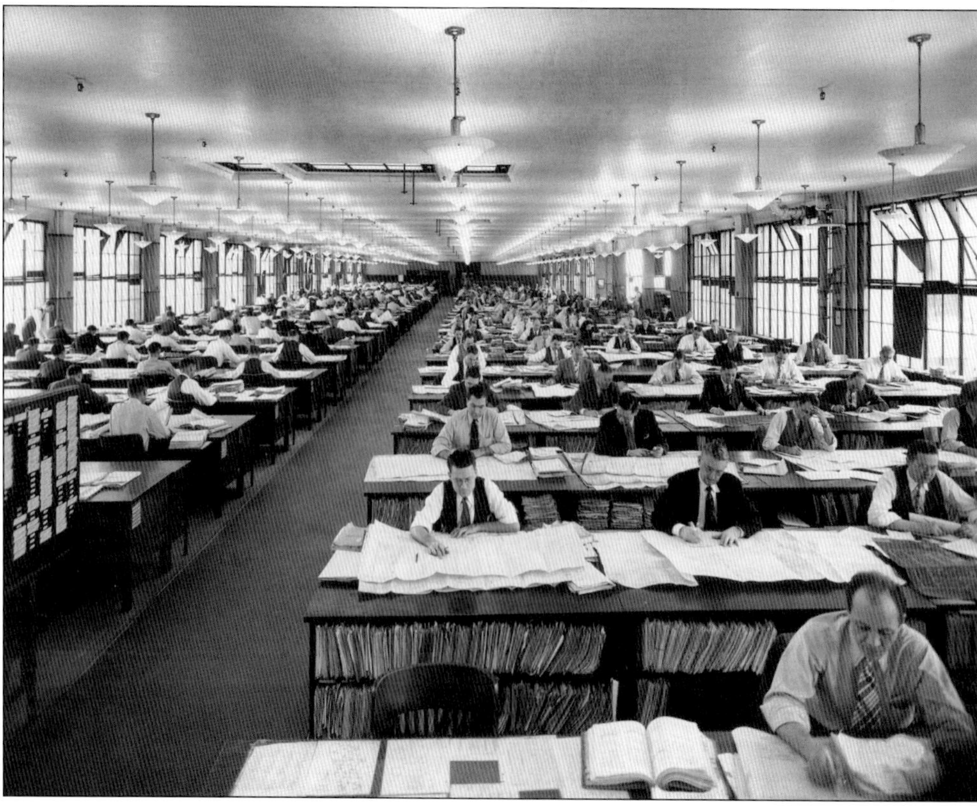

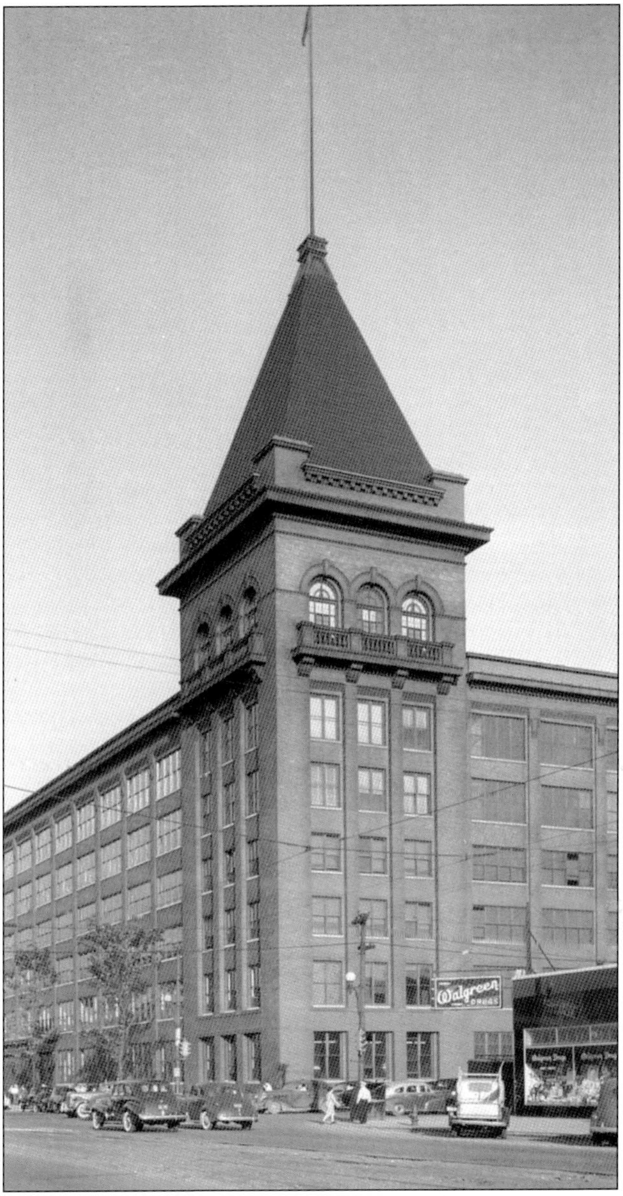

When it came to Hawthorne's architecture, form definitely followed function. Uniformly grim and utilitarian, the shops and offices were built for production, not show. Some employees jokingly referred to their workplace as the "Bohemian Bastille." However, behind these arched windows atop the landmark tower lay the exception: the ornate chambers of Hawthorne's "Mahogany Row," the home of the plant's executive offices. The Works cultivated a family atmosphere, but the company's father figures certainly enjoyed the privileges afforded by their rank. Henry Albright, the Works superintendent in the early 1920s, availed himself of all the perks at his disposal, arriving each morning via chauffeured limousine to find a private elevator waiting to lift him to his inner sanctum. Few rank-and-file Hawthorneites ever crossed this exclusive threshold. A golden anniversary or retirement party might bring an invitation to luncheon in the executive dining room, complete with prime rib and a hearty handshake from the exalted boss, but otherwise, the top floor remained off limits.

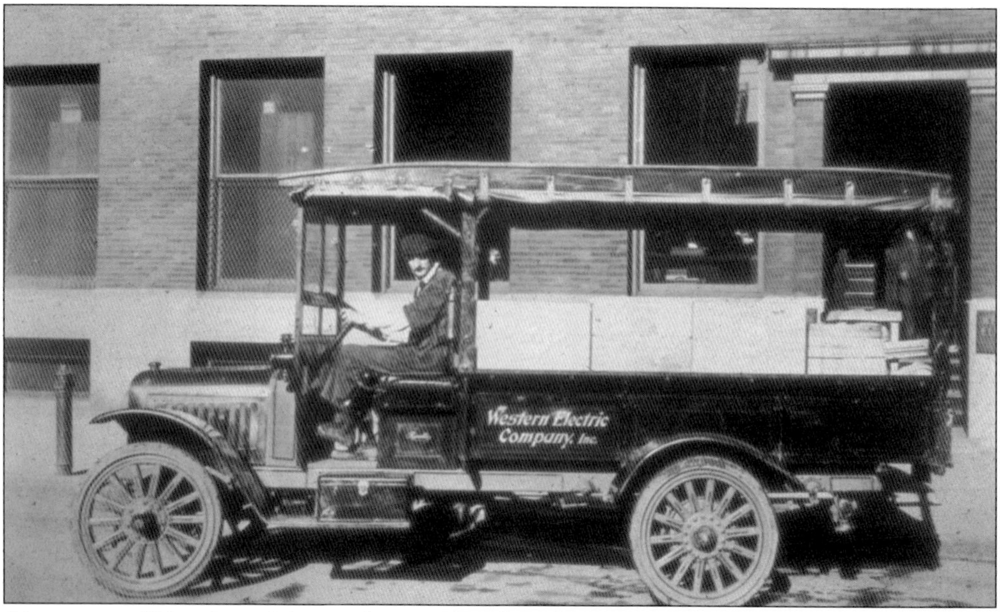

Above, one of Hawthorne's heavy-duty trucks takes a bow in 1924. The Works owned two dozen of the big haulers to transport freight around the plant. The Hawthorne motor pool included two sedans, two coupes, three roadsters, a pair of police motorcycles, and a limousine. Employees added their own traffic. About 1,200 commuters parked their automobiles around the Works each day. The automobile maintenance department repaired workers' cars and kept a mechanic on call to service stranded Hawthorne motorists. The company also offered auto insurance at reduced group rates. (Above, courtesy of *Western Electric News*; below, courtesy of the Simak collection.)

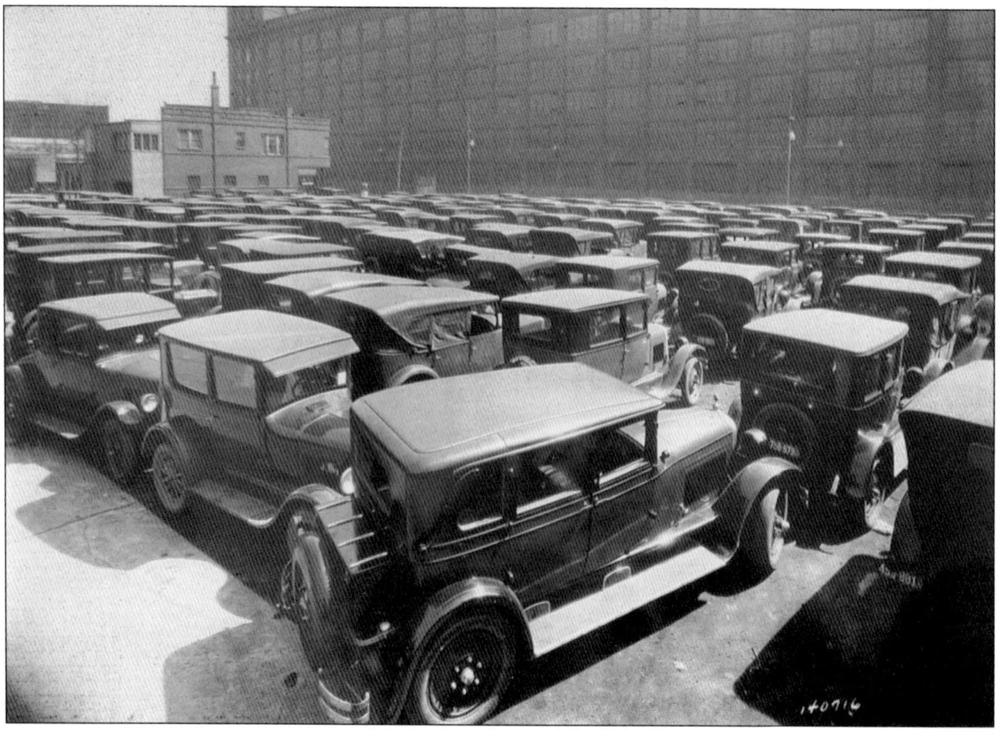

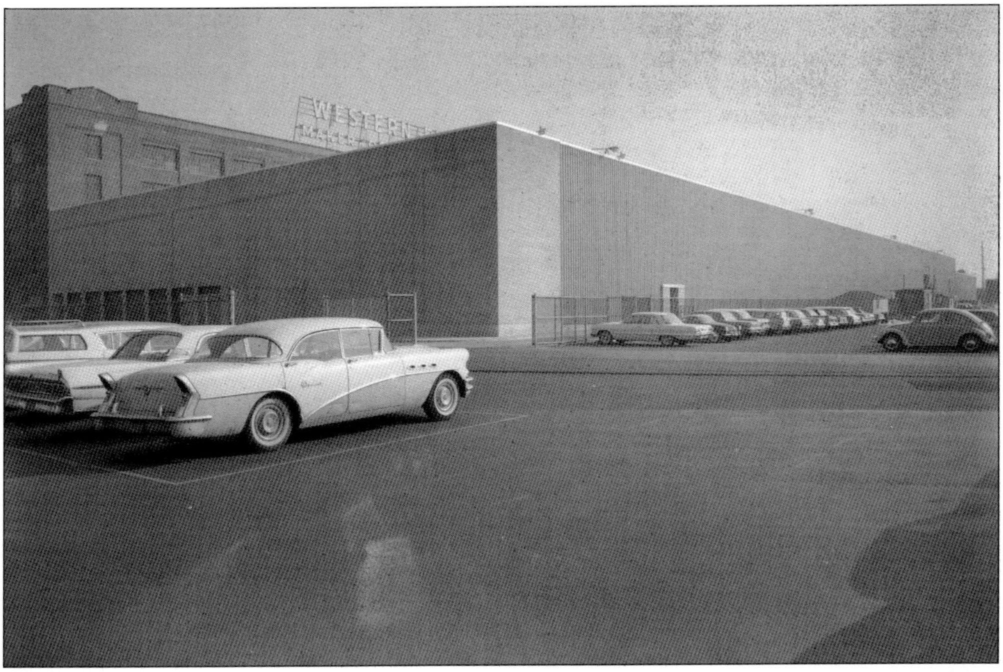

Parking a 1963 Volkswagen Beetle (right) was just as hard as finding a spot for a Ford Model A in 1929. Hawthorne's construction plans never included a multilevel employee garage, so anyone wanting a place in the company lots faced a long waiting list. As the workforce moved to distant suburbs, many employees used commuter railroads or carpooled.

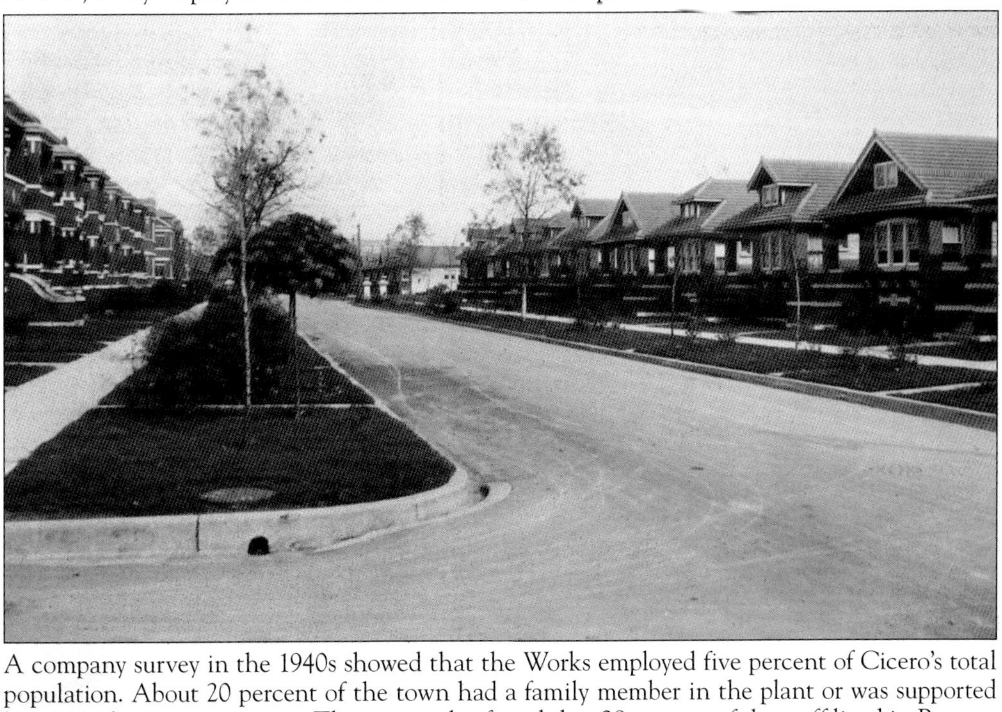

A company survey in the 1940s showed that the Works employed five percent of Cicero's total population. About 20 percent of the town had a family member in the plant or was supported by a Hawthorne wage earner. The survey also found that 28 percent of the staff lived in Berwyn and Cicero, while more than half (52 percent) lived in Chicago.

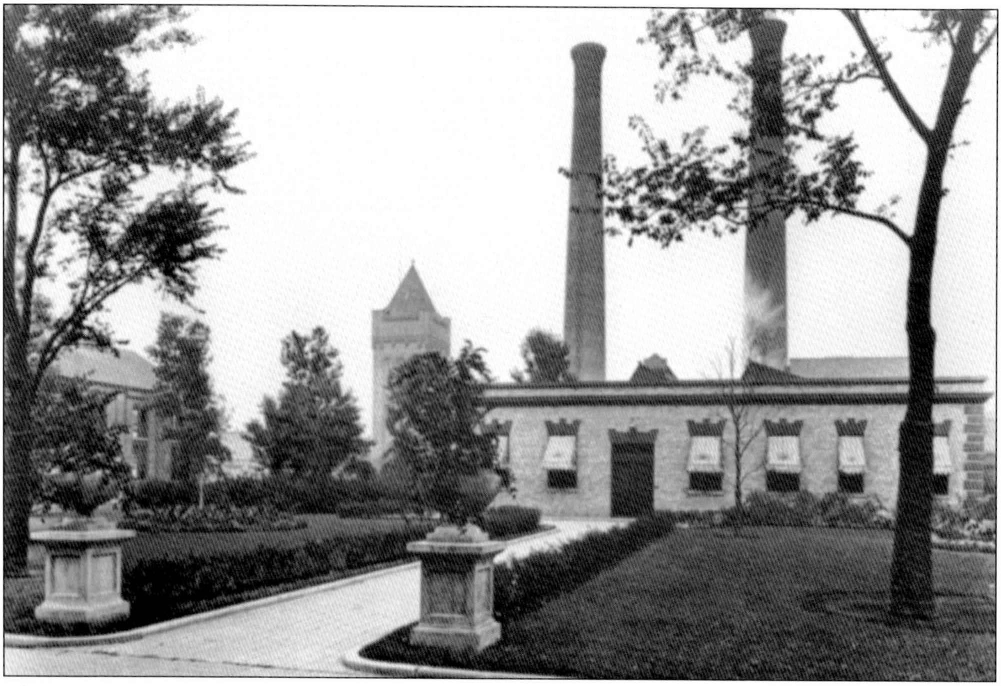

The hospital, seen above in 1916, functioned like every other department at the Works, with an eye toward quality, efficiency, and science-based methods. The professional staff (below) tended to the immediate needs of injured workers, but the on-site infirmary was much more than a mere first aid station. The staff helped prevent illness and injury by administering free inoculations, performing x-rays, conducting health screenings, and compiling health and safety statistics. On one occasion, the Hawthorne Works medical department collaborated with a Purdue University study by tracking the visual performance of workers in eye-straining jobs. The clinic maintained a full-time staff of doctors and nurses and remained up to date throughout its history.

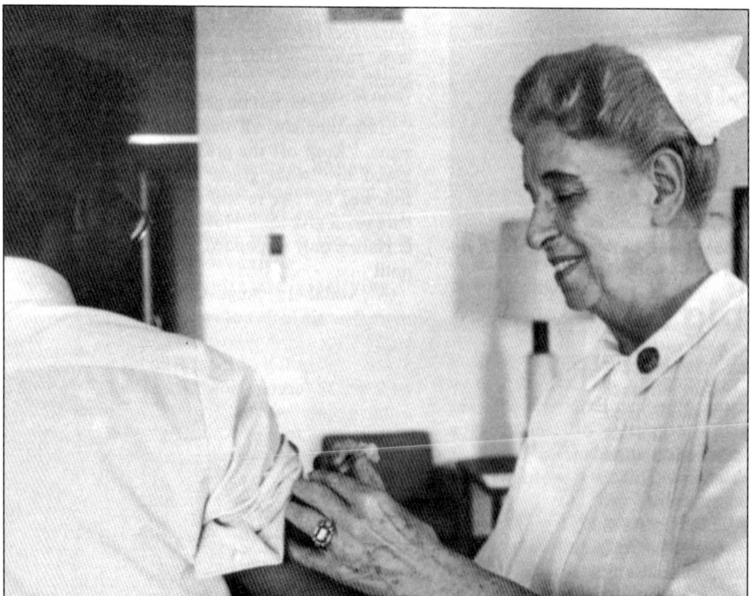

The athletic programs at Hawthorne developed world-class athletes. Cyril Coaffie, of Hawthorne's tool and machine division, ranked among the elite sprinters of the 1920s, earning a spot on two Canadian Olympic teams. At his peak, he held world records and dazzled coworkers at Hawthorne's annual employee sports meet. At the Paris Olympics in 1924, Coaffie's competitors included Britons Harold Abrahams and Eric Liddell, the subjects of the film *Chariots of Fire*. Abrahams edged out Coaffie (at right and below, far right) in a 100-meter semifinal heat on his way to the gold medal. But, in a series of post-Olympiad meets, Coaffie defeated Abrahams and outran Liddell. Coaffie returned to Hawthorne a hero, and his accomplishments earned him induction into the Canadian Sports Hall of Fame. (Both courtesy of the *Western Electric News*.)

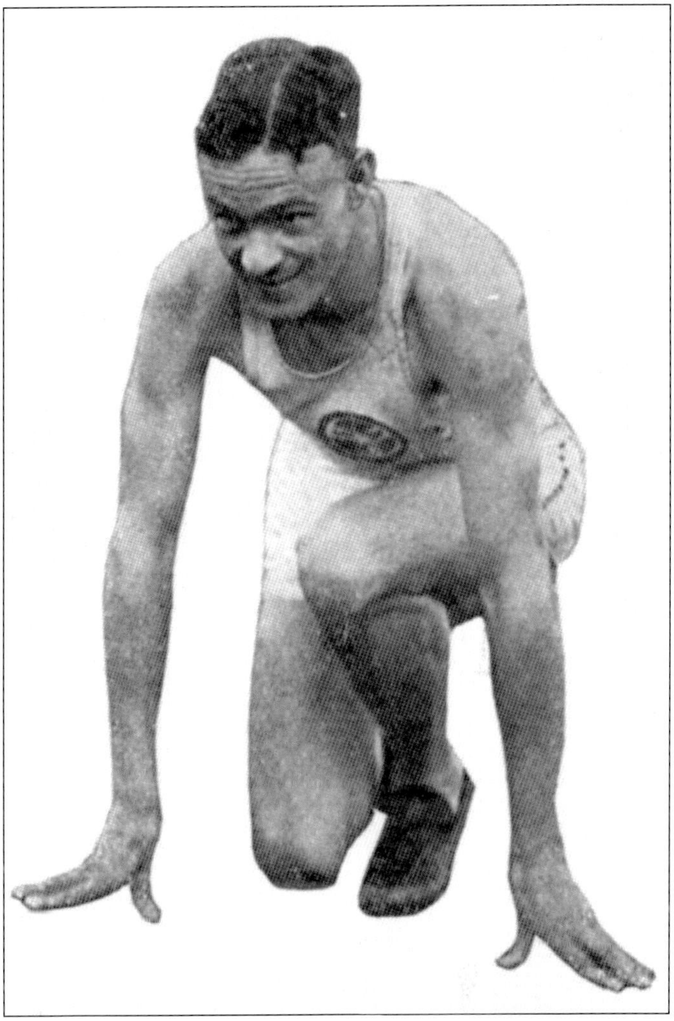

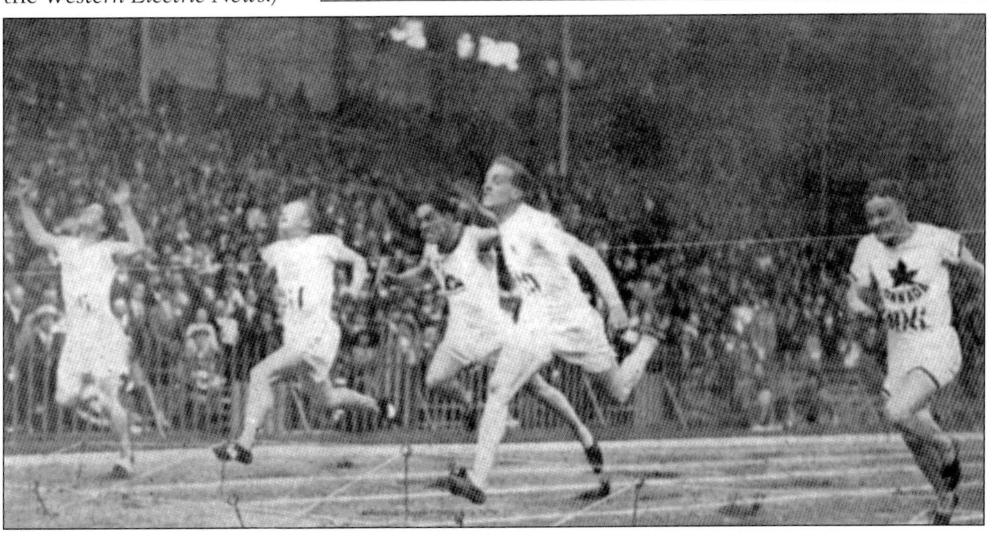

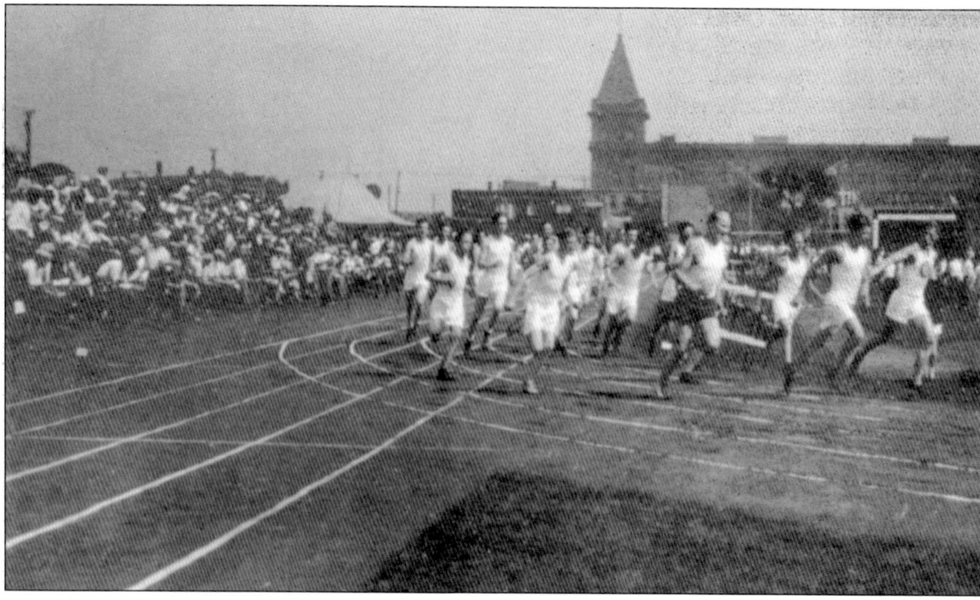

Fans cheer competitors rounding the turn at the Hawthorne Club–sponsored track meet at Memorial Field on September 18, 1926. Winners received coupons worth $7 in club store merchandise. The Albright Gymnasium was erected on this spot the following year. Just two days after this meet, the buildings visible in the center background were riddled with bullets when Al Capone's rivals attempted a drive-by assassination. (Courtesy of the *Western Electric News*.)

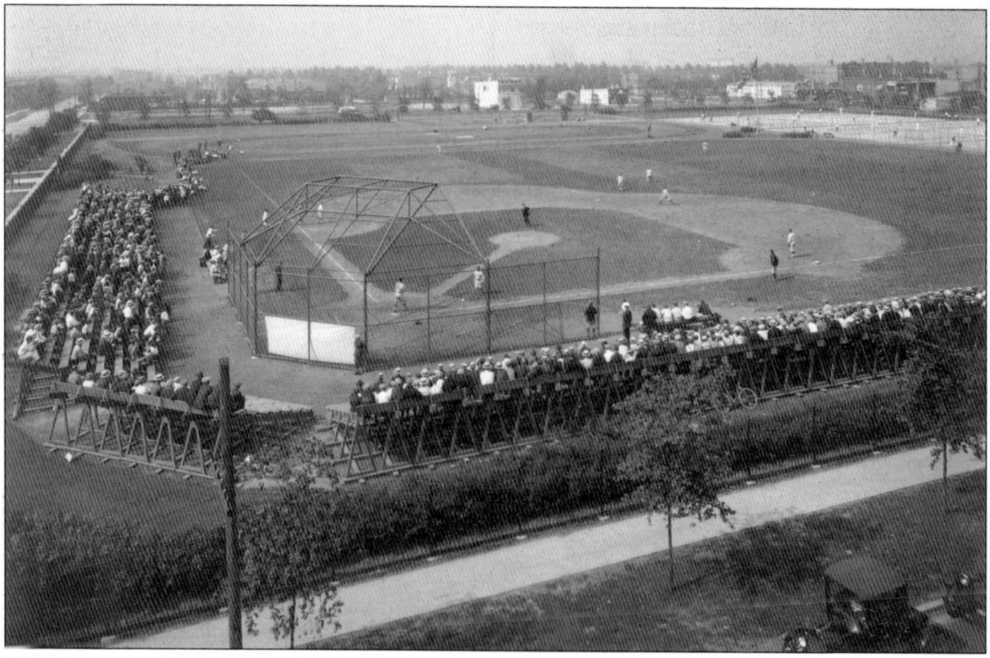

The Western Electric baseball team hosts a squad from Peoples Gas Company at Memorial Field in 1923. Lou Fiene, a former Chicago White Sox pitcher, managed the Hawthorne side to three consecutive Chicago Industrial League titles in the early 1920s. The lineup included a number of former professional, semiprofessional, and college stars, an indication of just how seriously Hawthorne took its sports. (Courtesy of the Jezek collection.)

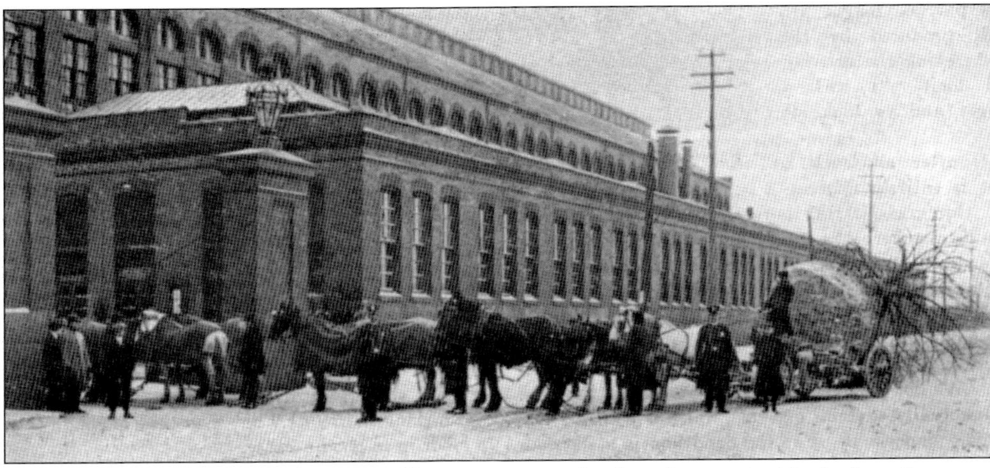

The Hawthorne Works employment office was next to the foundry, just inside the busy Entrance No. 1 on Cicero Avenue. Interviewers carefully scrutinized the endless stream of applicants, weeding out those with poor work records and "floaters," those who drifted from job to job. Turnover posed the biggest problem for the worker-hungry plant; 10 percent of new employees left within six months. (Courtesy of the *Western Electric News*.)

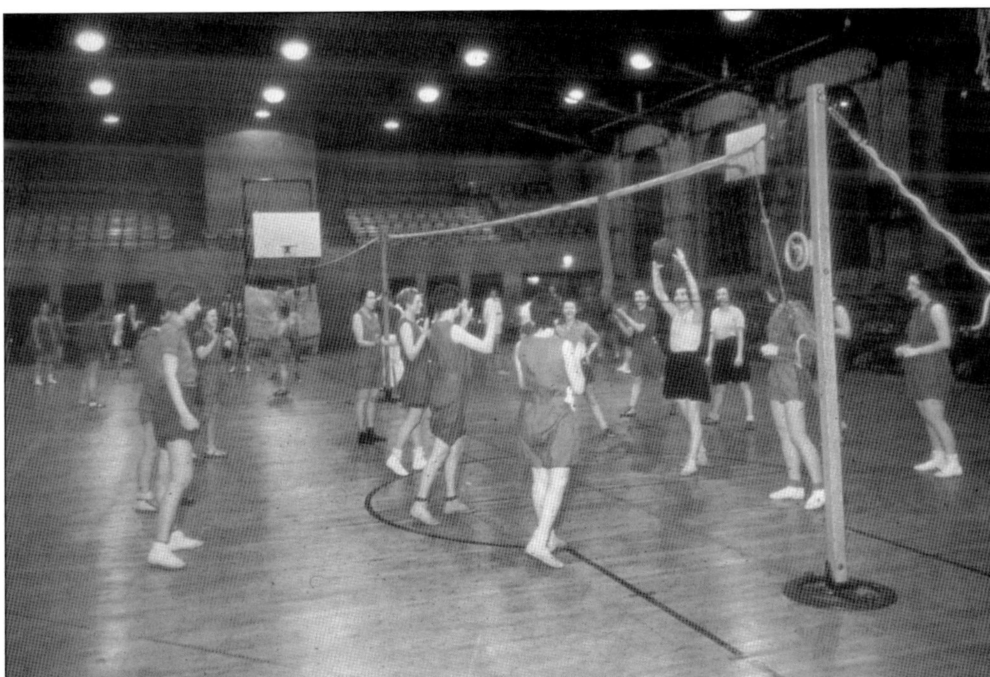

Young ladies learn the finer points of volleyball inside the new Albright Gymnasium. The Hawthorne Club encouraged athletic activities for both men and women as a healthy way to build self-confidence and community spirit. With about 8,000 active members in the 1920s, the sports program grew into the largest at any American industrial plant.

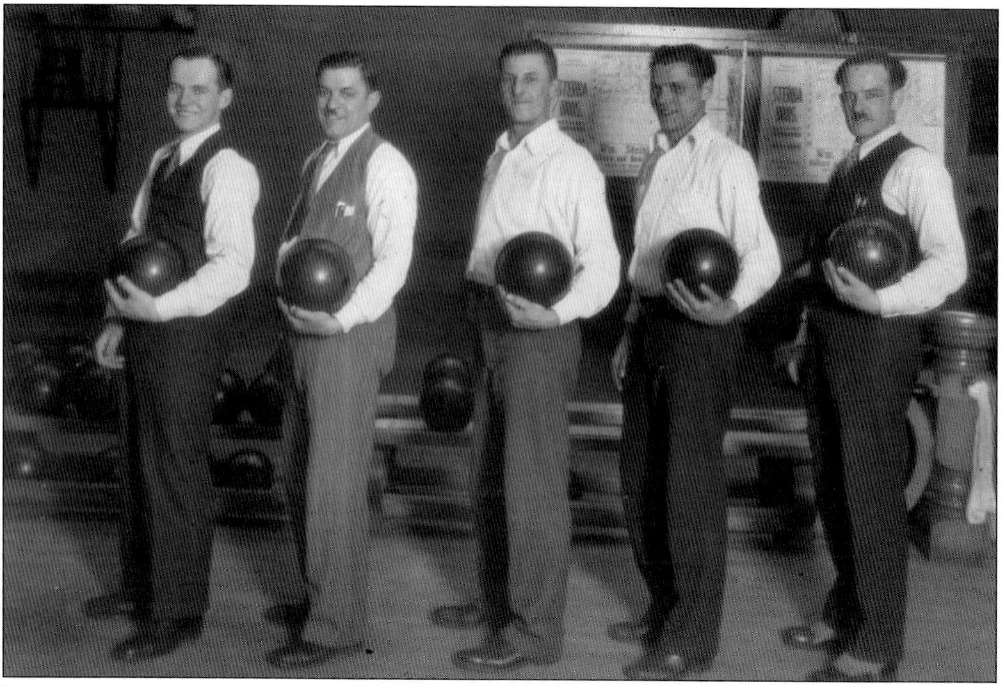

Bowling is a great way to sharpen hand-eye coordination, balance, and upper-body muscle tone, or maybe just an excuse to hang around and down some brews after work. Either way, Hawthorne folks kept the alleys busy, with 2,000 men and women participating in 32 leagues by 1940. The pastime ranked among the more popular team sports with the Works family, along with softball and basketball.

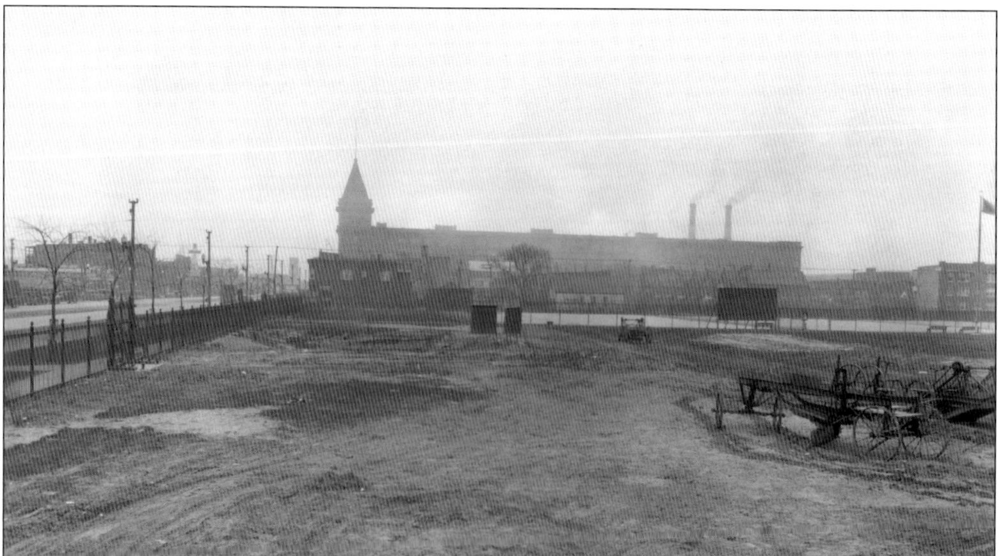

Expansion in the 1920s robbed the Works of recreation space. To replace the lost athletic grounds, the company looked two blocks west on Twenty-second Street. A mere 8,000 tons of soil turned farmland into the impressive Memorial Field, dedicated in 1921. Six years later, a portion of the site was cleared again to make way for the Albright Gymnasium.

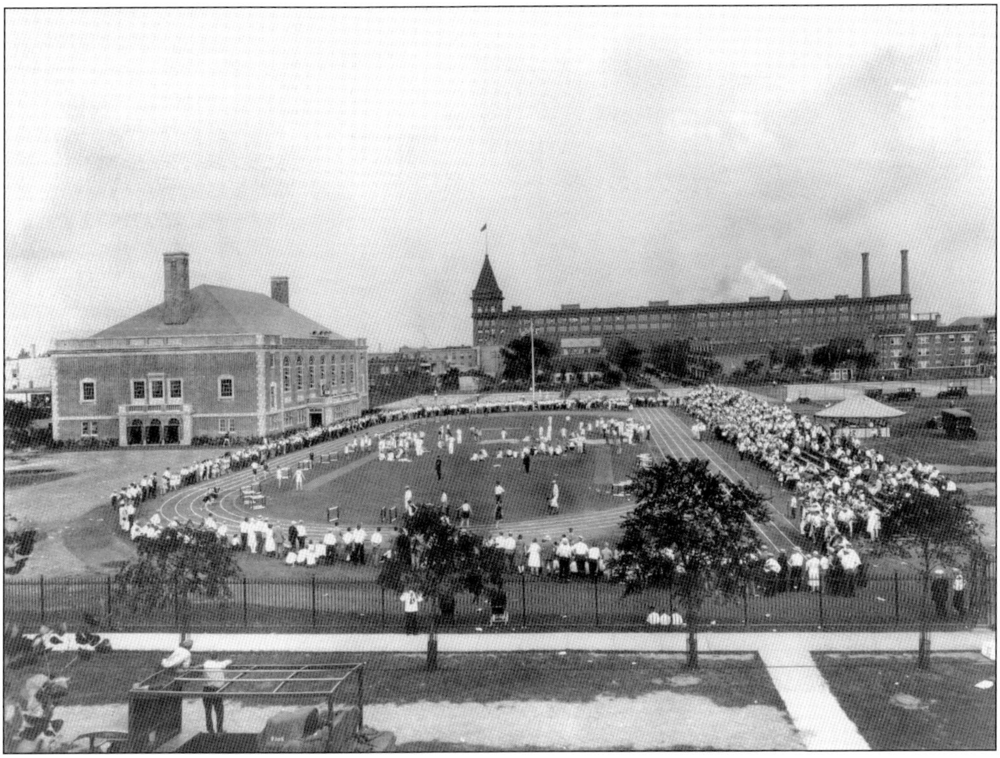

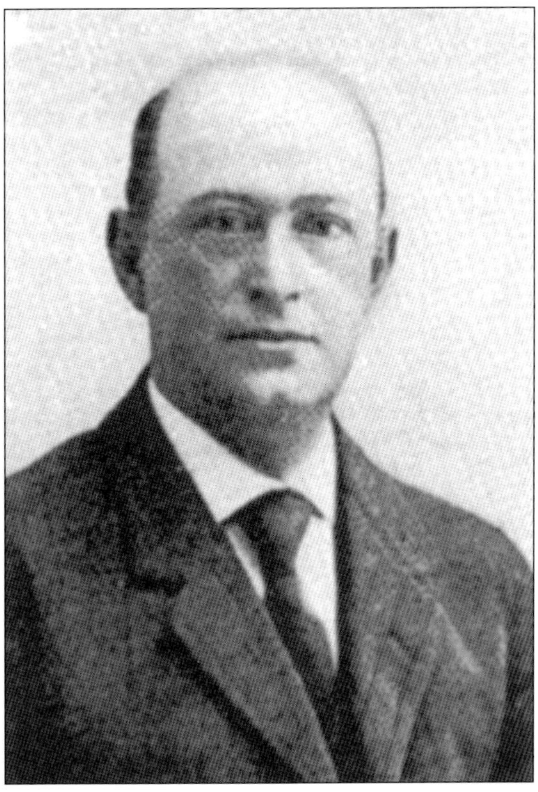

The Albright Gymnasium (above) opened in 1927. The building was named in honor of Henry F. Albright (right), the Works superintendent from 1908 to 1926. Situated on a 10-acre parcel of land, the gym served as a civic center for the Works family, hosting concerts, club exhibitions, athletic events, and even equestrian performances. After Hawthorne's closure in the 1980s, ownership of the facility passed among the local school district, the park district, and the Town of Cicero. Upkeep proved costly, and the once-grand social center fell into disrepair. Finally, in 2006, the town demolished the old gym and replaced it with a new town center complex that opened in 2008. (Above, courtesy of AT&T Archives; right, courtesy of the *Western Electric News*.)

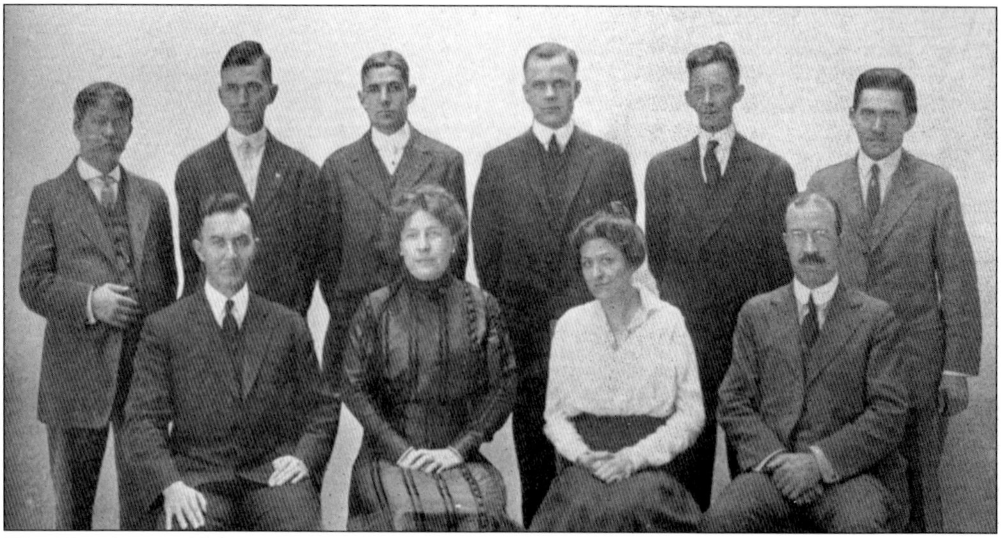

The Hawthorne Club evening school faculty pose for a 1915 portrait. The club started its first evening classes in the fall of 1913. Most employees lacked anything more than a basic formal education and joined eagerly. Within two years, enrollment reached 710 students. Courses included practical mathematics, mechanical drawing, manufacturing principles, and English. (Courtesy of the *Western Electric News*.)

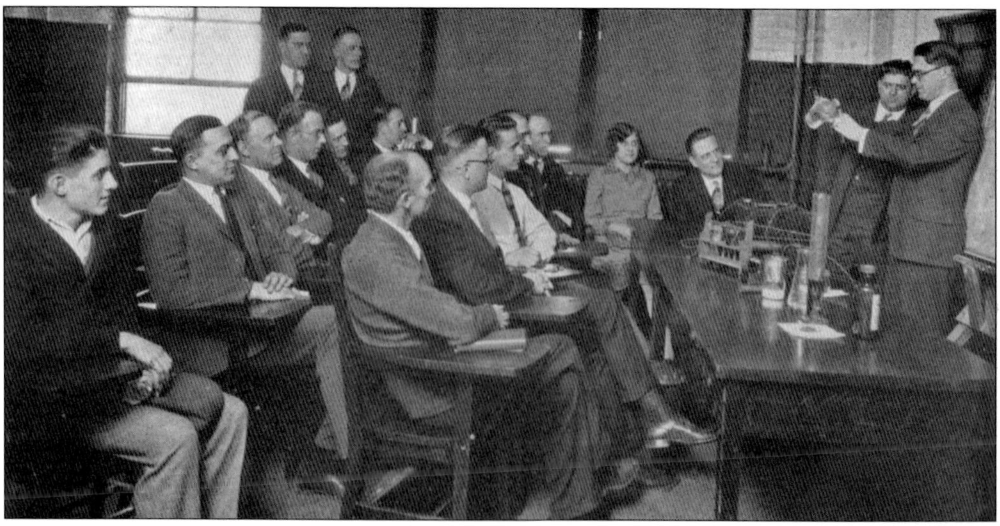

By 1927, the Hawthorne evening school graduated 1,350 students and enrolled 3,736. Certificates were awarded to those who completed the original core curriculum courses. By its 14th year, the school had added a dozen additional subjects, including chemistry (seen here), blueprint reading, and radio principles. All of the courses taught skills applicable to Hawthorne's workshops.

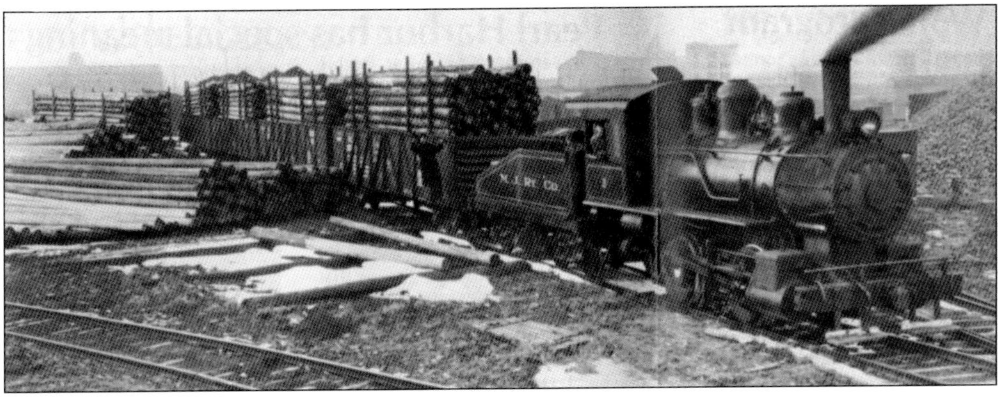

The Manufacturers' Junction Railroad, founded in 1903 and owned by Western Electric, ran on 13 miles of track connecting the Works to other short-line railways, hauling in tons of raw materials and carting away more tons of scrap. At its peak in the 1920s, the railroad employed 123 crewmen and owned four steam locomotives, which were eventually replaced by diesel-powered engines in 1947. The 1925 photograph above shows one of the old steamers hauling away carloads of telephone poles, brought to Hawthorne to be treated with preservative. Below, the Manufacturers' Junction was still rolling past the Works in 1973. The rail line marked the boundary between Cicero and Chicago. (Both courtesy of the *Hawthorne Microphone*.)

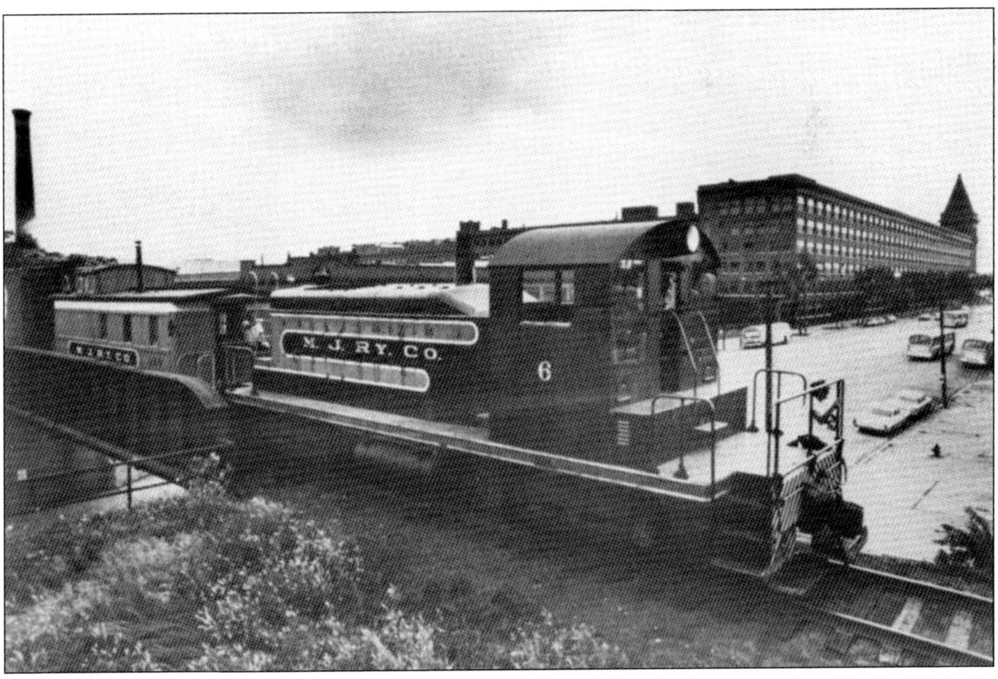

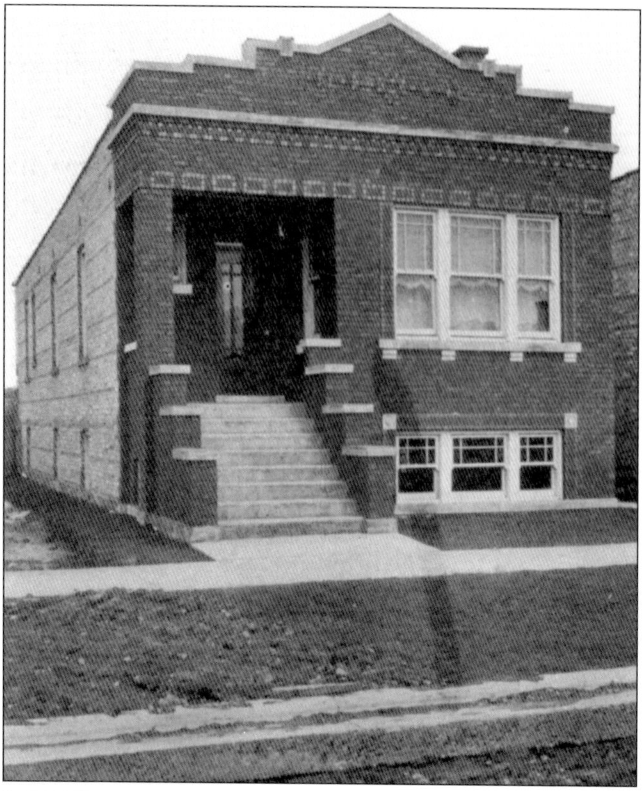

World War I interrupted civilian home construction and tightened the housing market. In response, the Hawthorne Club Building & Loan Association was created, funded by employees' payroll deductions. Just three years after its opening in 1920, the group was financing the construction of a dozen homes each month, like the sturdy Cicero bungalows seen here. Thousands of thrifty Hawthorne staff joined the association for its savings plan and built up reserves for a rainy day that appeared unlikely during the booming 1920s. By 1929, the Hawthorne Club Building & Loan Association had increased its capitalization to $20 million, making it the largest such organization in the country. (Both courtesy of the *Western Electric News*.)

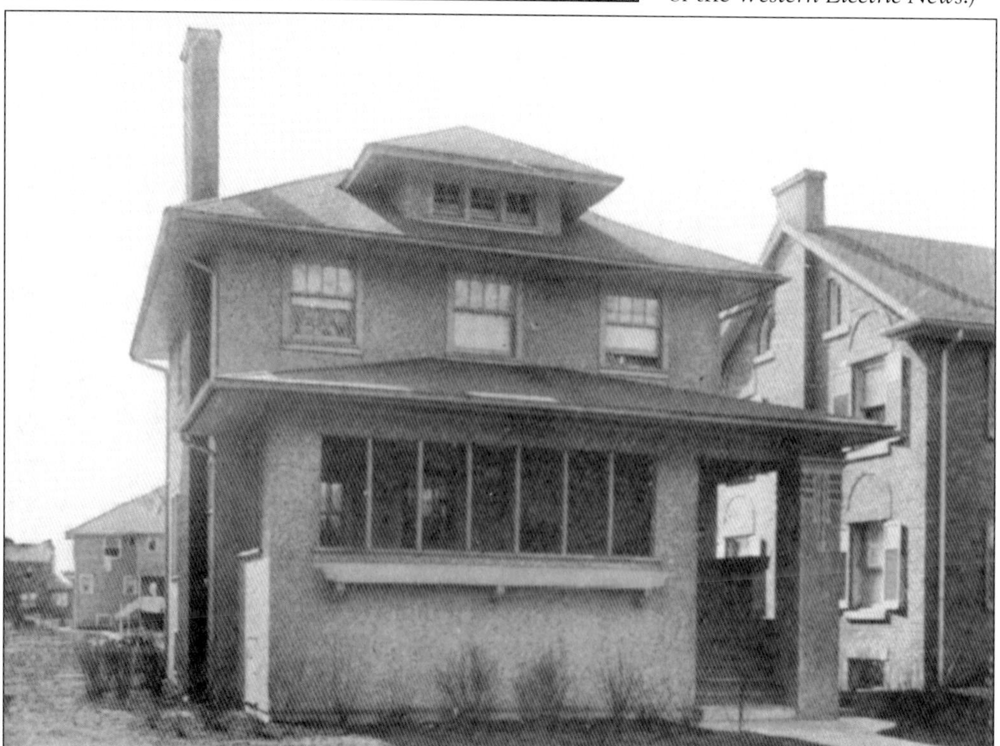

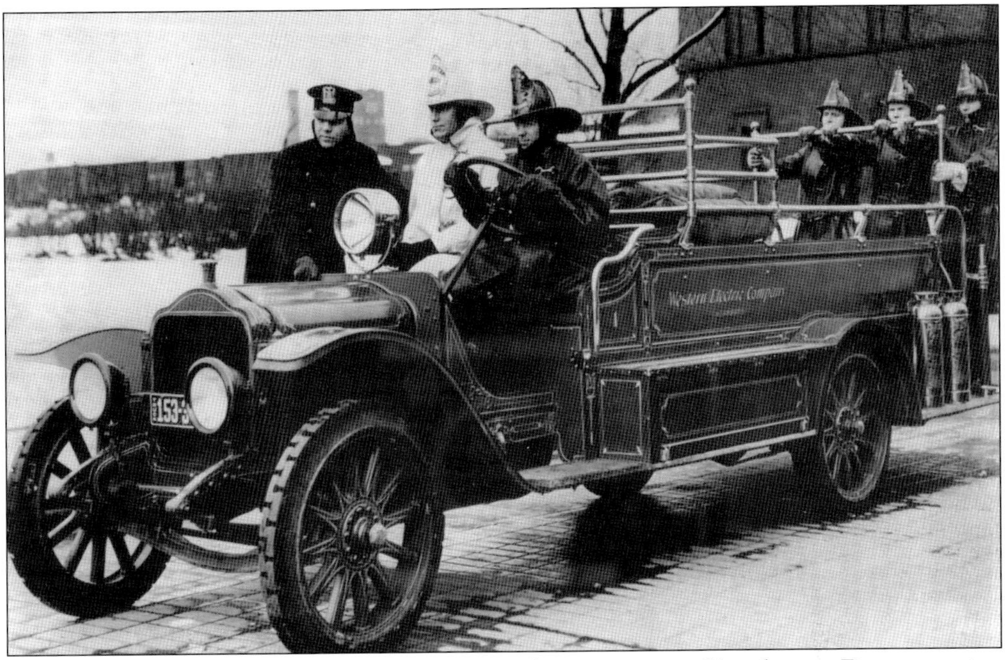

The water tower and firehouse predated every other structure at Hawthorne. Fire prevention mattered at the Works, and every building design incorporated fire doors and enclosed stairways. Fire department equipment evolved over the years. The 1925 fire truck above conducted constant drills, while the 17-man crew maintained the many hydrants, sprinklers, and alarm boxes around the plant. By 1979, the Works' three-shift, 75-man team operated from the brand-new Ford truck seen below. While 11 miles of water mains and 99 hydrants stood ready, prevention remained the watchword. Fire captains reported hazards and employees practiced evacuations. The Works reported only five fires with over $100 damage in the last half of the 1970s. (Both courtesy of the *Hawthorne Microphone*.)

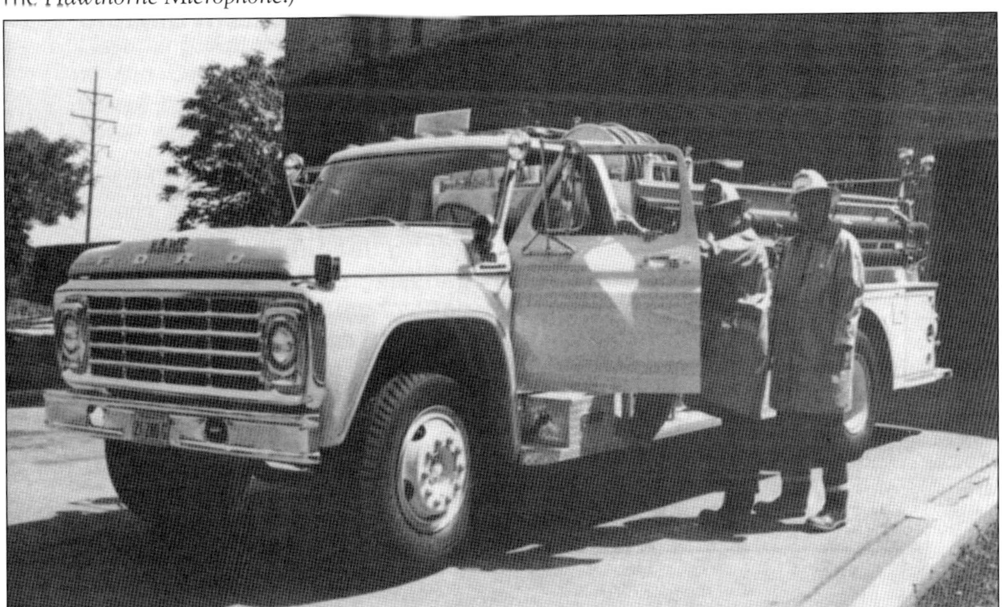

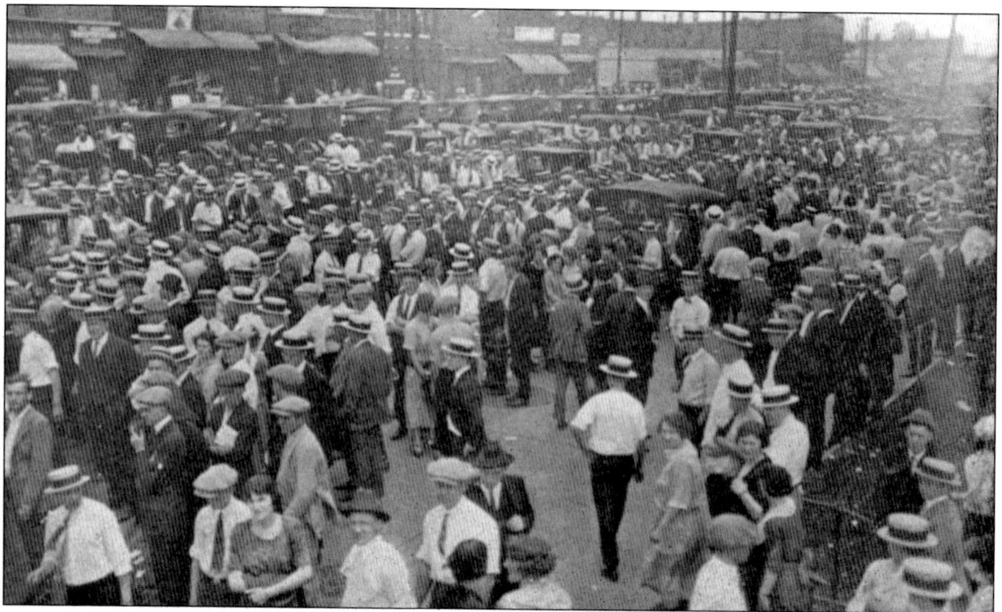

A happy crowd fills Twenty-second Street for the Hawthorne Club candidates' parade. The hopefuls ran their campaigns like politicians, with slogans, posters, and speeches. Formed as the Hawthorne Men's Club in 1911, the group reorganized four years later as the Hawthorne Club, admitting women as members and officers. The organization ran the plant's social, athletic, financial, and educational activities. (Courtesy of the *Western Electric News*.)

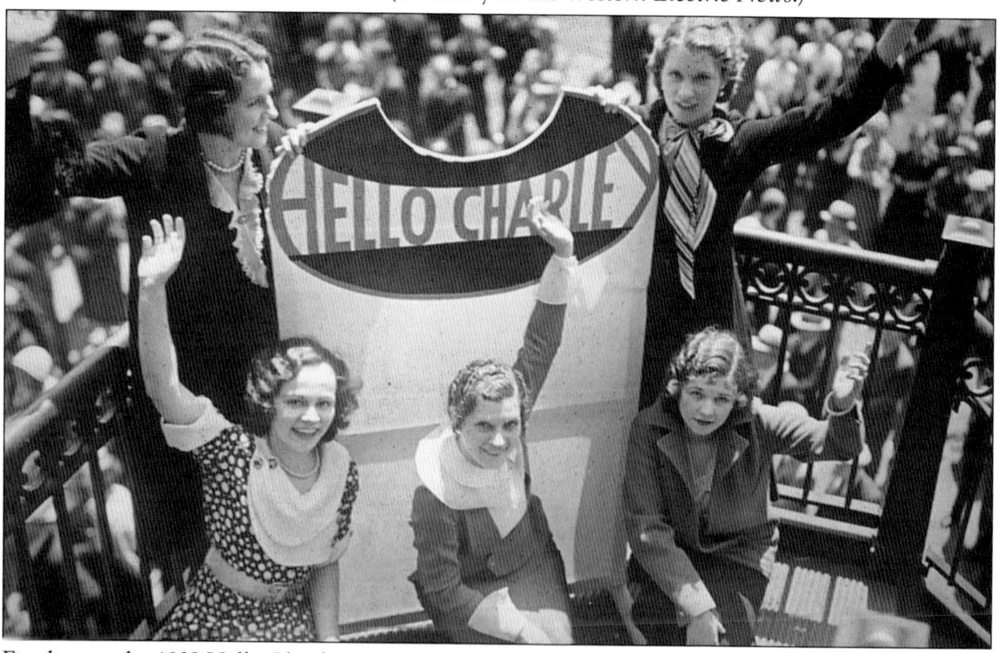

Finalists in the 1932 Hello Charley Girl contest smile for the photographer. Alma Klaud (standing, left) took the honors that year, but she was the last to hold the crown until 1935. Hard times and a decimated, dispirited membership forced the Hawthorne Club to halt the contest. The Depression reached its nadir in 1933, when a relatively scant workforce of 6,000 clung to their Hawthorne jobs.

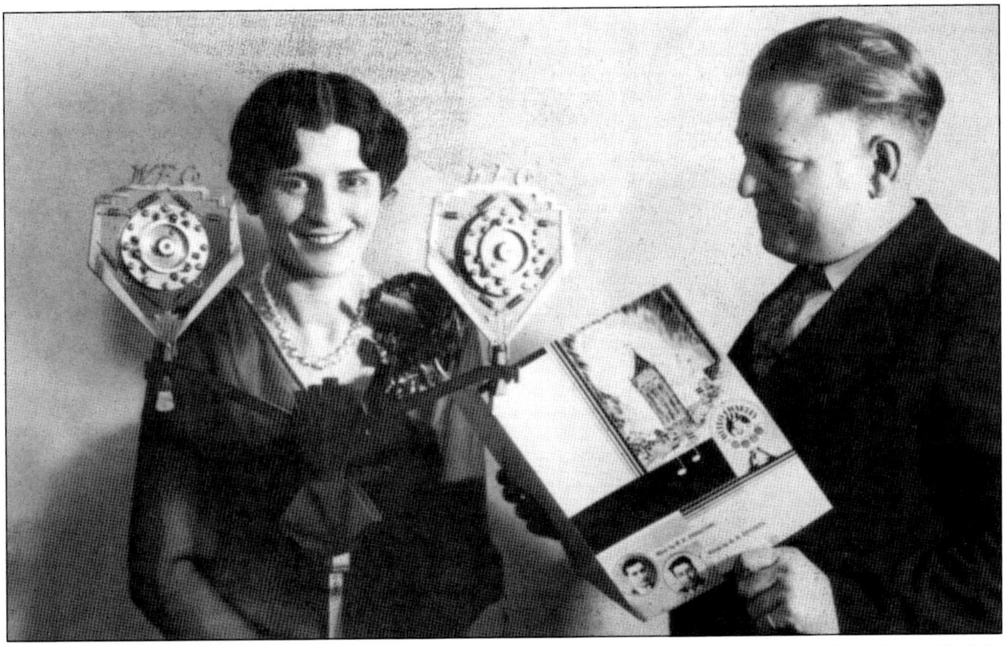

Above, Jean O'Rourke, the winner of the inaugural Hello Charley Girl crown in 1930, poses with lyricist and Hawthorne employee R.H. Epstein. Along with coworker W.J. Ferguson, Epstein penned the words to a song honoring the new beauty queen. The tune went: "Let's stand right up and loudly sing / And let our smiles and laughter ring / As we shout the Charley way." It did not catch on, and the song was forgotten until the sheet music was donated to the Hawthorne Works Museum. The name of the contest originated with a postcard mailed to the Works addressed to "Charley at Hawthorne." The card found its way to the correct recipient, and, from then on, all Hawthorne employees were nicknamed Charley. Winners were pictured on bumper stickers and luggage tags distributed to Hawthorne workers.

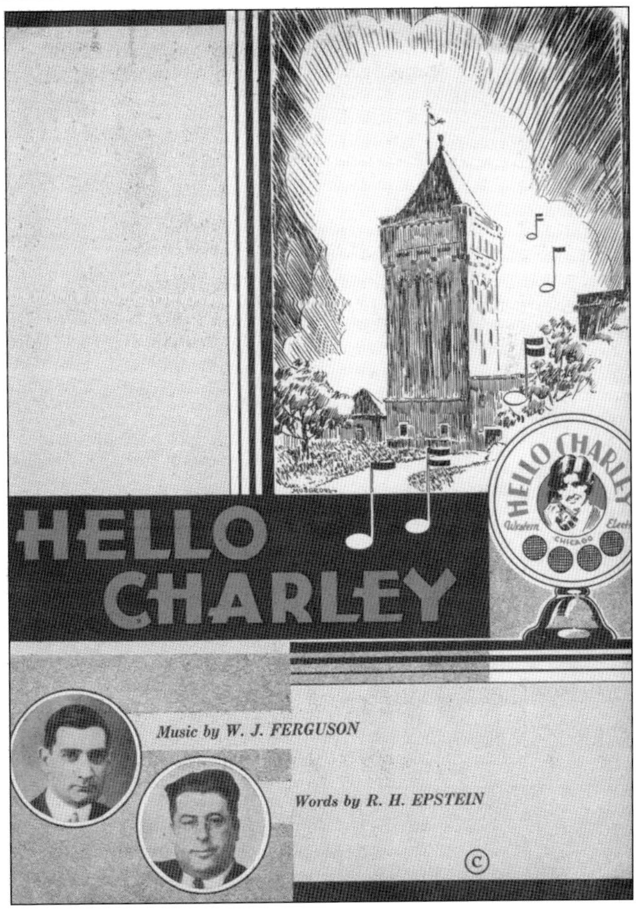

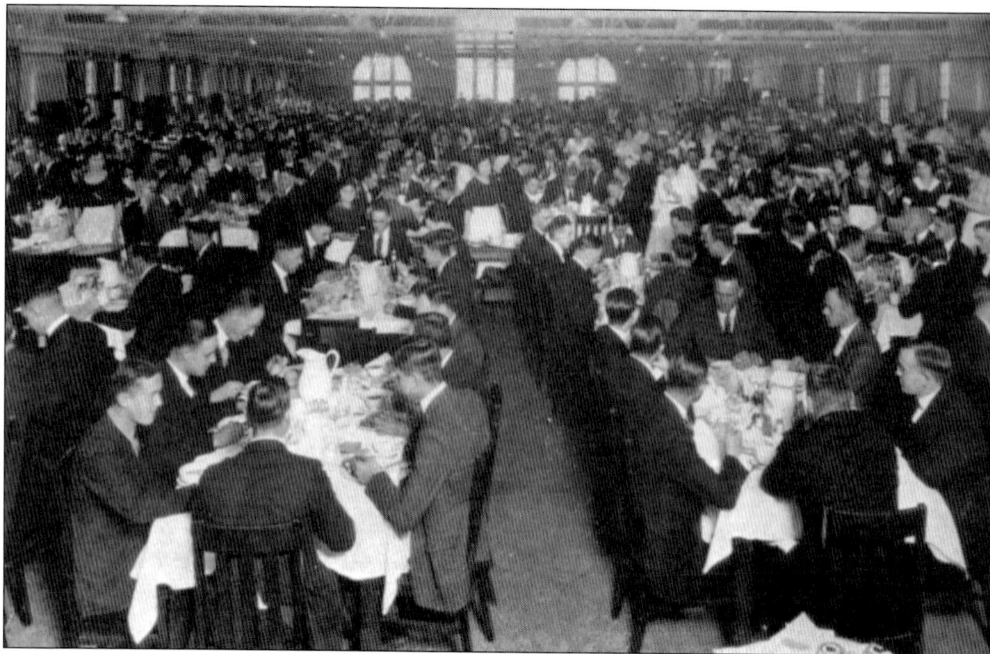

The nation's telephone makers worked up an appetite, and, every day for 75 years, the Works fed a horde of hungry Hawthornites. In the 1920s, the nonprofit restaurant served 3,000 lunches a day. During the hectic days of World War II, a kitchen staff of 420 prepared 1,000 meals an hour and 180,000 per week in 10 separate cafeterias. The grocery list for one year in the 1950s included 220,000 pounds each of beef and potatoes, 88,000 pounds of pork, 36,000 pounds of lettuce, and 3.7 million cups of coffee. Two staff dietitians organized the daily menu. The last new cafeteria (below) opened in the central manufacturing buildings in 1979. Smaller and more sedate, the comfortable eatery still served economical, nutritious meals. (Above, courtesy of *Western Electric News*; below, courtesy of the *Hawthorne Microphone*.)

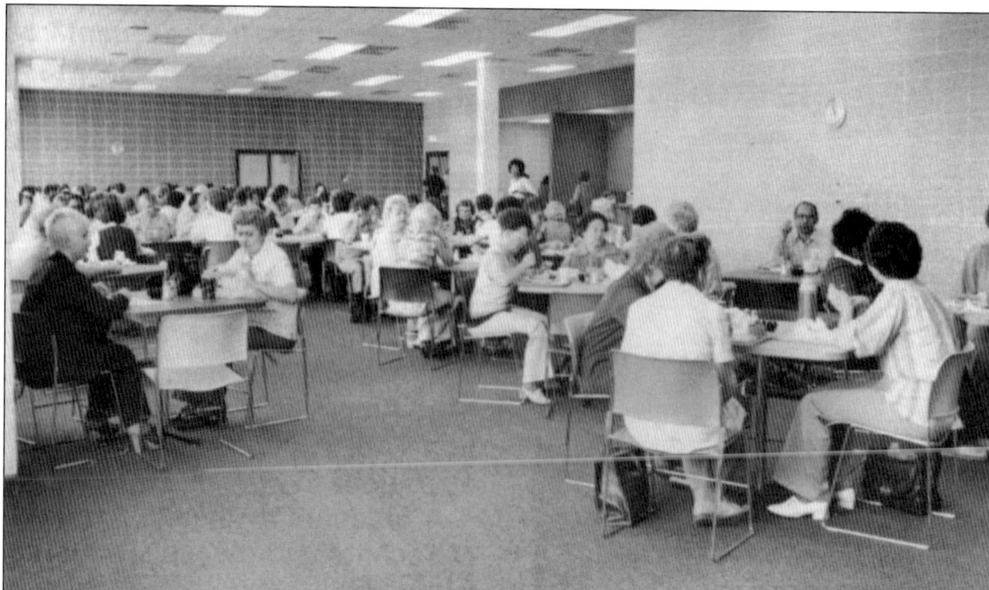

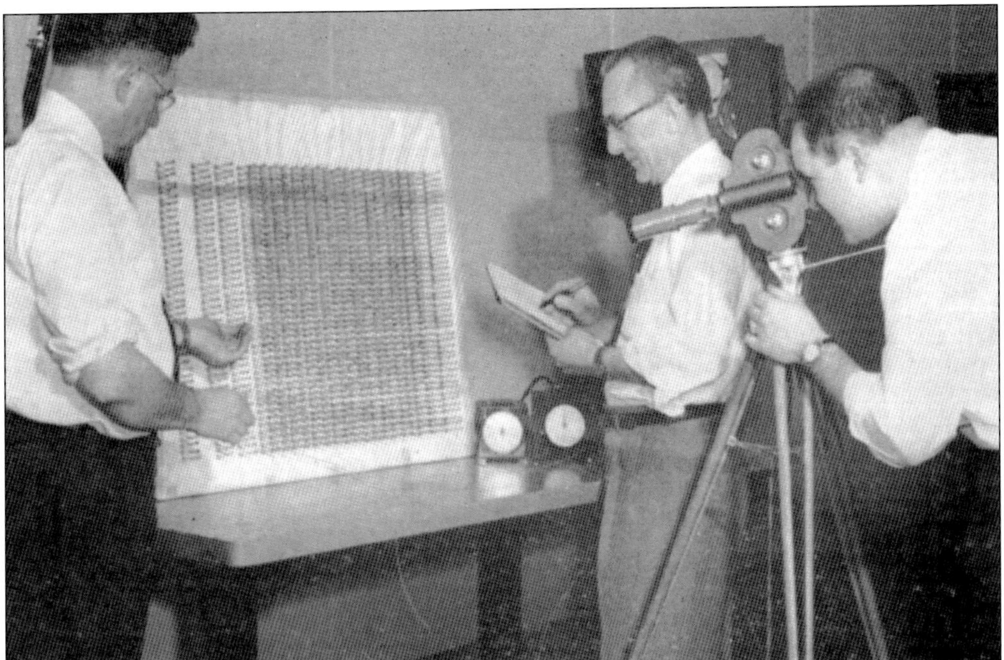

Always keen on statistics, the Hawthorne Works compiled data to support its manufacturing methods. In 1959, these three industrial engineers employed a movie camera and electric timers to test the limits of human memory while wiring complicated switchboard equipment. Engineering students from around the world toured Hawthorne for a look at the most advanced production techniques. (Courtesy of the *Hawthorne Microphone*.)

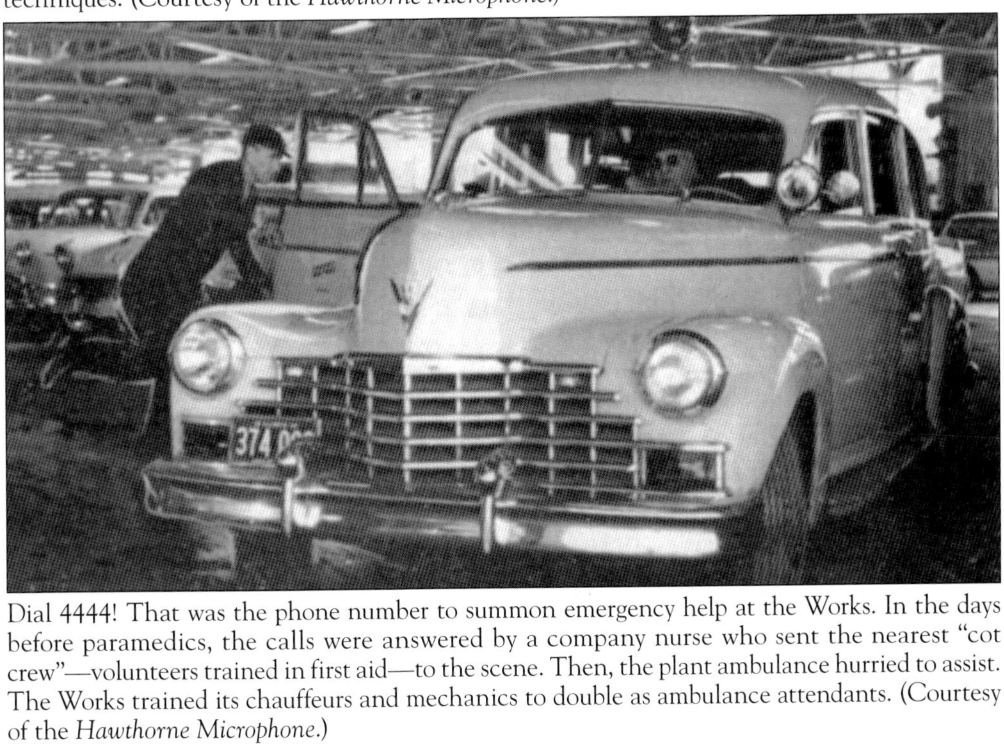

Dial 4444! That was the phone number to summon emergency help at the Works. In the days before paramedics, the calls were answered by a company nurse who sent the nearest "cot crew"—volunteers trained in first aid—to the scene. Then, the plant ambulance hurried to assist. The Works trained its chauffeurs and mechanics to double as ambulance attendants. (Courtesy of the *Hawthorne Microphone*.)

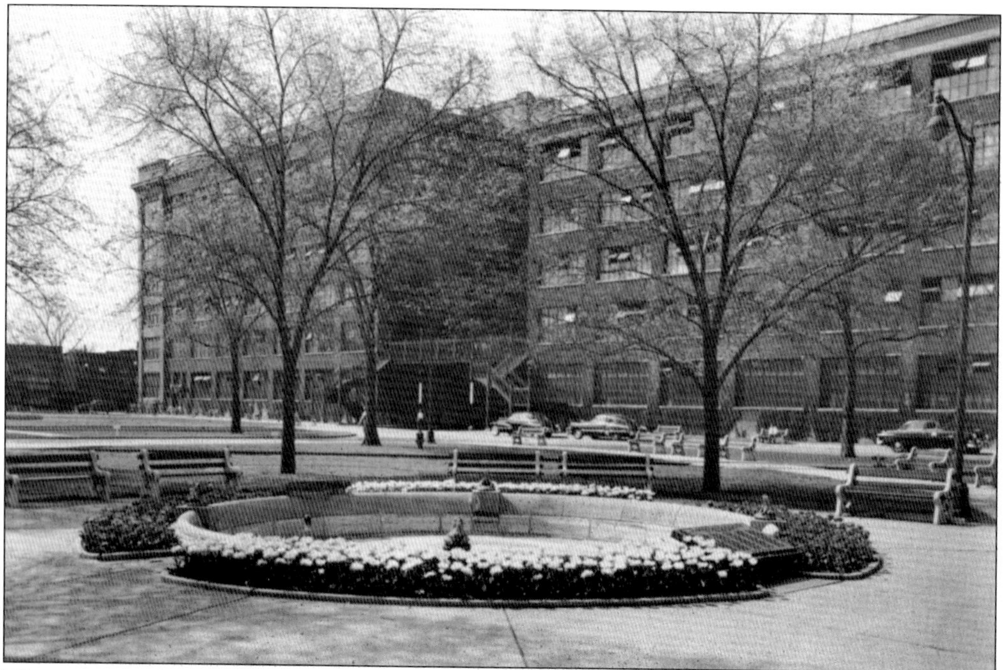

These views of Hawthorne's courtyard in the 1950s reflect the popular image of that decade: tranquil and orderly. But, then as now, people faced difficulties on the job and in their personal lives. The medical department at Hawthorne acknowledged this fact and established a confidential alcoholism treatment program well before society at large came to regard substance abuse and addiction as medically treatable conditions. Instead of punishment, the company offered medical intervention and only resorted to disciplinary action when an employee refused treatment. By the 1970s, Hawthorne had formed a labor-management committee to oversee alcoholism education and referrals. Just over 100 employees belonged to the plant's Alcoholics Anonymous group. The health insurance plan paid for up to four weeks of inpatient care for employees with more than six months service.

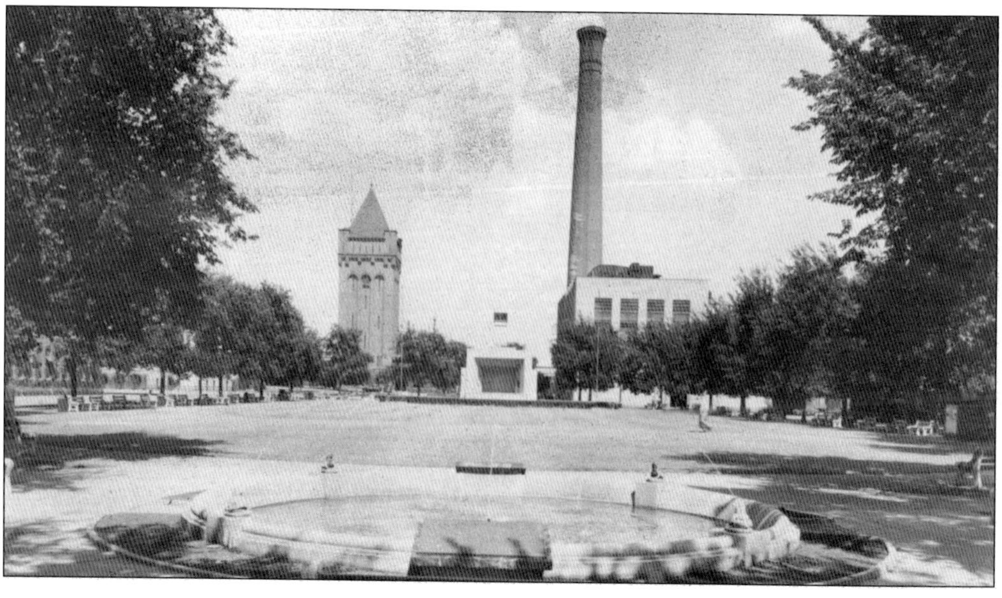

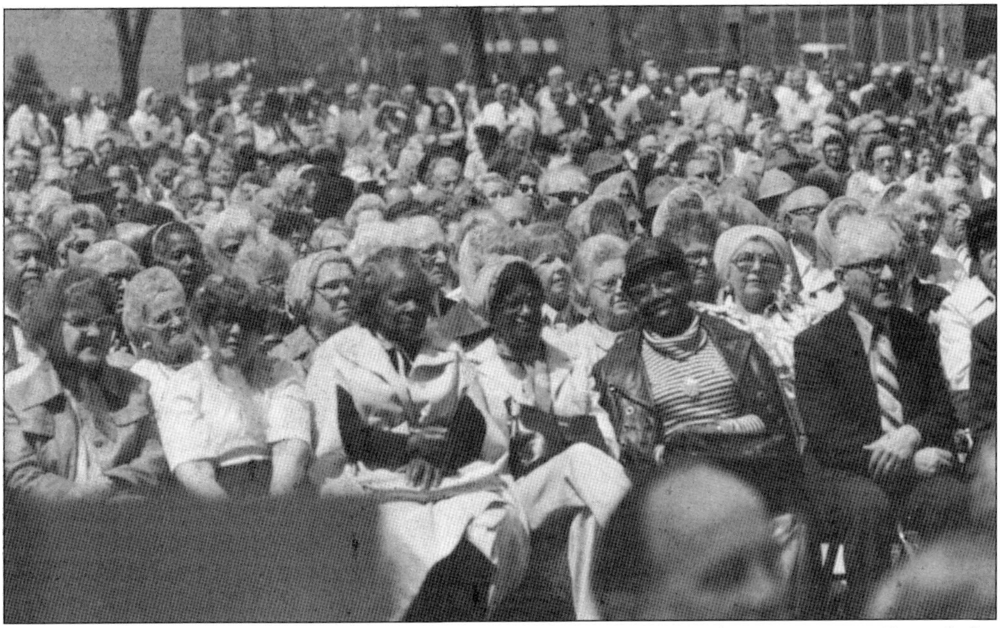

By the time Hawthorne celebrated its 75th anniversary in 1978, these retirees reflected the workforce's racial diversity. Such was not always the case. Prior to World War II, the Works hired few African Americans, in part to keep them from seeking homes in white neighborhoods. In 1930, out of 66,000 residents, Cicero had only five African Americans. Western Electric's personnel policy also discouraged hiring men over 35 years old or women over 30. Practices changed during World War II, when Executive Order 8802 required integrated hiring on government-contract jobs. After the war, an increasing number of African Americans found jobs, education, and promotion at the Hawthorne Works. However, a racially integrated workplace did not lead to an integrated community. As late as 1980, African Americans still made up only one percent of Cicero's population. (Both courtesy of the *Hawthorne Microphone*.)

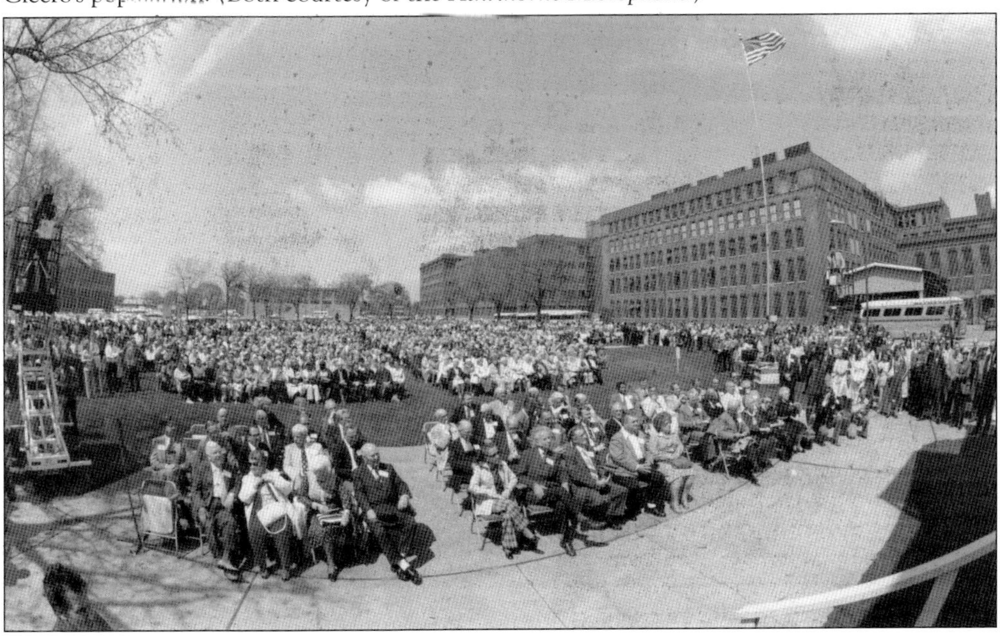

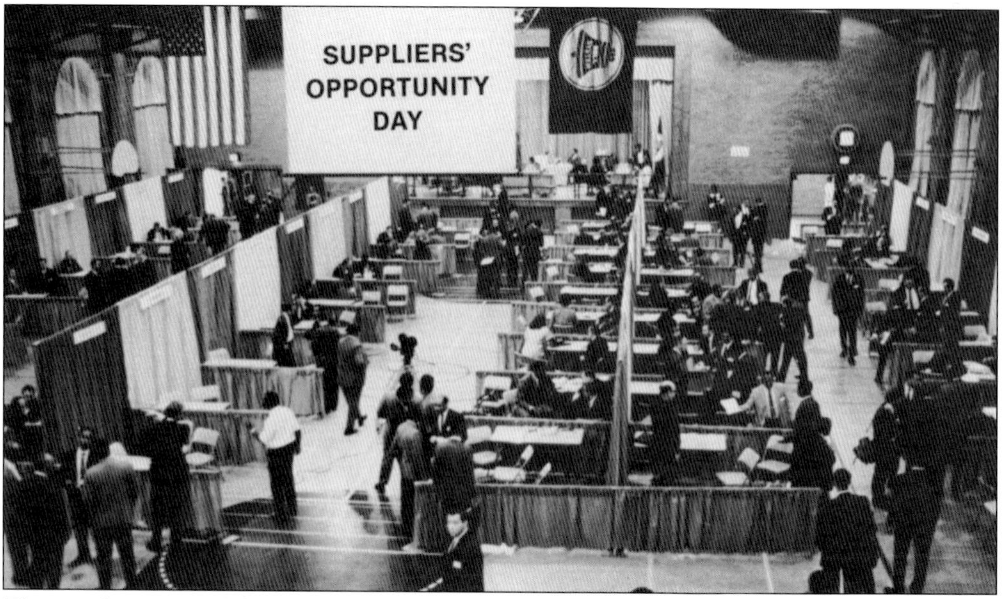

The social activism of the 1960s forced corporate America to address calls for increased minority business opportunities and inclusion in the workplace. AT&T and the Bell System companies responded by applying personnel management methods based on the Human Relations theory, which stressed sensitivity to workers' concerns and offered counseling and education as remedies. The Bell System initiated minority hiring and training plans and designed courses to address fears and misconceptions of workers interacting for the first time with members of another race. In September 1968, Hawthorne hosted the Suppliers' Opportunity Day conference at the Albright Gymnasium for minority small-business owners and purchasing agents for 50 large corporations to discuss forming supplier relationships. Co-sponsored by Western Electric and the Chicago Urban League, the conference grew into the annual Chicago Business Opportunity Fair. (Both courtesy of the *Western Electric News*.)

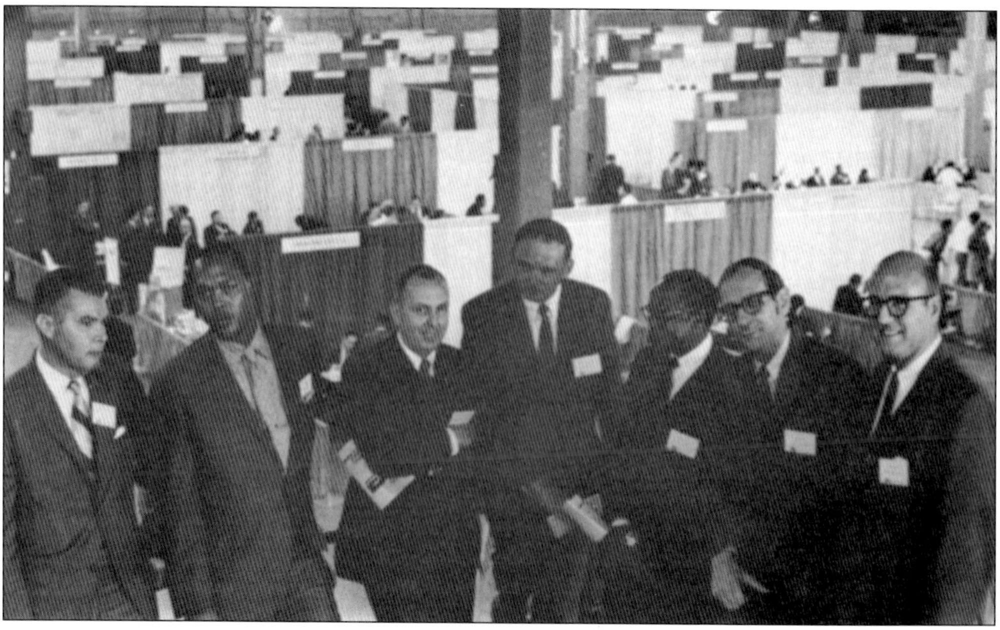

Seven

World War II
Victory Producers

The Hawthorne Works and the Bell System joined in the national recovery as production rates and employment numbers crept back toward pre-Depression levels. But as the country's wounded economy slowly regained momentum, a new and greater threat arose in Europe and East Asia. Americans watched in horror as the armies of Hitler's Germany overran the European continent with stunning ease. Japanese forces brutally assaulted the Chinese mainland and threatened American possessions in the Pacific. By 1940, Britain stood alone, while an ill-prepared America hoped two vast oceans would afford protection against attack and allow the nation to continue its recovery in peaceful isolation. Everything changed on December 7, 1941.

Even before the attack, Western Electric had begun refocusing its efforts toward defense. The government became its primary customer, overriding the civilian needs of the Bell System. Automakers and steel mills followed suit, retooling their plants for military needs. But once the United States entered the conflict, it was clear that this crisis would demand more of the nation and its industries than anything previously imagined. The daunting mission: to train, arm, supply, transport, and electrically connect a modern military machine.

America's armed forces carried obsolete weapons at the beginning of the war, but within factories like the Hawthorne Works lay the means to erase that deficit: the manpower, machinery, and know-how of the world's largest industrial economy, ready to mobilize to face any trial. These plants, far from the battlefront but once again operating 24 hours and seven days a week, constituted America's most formidable weapon. The Electrical Capital of America transformed itself into the Arsenal of Communication for the duration.

During the war years, the mission, minds, and machinery of the Hawthorne Works combined to meet a monumental challenge. Its crew assembled, tested, and shipped the most sophisticated weapons under tight security. On land, sea, and air, Western Electric products functioned effectively, earning praise for brilliant design and consistent quality. Once again, women stepped up to perform every task needed to put a well-equipped soldier in the field, while thousands of Hawthorne's men marched off to war. More than 100 never returned.

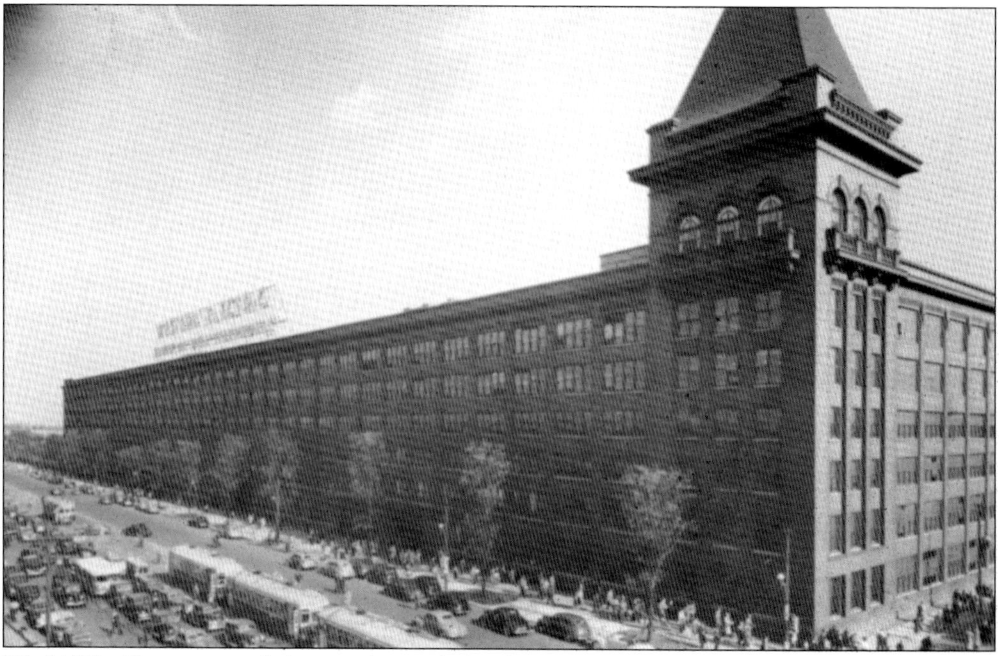

World War II jumpstarted America's crippled industries. In 1940, Western Electric's sales to the US government amounted to $3.5 million. The next year, that number skyrocketed to $41 million. Defense contracts accounted for one third of Western Electric's output by the time of the attack on Pearl Harbor. By June 1942, the peacetime telephone maker had transformed itself into the Arsenal of Communication.

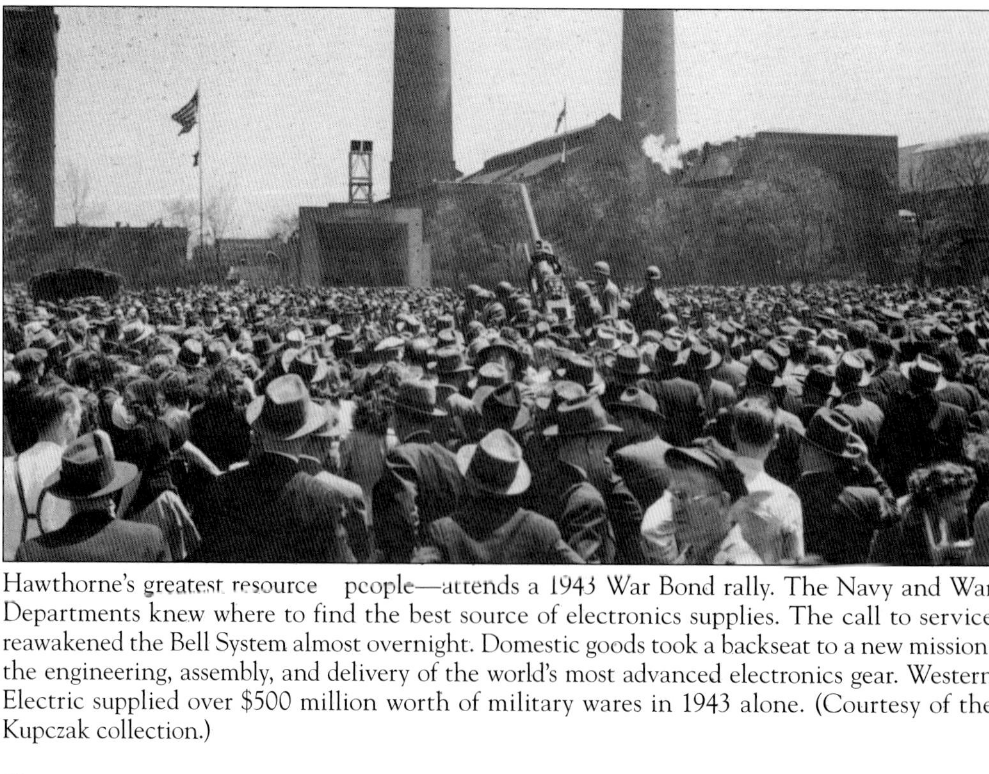

Hawthorne's greatest resource people—attends a 1943 War Bond rally. The Navy and War Departments knew where to find the best source of electronics supplies. The call to service reawakened the Bell System almost overnight. Domestic goods took a backseat to a new mission: the engineering, assembly, and delivery of the world's most advanced electronics gear. Western Electric supplied over $500 million worth of military wares in 1943 alone. (Courtesy of the Kupczak collection.)

Clarence G. Stoll, the president of Western Electric during the war, oversaw the company's swift transformation into a key military supplier. Like many WE executives, Stoll spent his entire career with the company, starting as a freshly minted engineer out of Penn State in 1903. By 1912 (right), the fast-rising junior executive was placed in charge of the Antwerp plant. He then served as the general superintendent of the Hawthorne Works from 1923 to 1926 before assuming leadership of the company in 1940. "Whether we are soldiers in uniform or soldiers of production," he wrote his employees in 1944, "we are in the fight just the same . . . Every Western Electric employee is a victory producer." Seen below after the war, Stoll won a commendation from Pres. Harry Truman and retired in 1947.

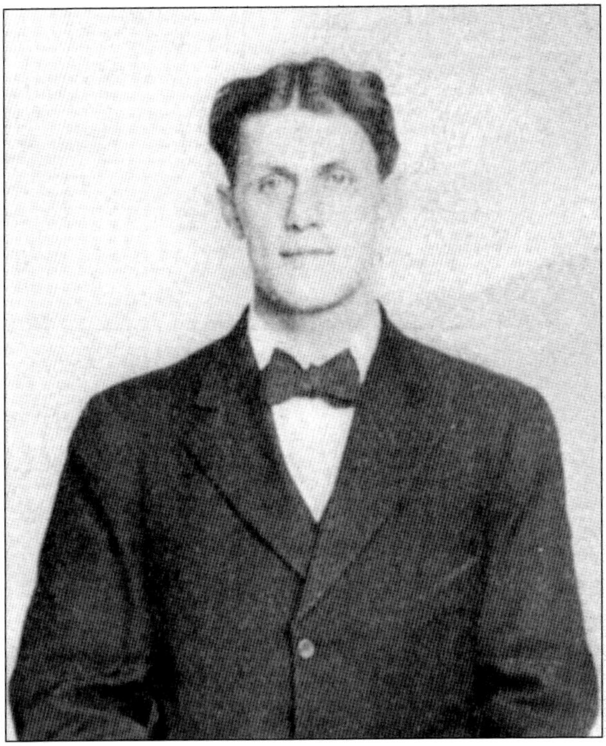

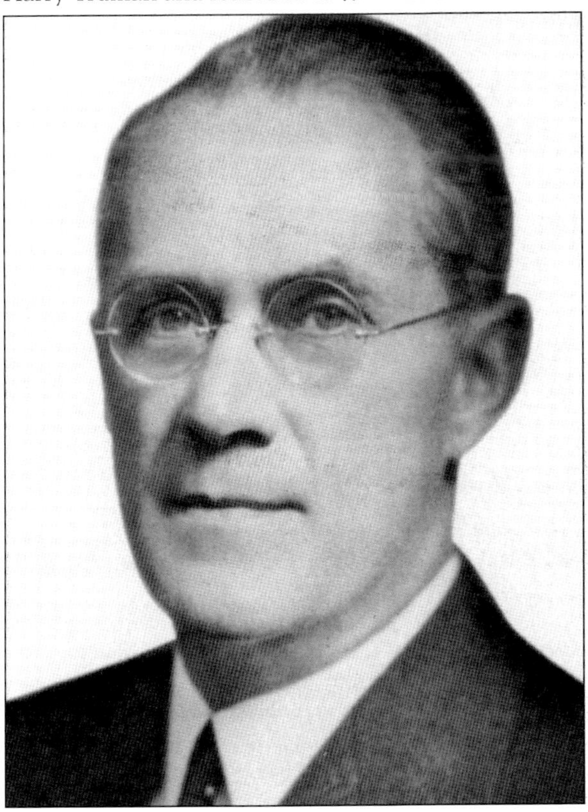

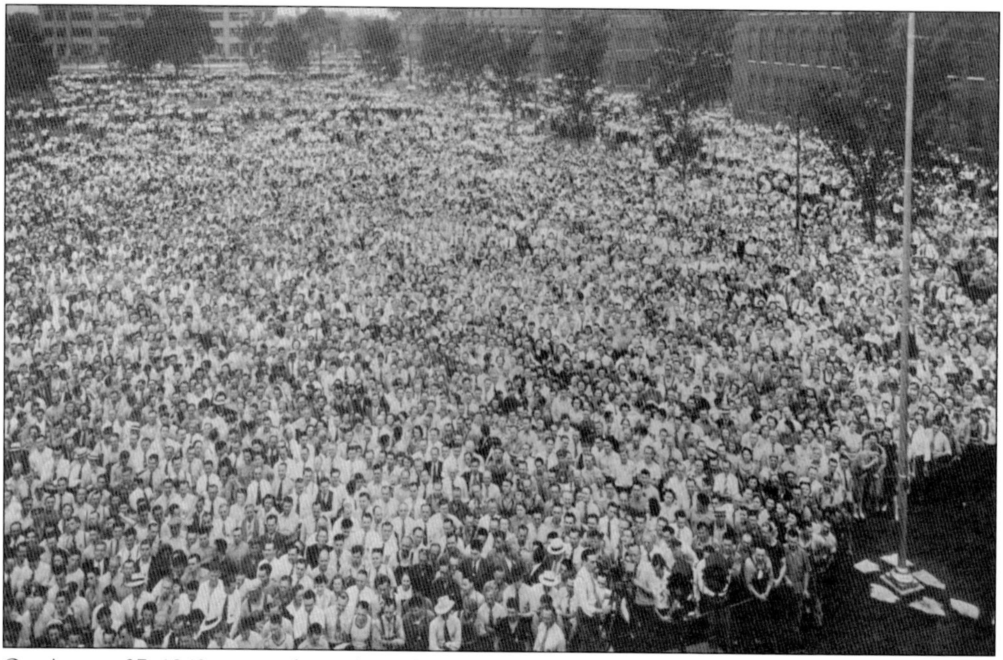

On August 27, 1942, a sea of proud employees filled the Hawthorne Works courtyard to witness the presentation of the Army and Navy "E" Awards, granted for "exceptional performance in the production of war equipment." The Works supplied billions of dollars worth of field telephones, aviation radiotelephones, and ship-to-shore transmitters and receivers. Designed by Bell Labs, assembled and tested by Hawthorne and its sister factories, and then shipped safely overseas, Western Electric's equipment proved durable and reliable in the most trying conditions. The company also played a key role in the development and production of one of the most advanced tools in the Allied arsenal: radar. By war's end, Western's plants had turned out more than half of all of America's radar sets.

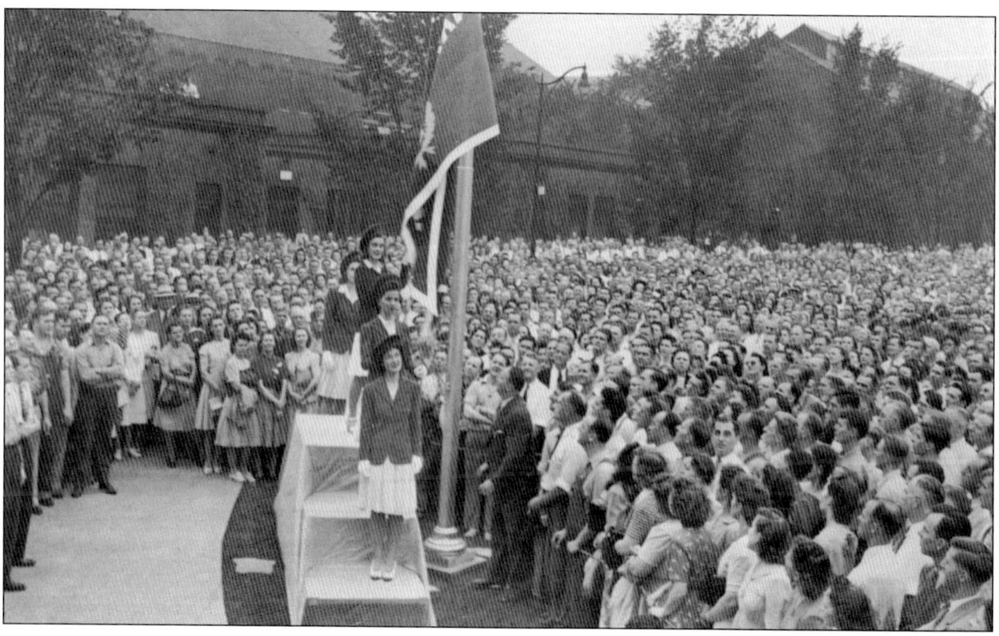

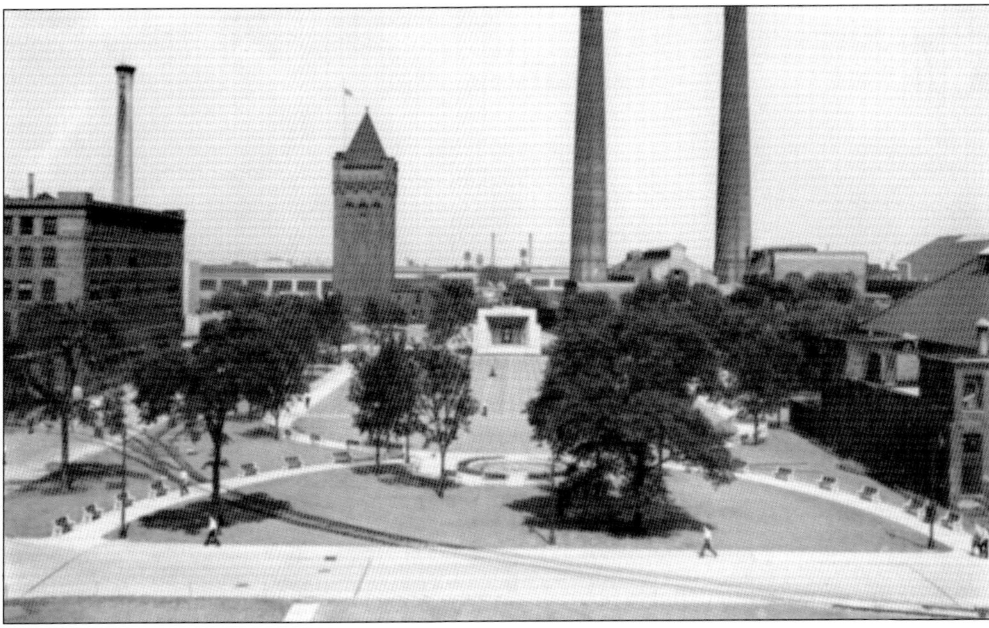

By July 1944, American troops were locked in fierce combat across the globe: in France, in Italy, and on sweltering Pacific islands. But at home, this was the peaceful scene at the Hawthorne Works. Safe, secure, efficient factories running at full tilt thousands of miles from the battlefront gave the United States an insurmountable advantage.

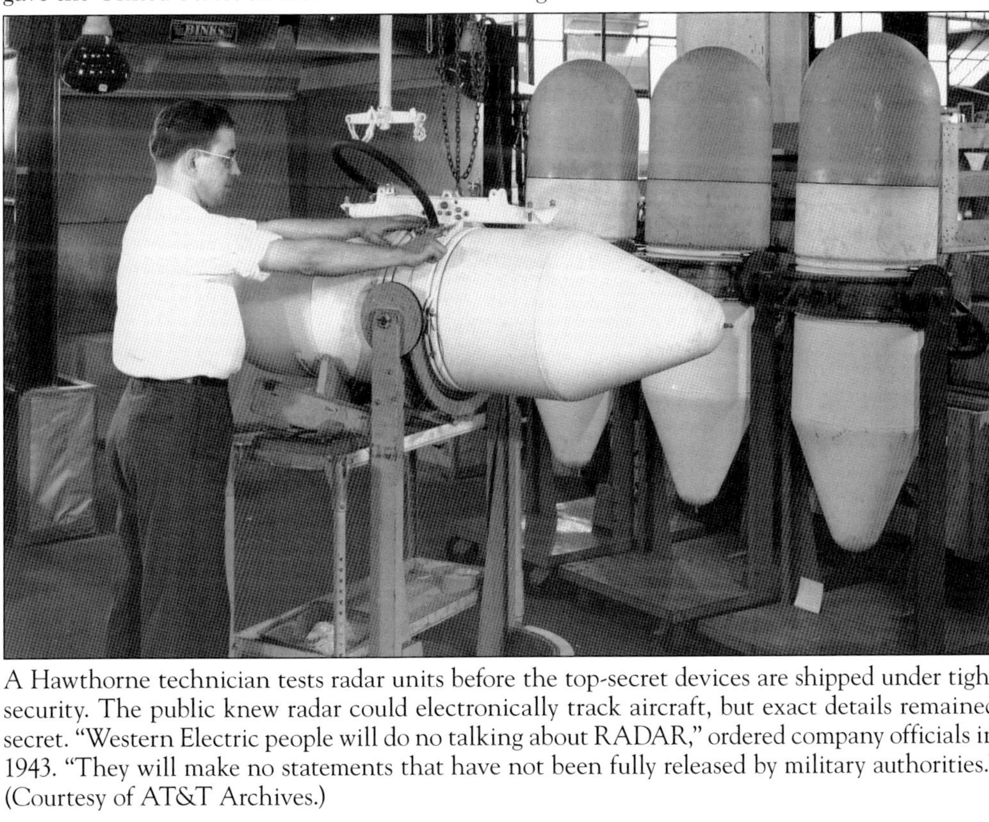

A Hawthorne technician tests radar units before the top-secret devices are shipped under tight security. The public knew radar could electronically track aircraft, but exact details remained secret. "Western Electric people will do no talking about RADAR," ordered company officials in 1943. "They will make no statements that have not been fully released by military authorities." (Courtesy of AT&T Archives.)

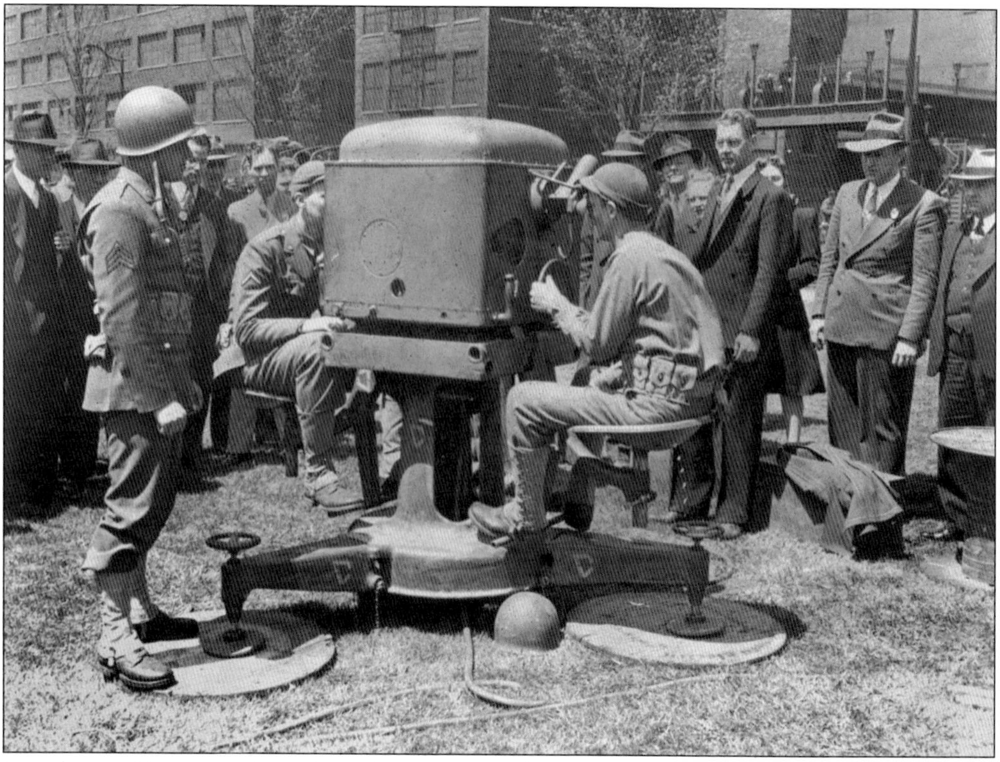

Hawthorne Works superintendent David Levinger (above, third from right, with glasses) observes as Army personnel demonstrate the tracking element of an M9 gun director for the people who built it. Below, the tracker is shown deployed with the complete M9 unit, including a mobile analog computer, a radar screen, and a 120-millimeter antiaircraft gun. Hawthorne's handiwork helped American defenders halt air attacks on battlefields all over the world. Radar spotted incoming enemy aircraft and the tracker determined its speed, altitude, and direction and then relayed the information to the computer, which calculated the proper trajectory and fuse setting. (Above, courtesy of *Western Electric News*; below, courtesy of AT&T Archives.)

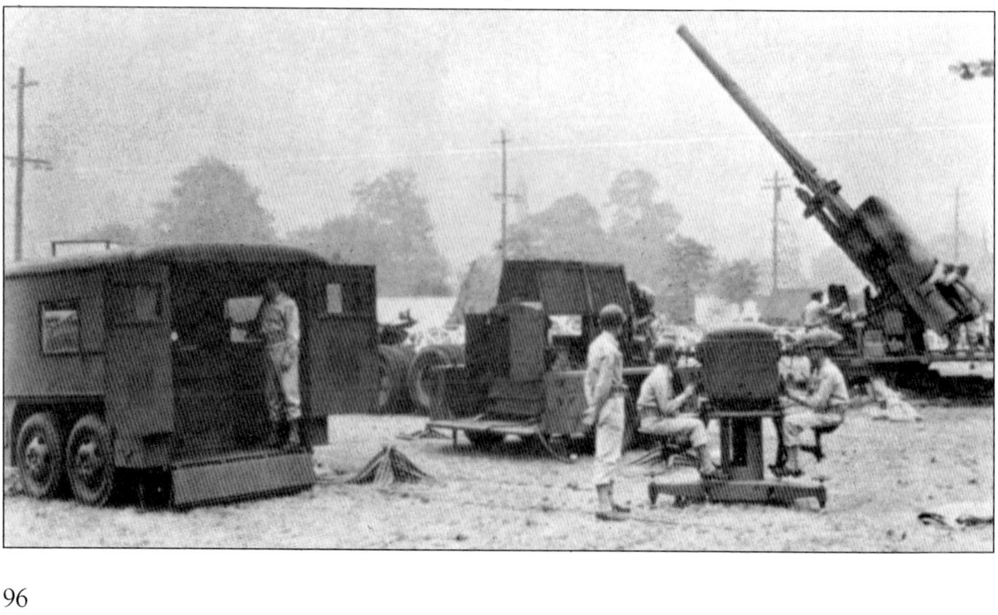

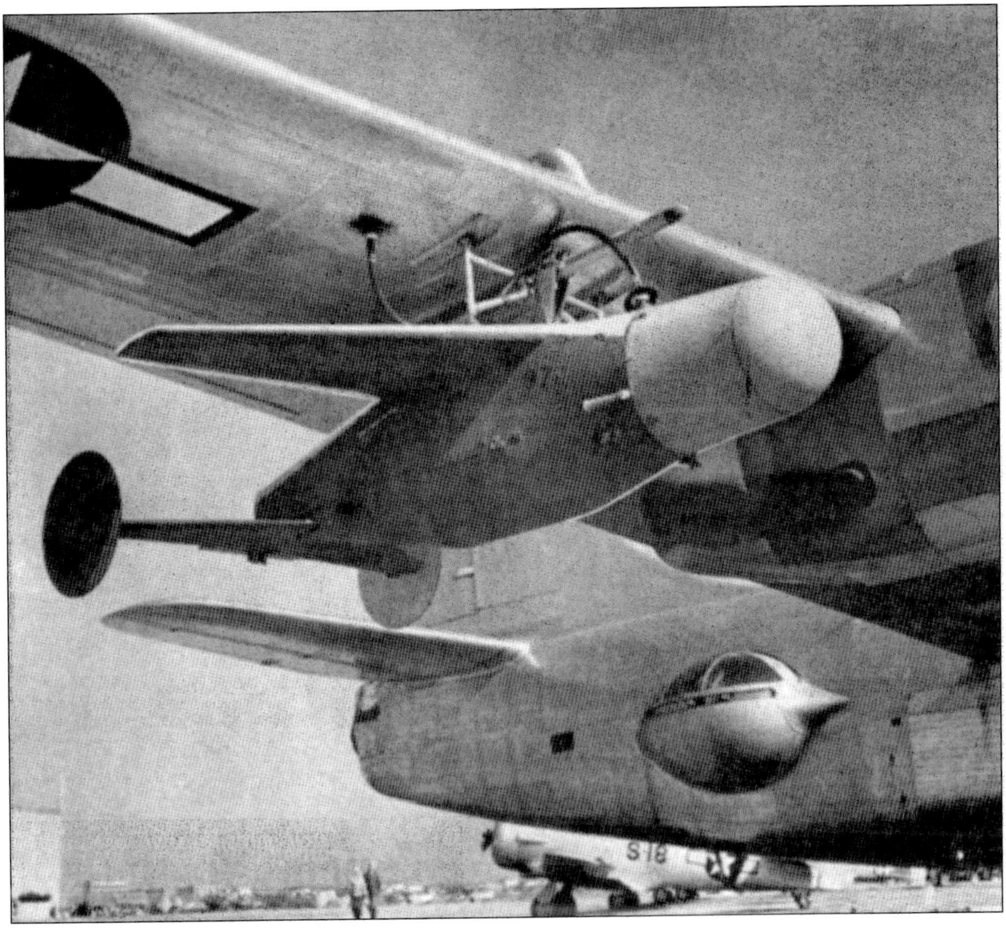

Tucked under the wing of a Navy bomber, Hawthorne's Project 70 looked more like a bowling pin than a lethal weapon. Dubbed the "bat bomb," it was actually the first successful radar-controlled aerial missile. The 12-foot glider carried a load of explosives and a small guidance radar unit made at Hawthorne. When launched, the glider's radar locked onto an enemy target and impacted at high speed. Like more than one-third of Hawthorne-made military goods, Project 70 was classified top secret.

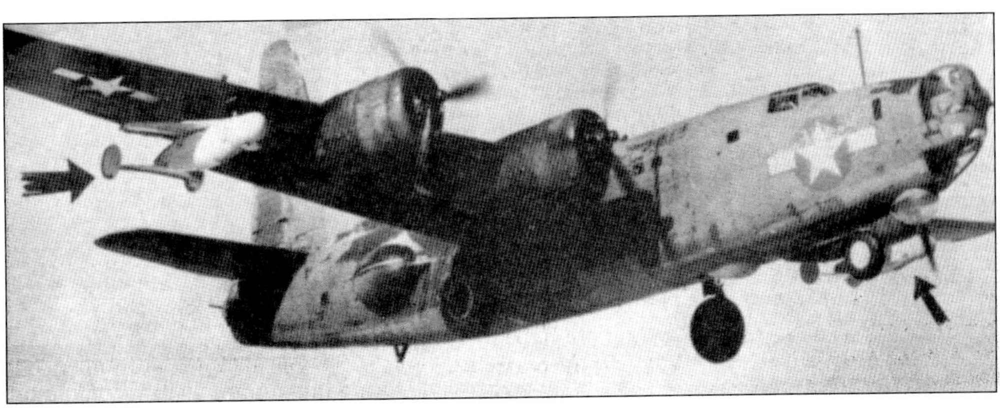

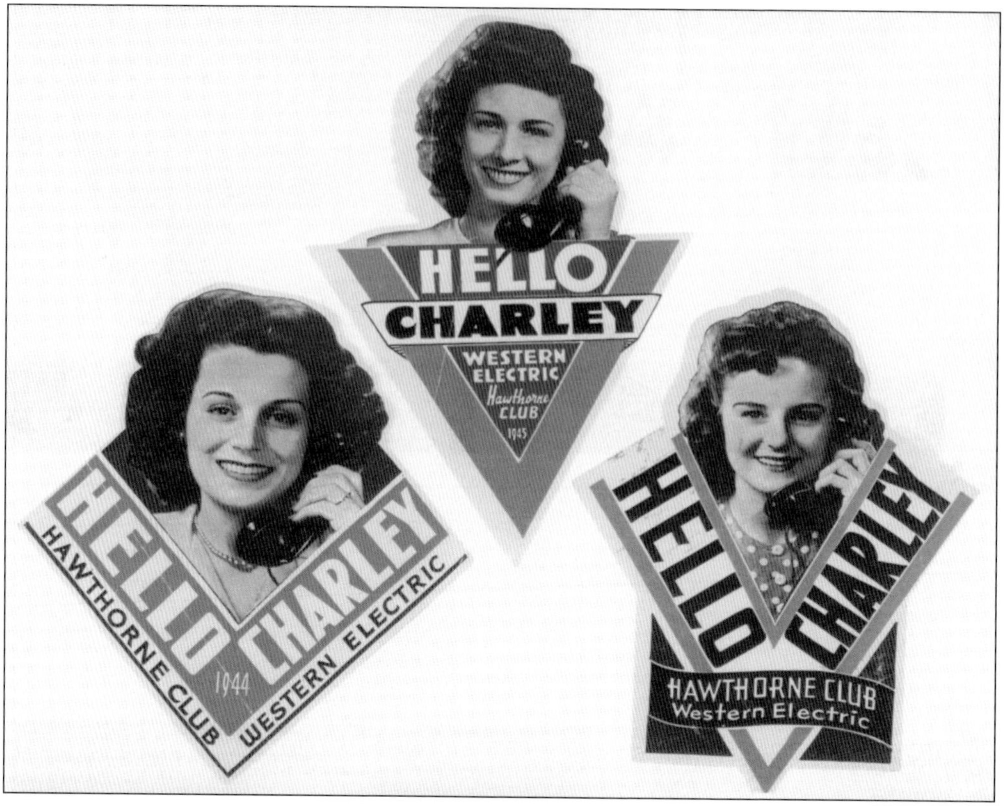

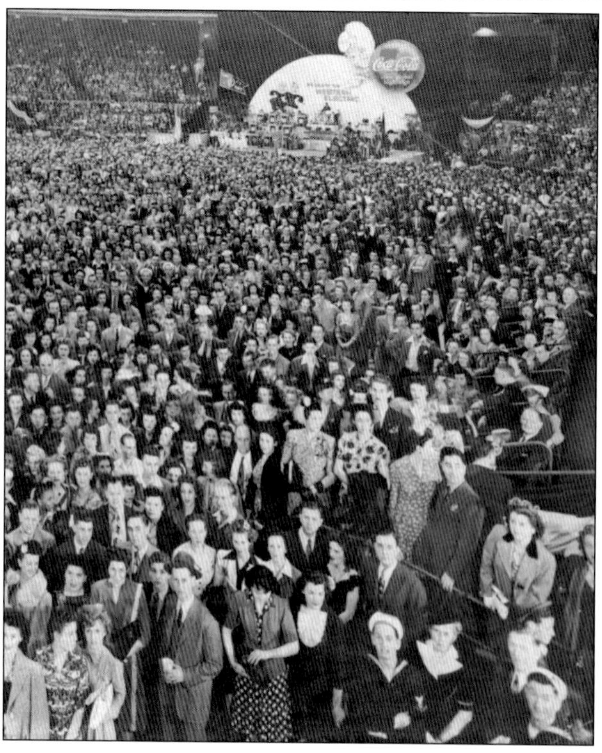

Even world war could not slow Hawthorne's busy social scene. Sports leagues and clubs carried on, lifting the spirits of the hardworking staff. The activities relaxed employees worried about loved ones or coworkers in uniform, of which there were nearly 5,000 in 1944. The annual Hello Charley Girl competition went on uninterrupted, with one wartime twist: the winner added the title "Victory Girl." Even Uncle Sam threw a party for the Hawthorne crew. In May 1944, the War Department treated its best supplier to a swinging night at Chicago Stadium (left) featuring Tommy Dorsey's Big Band, with Chicago's own Gene Krupa on drums.

Winning the Hello Charley Girl competition would be the highlight of most Hawthorne stories, but for Virginia "Ginny" Scharer (right), that honor was just the beginning of a remarkable lifelong journey. In 1941, coworkers named her the plant's beauty queen, a role tailor-made for the bright-eyed brunette. Meanwhile, another local product was making a name for himself on the world's stage. Cicero's Robert Brouk (below), an Army fighter pilot, joined the famed Flying Tigers in 1941. In 10 months, Brouk's P-40 downed four Japanese planes over China. After being wounded in early 1942, the decorated veteran returned to his hometown a hero. (Both courtesy of Virginia Davis.)

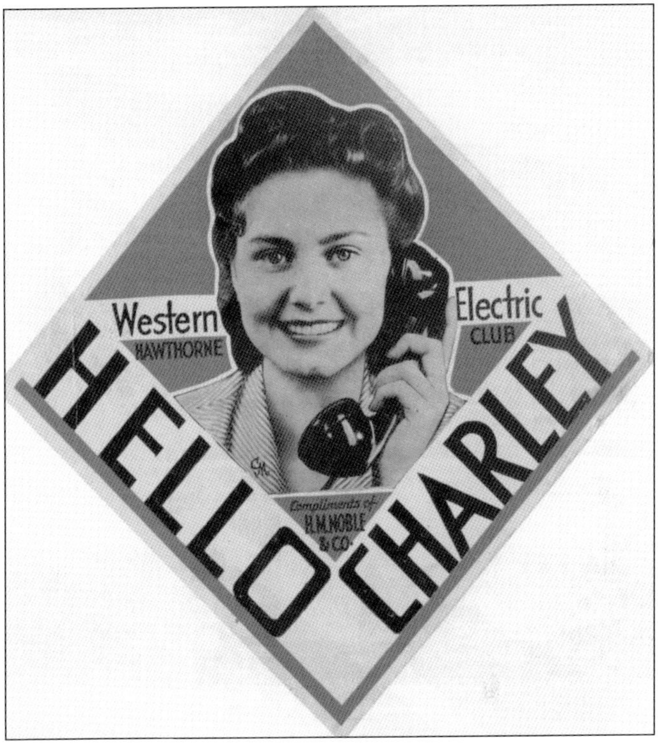

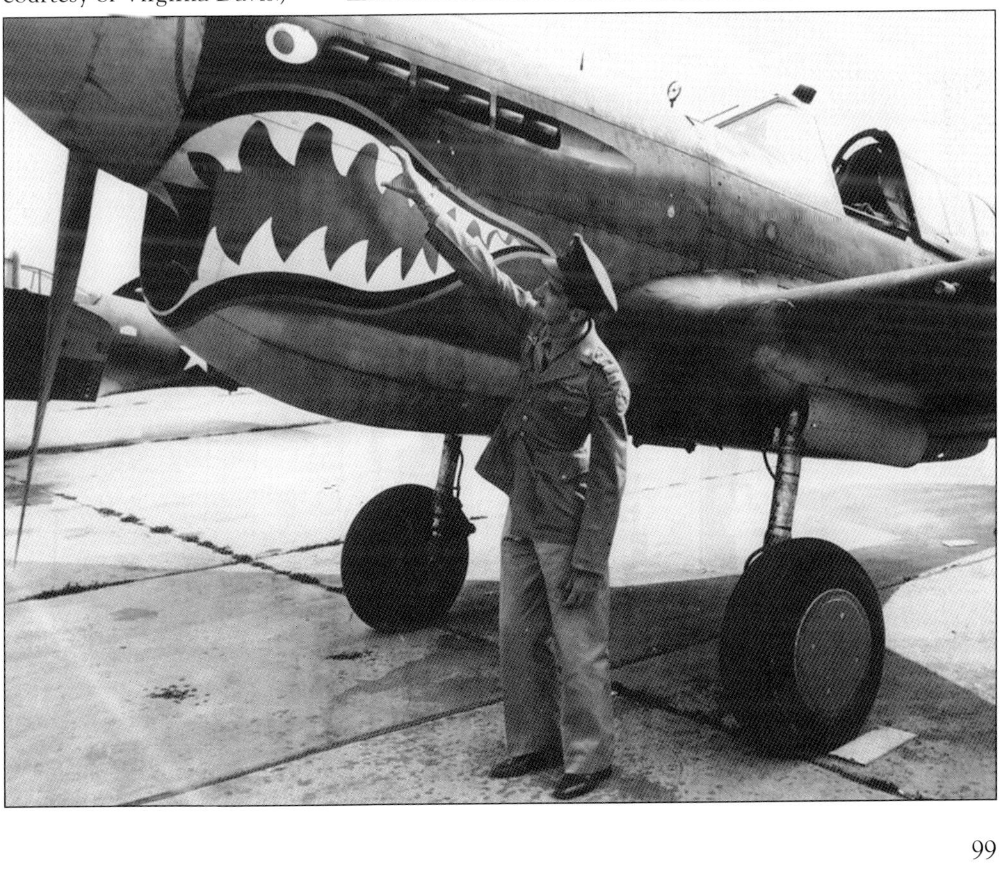

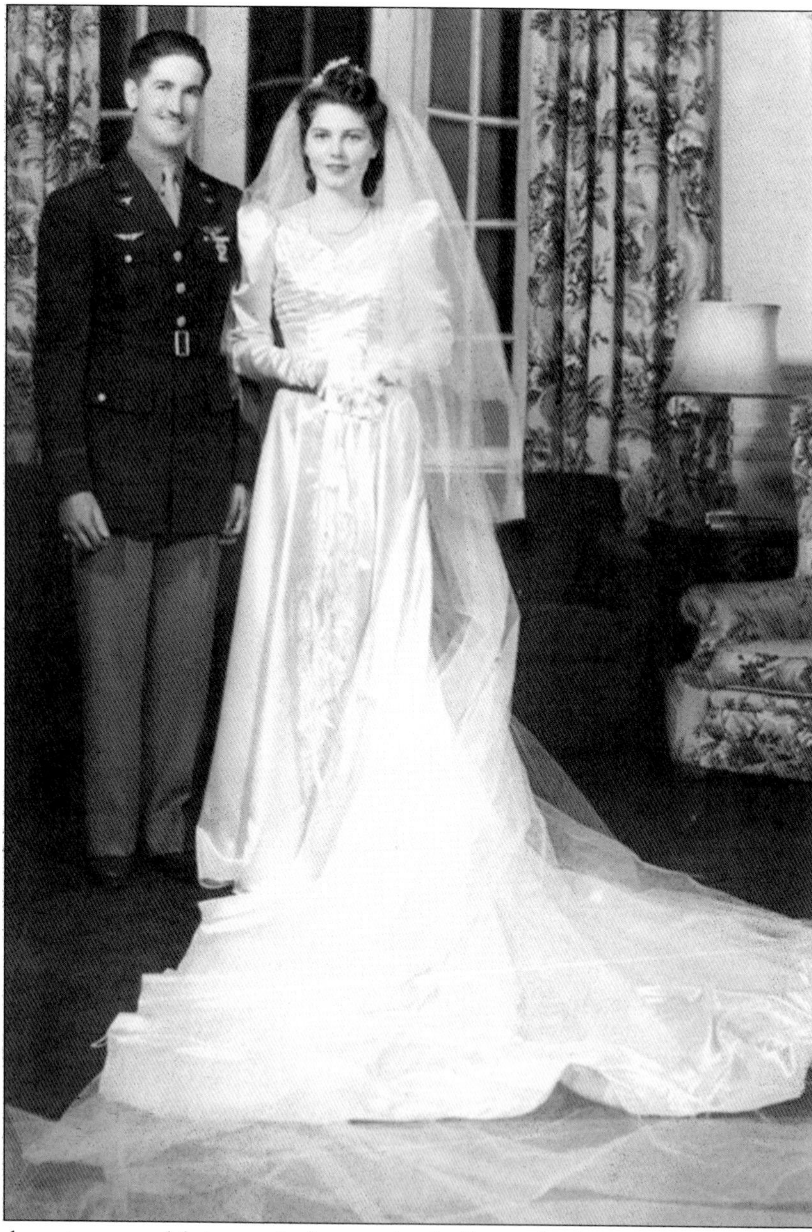

Bob Brouk, an instant celebrity, made the rounds of rallies and radio interviews. Cicero celebrated Bob Brouk Day on August 2, 1942, with a Cermak Road parade to Hawthorne's Memorial Field. A few days earlier, Brouk had toured the Hawthorne Works escorted by none other than Virginia Scharer. They met for tea later, just the two of them. Maybe it was inevitable they would hit it off, the war hero and the beauty queen. They kept in touch despite Brouk's hectic schedule, and, three months after they met, Brouk called from his base in Florida to propose. She said yes. Their November wedding made the papers, a charming diversion amid wartime anxiety. But war is ultimately an ordeal of shattering loss, making no exceptions for love or goodness. Three weeks after their wedding, a training accident claimed Bob Brouk's life. His young widow restarted her life by joining the Army. While serving in the Middle East, Virginia met Harvey Davis, the man who would become her new husband, in a marriage that lasted 57 years. (Courtesy of Virginia Davis.)

Eight

Postwar Countdown

The end of the war found Western Electric and the Hawthorne Works once again vigorous and running at full capacity, with their confidence rebuilt and their reputations unequaled. No job was too big for the Arsenal of Communications. In the postwar years, Western Electric's world was dominated by revolutionary technology, the demands of an eager public, and a partner-adversary relationship with government. The times presented formidable challenges and major opportunities, not unlike every other chapter in Hawthorne's history. The Works had always proved equal to these problems, an adaptable survivor. Smart money was betting on Western Electric and the Works to stay on top for a very long time.

With victory secured in 1945, Americans looked to turn their swords back into plowshares—and automobiles, radios, television sets, and telephones. Years of privation and sacrifice, dating back to the end of the 1920s boom years, gave way to a spirit of great expectations. Returning GIs pursued domestic tranquility through education, careers, families, and homes furnished with a host of consumer goods. The Hawthorne Works helped provide employees with disposable income and a reason to spend it.

But not all was tranquil. The Cold War kept Western Electric busy with defense contracts, but new government lawsuits reshaped the company again. The social turmoil of the 1960s came right to Hawthorne's doorstep, and changing technology shrank Hawthorne's payroll. Nevertheless, the Works fought to remain vital. Rising production figures and equipment upgrades testified to continued confidence in the plant's long-term future.

But no amount of effort could slow a changing world. Skyrocketing energy costs handcuffed modernization efforts, and Hawthorne's vast buildings, once an asset, became a serious liability. Some came down, and a streamlined Works battled for position among more modern plants around the country. Eventually, more and more jobs slipped away until a mere skeleton crew remained. The countdown commenced. Finally, the empty, silent buildings disappeared, along with the age they had helped create. A new telecommunications revolution swept the world, but this time without the sense of humanity and fairness that made Hawthorne's name.

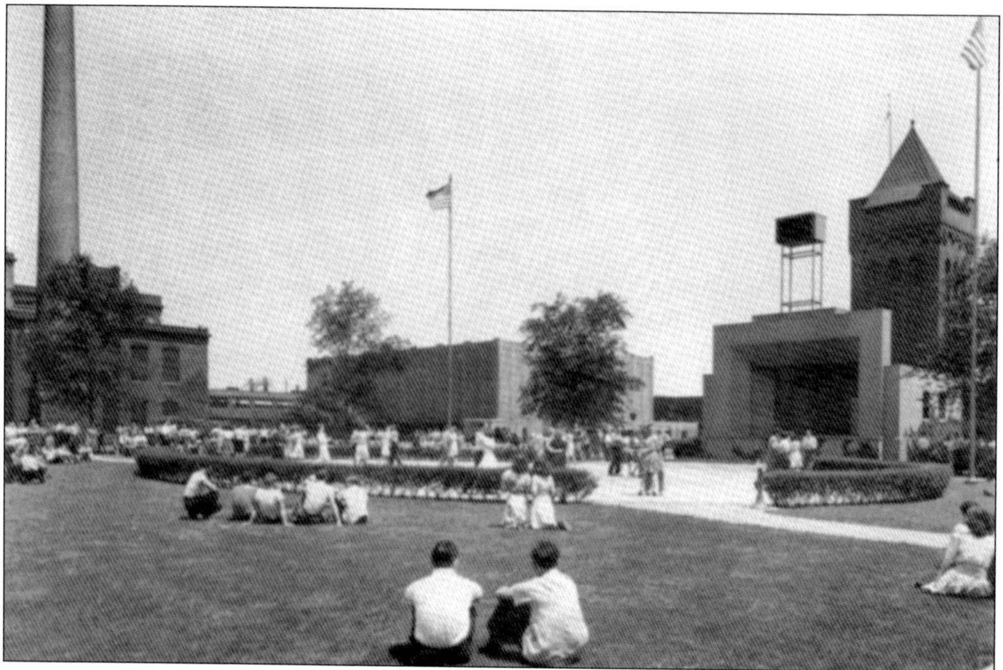

It is 1946, and the war's end signaled a return to peacetime routines like noontime dances at the band shell, as seen in these photographs. But the sudden surge in civilian demand put Hawthorne to the test yet again. In mid-1944, the war production board had authorized production of 800,000 civilian telephones, but, the next year, two million home telephone orders awaited fulfillment, with even more on the horizon. In the last quarter of 1945, Hawthorne turned out 600,000 new phones; in 1946, it made four million more. The Works pleaded for 1,000 women to take on inspection and light assembly work, enticing them with a $1 per hour starting wage.

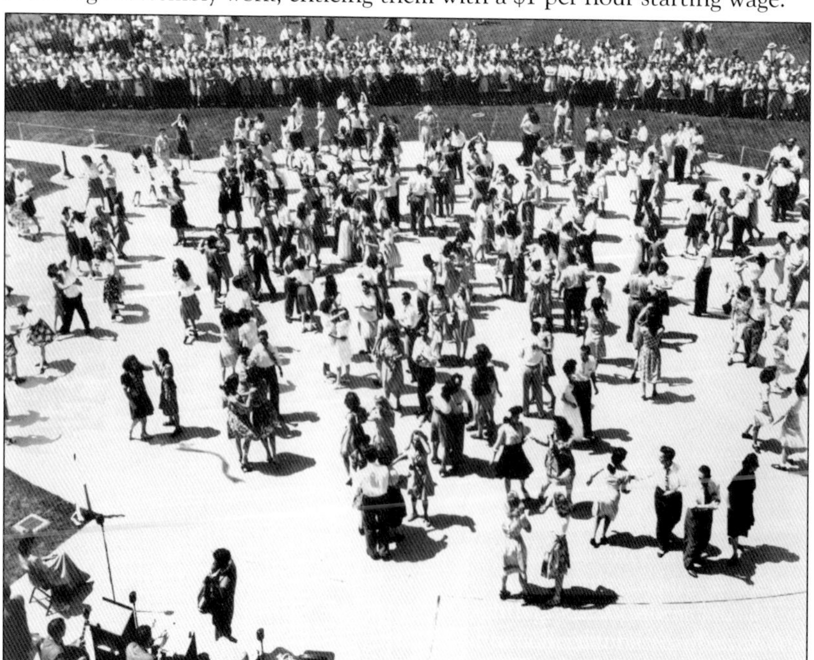

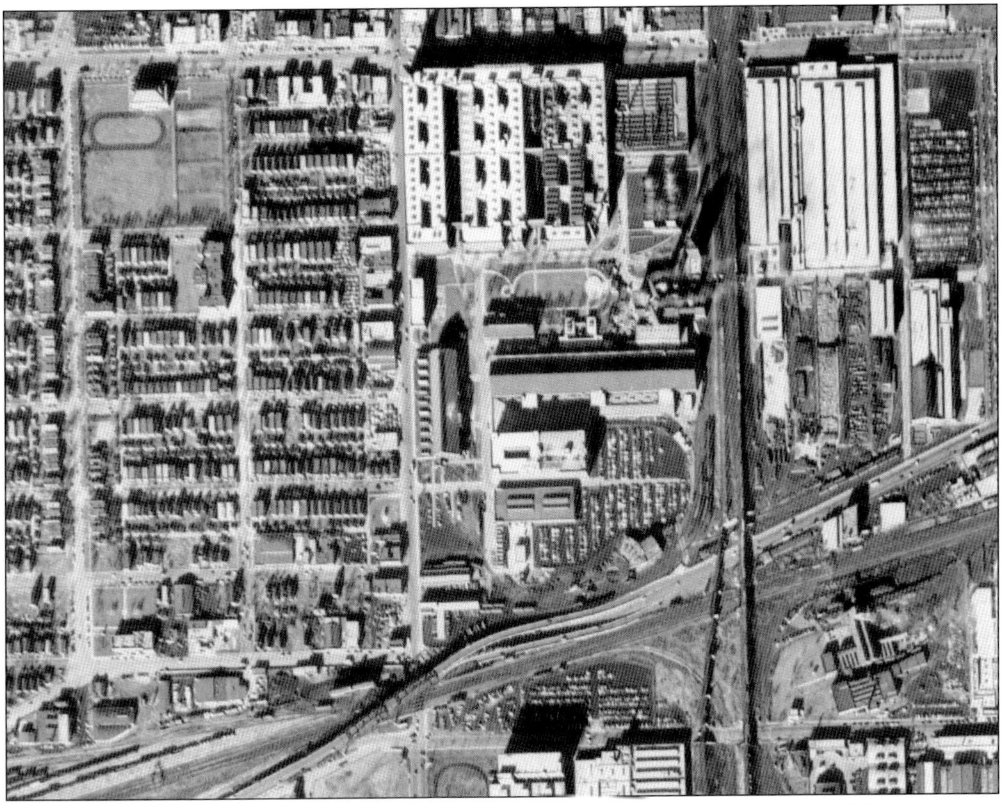

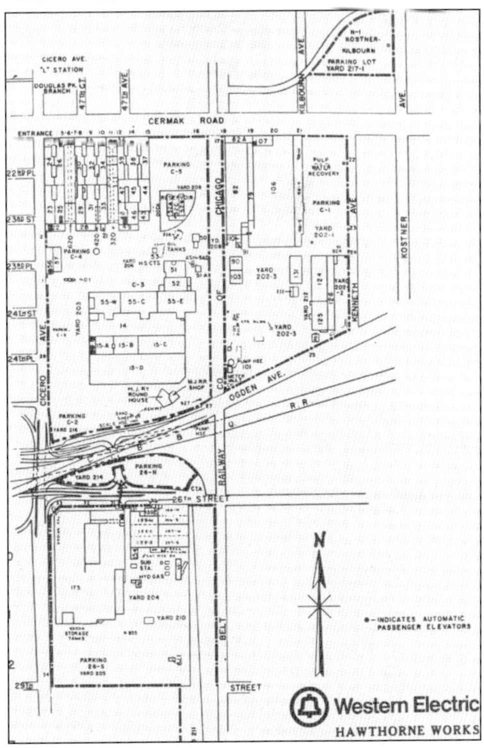

The 1951 aerial shot above captures the Works at its peak. Nearly 25,000 workers occupied the maze of shops and offices, busy supplying the nation's continually growing communications needs. American homes and businesses leased over 33 million telephones by mid-century. The postwar boom made the city of stockyards the new telecommunications capital of the world. Companies like Zenith, Motorola, and Automatic Electric assembled radios, record players, and that new sensation: television. Telephone handset production moved to Indianapolis in 1951, but the need for switching equipment kept the wheels turning at Cicero Avenue and Cermak Road. Western Electric maintained its trusted relationship with the Defense Department during the Korean War, even as the Justice Department filed an antitrust lawsuit against the Bell System in 1949. (Above, courtesy of historicaerials.com.)

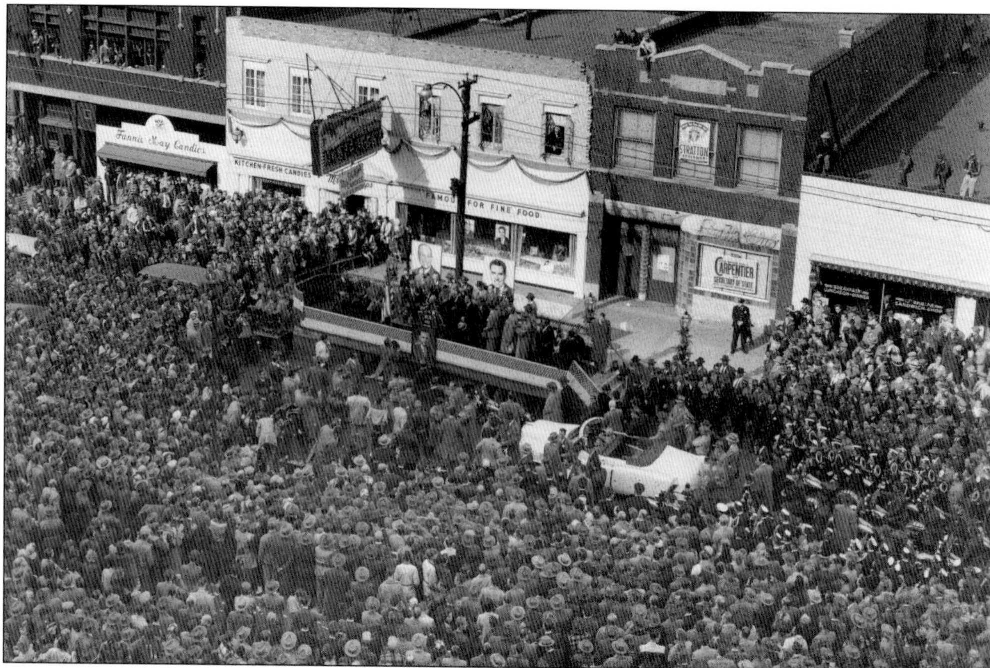

On October 31, 1952, Gen. Dwight D. Eisenhower's presidential campaign rolled into Cicero. An estimated 45,000 supporters jammed Cermak Road (formerly Twenty-second Street) outside the Hawthorne Works to welcome the Republican nominee and World War II hero. In his brief remarks, "Ike" lamented the loss of Czechoslovakia to Communist rule, a message sure to resonate in the heavily Bohemian neighborhood. Just four days later, Eisenhower and his running mate Richard M. Nixon won a landslide victory. The Eisenhower administration kept companies like Western Electric busy building Cold War–era electronic defense systems. But, at the same time, the Justice Department continued to pursue its antitrust lawsuit against AT&T, which ultimately forced the company to withdraw from all non-telephone businesses.

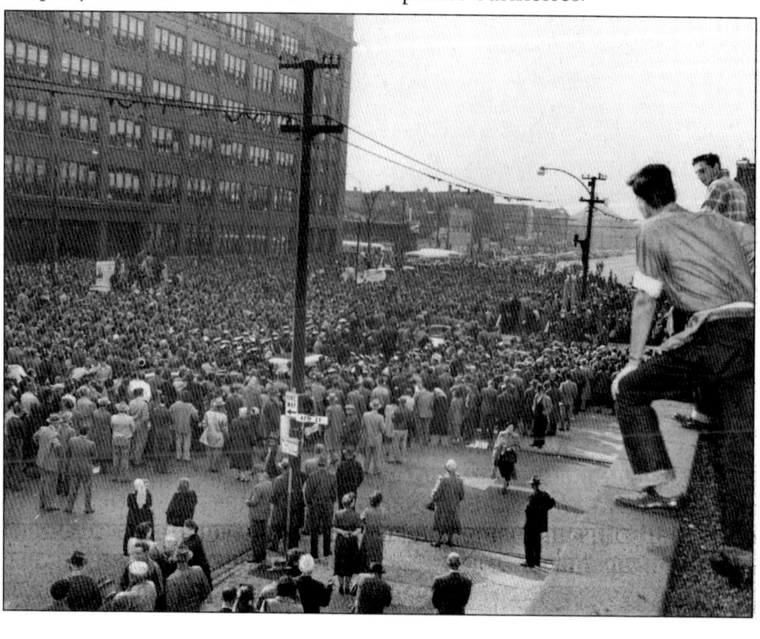

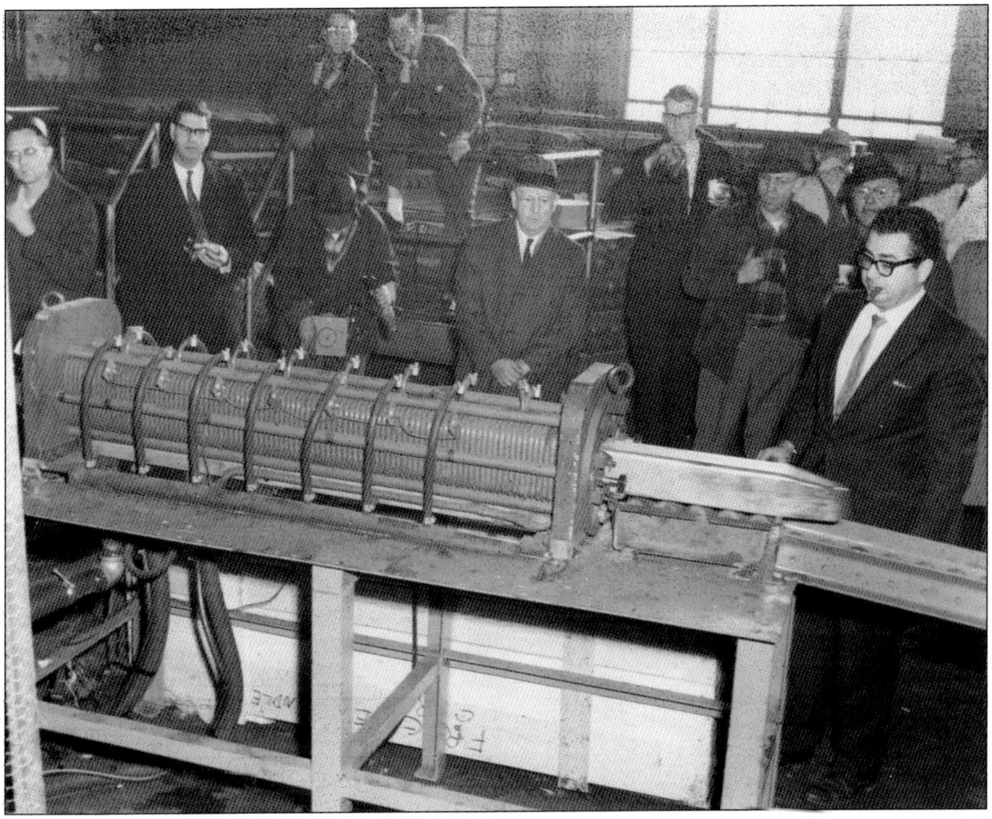

Above, a group of cable plant employees appear impressed by an early 1960s demonstration of a new electric heating element designed to prepare copper billets (ingots) for transformation into miles of telephone cable. Into its 75th year, Hawthorne was still setting new production records for cable, copper rod, and thin-film circuit packs. The plant turned out 78.5 billion feet of cable in 1979 alone.

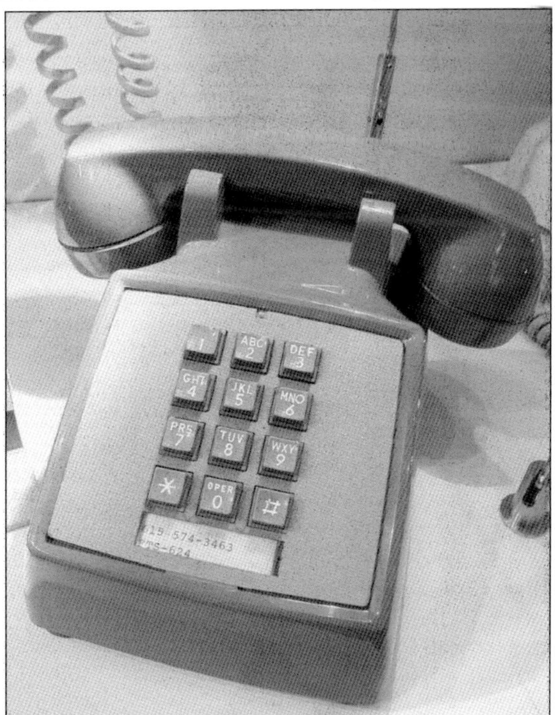

About 40 years after adopting the rotary dial, Bell System designers came up with a new way for customers to connect: the push-button telephone. An early prototype developed in 1959 underwent field testing in 100 homes and businesses in Elgin, Illinois, and evolved into the familiar touch-tone phone seen here. It was introduced in 1963. Combined with the Hawthorne-built Electronic Switching System, the keypad sped up direct-dialed long-distance calling.

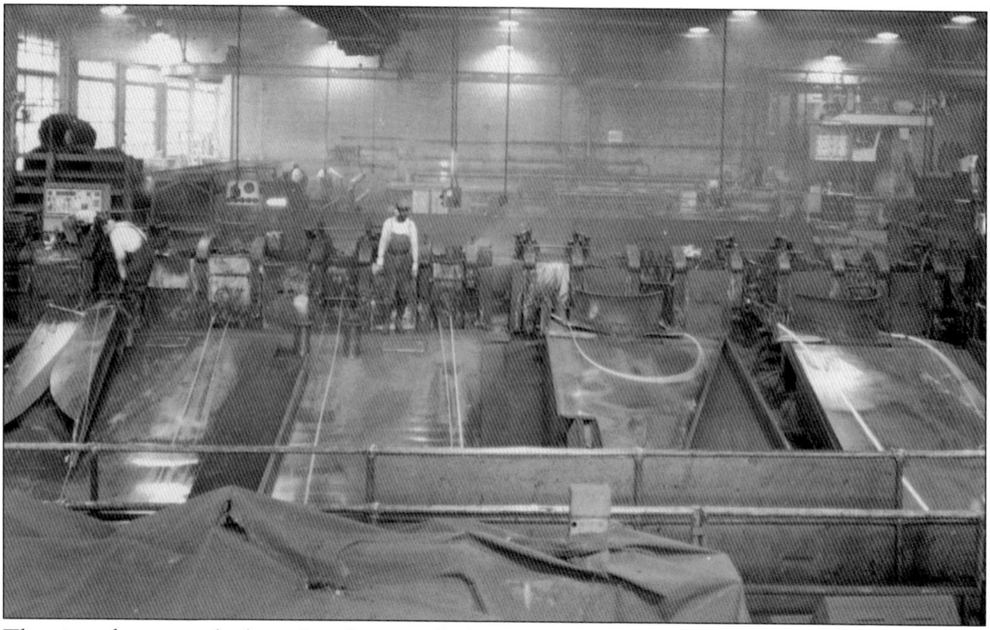

The view above, inside the rod and wire mill, shows the initial steps in the telephone cable-making process. First, 150-pound pure copper ingots were softened by heating them to 1,800 degrees Fahrenheit. The glowing metal was then squeezed through a series of progressively narrower motorized dies. Operators used steel tongs to feed the red-hot rods into the next smaller die. The resulting 5/16-inch-diameter rod cooled and was then "pickled" in an acid bath to remove surface oxides. In an adjoining room, drawing machines further reduced the cable down to usable, thinner diameters. The looping machinery in the mill turned out telephone cable this way, virtually nonstop for decades, until it was replaced by more efficient and safer continuous casting equipment (below) in the 1970s.

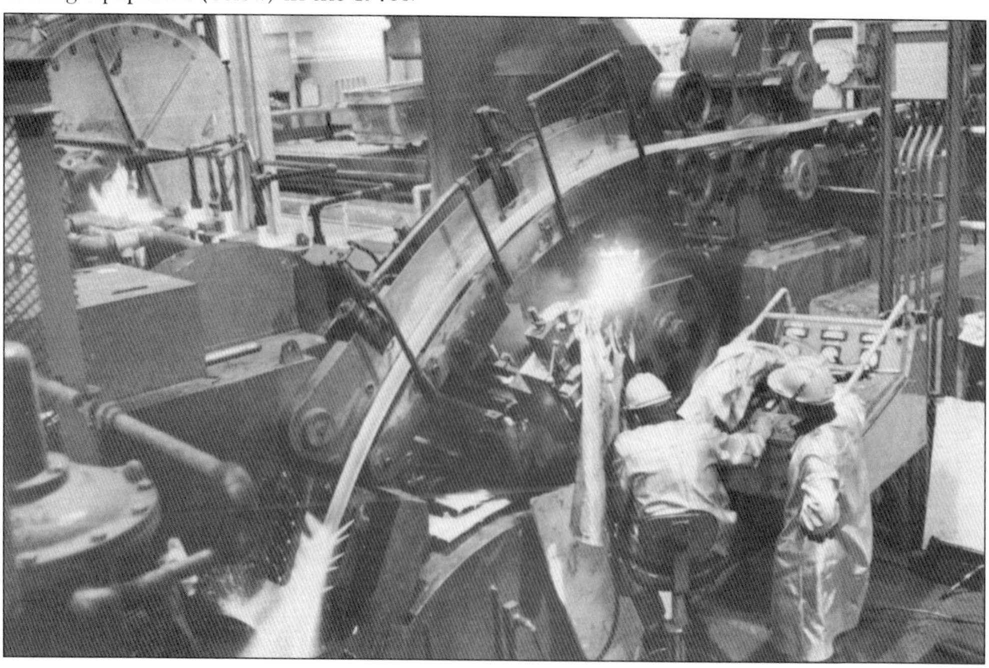

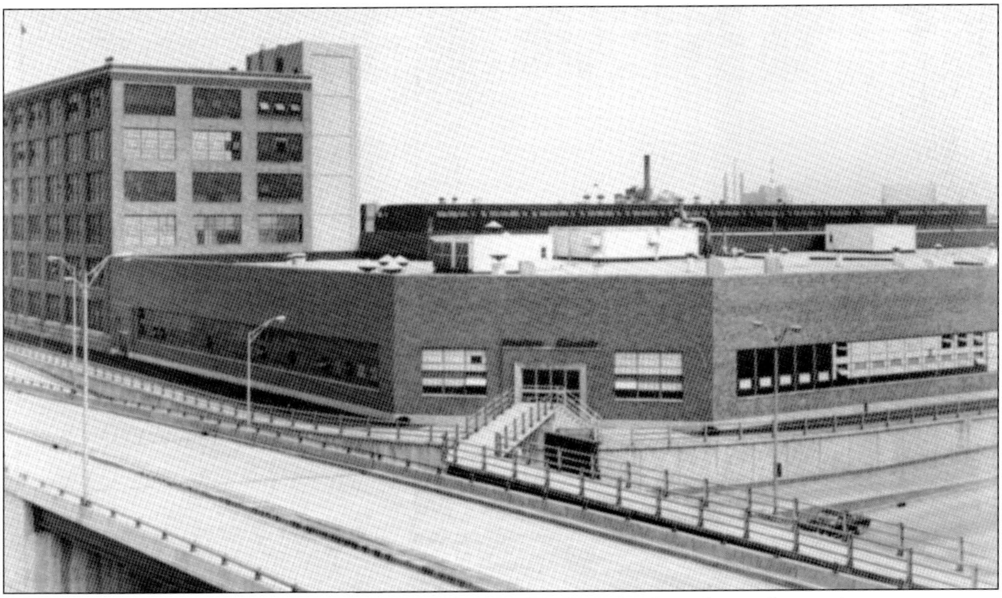

Erected in 1958, the single-story addition to the Works above looks rather ordinary, but it represents Hawthorne's response to the changing requirements of modern manufacturing. Assembly in the older multistory buildings included interruptions to move items from floor to floor by elevator or cart. These old-fashioned spaces lacked the long, open layout needed to produce smaller components like the transistors that were quickly replacing vacuum tubes. Some product lines were transferred to newer Western Electric plants in Omaha, Oklahoma City, and Columbus. By the late 1950s, it was clear that Western Electric's oldest facility needed to undergo major renovations or face possible closure. In 1960, Western Electric committed to a five-year, $30 million modernization program at Hawthorne to add streamlined, flexible workspaces, like the conveyor line below in the metals mill. (Both courtesy of the *Hawthorne Microphone*.)

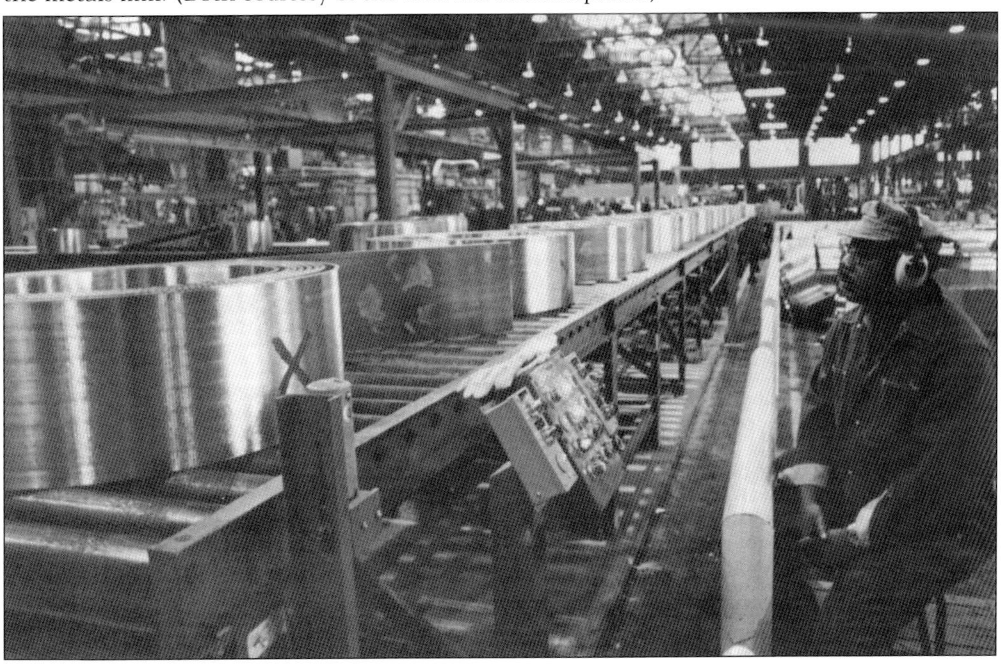

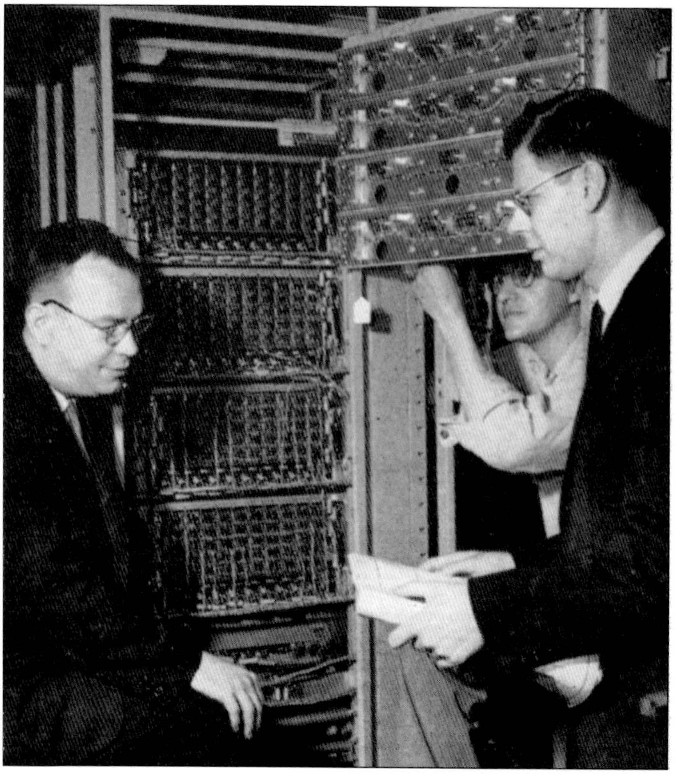

Engineers inspect the wiring in an Electronic Switching System (ESS) cabinet in preparation for shipping and installation in 1960. Hawthorne worked closely with Bell Labs for four years to develop the improved apparatus, which employed transistors to replace many of the metal parts required in the Step-by-Step and Crossbar varieties. Even at this late date, Hawthorne handled production of some of the most up-to-date telecommunications equipment. (Courtesy of the *Hawthorne Microphone*.)

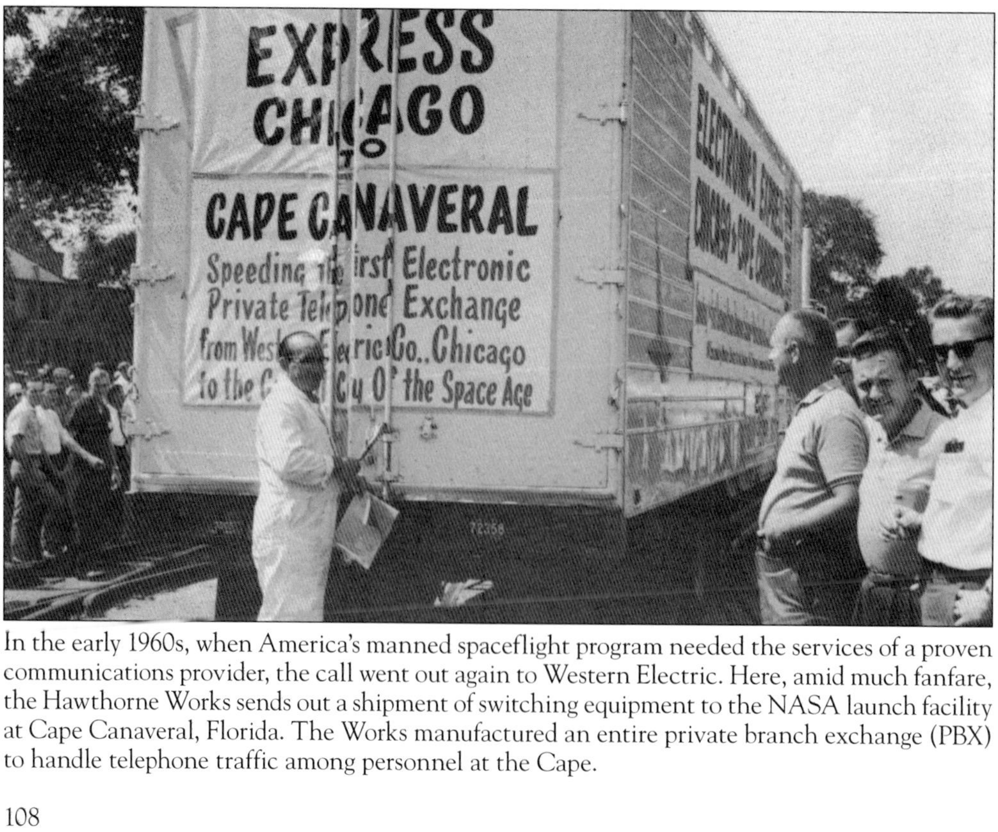

In the early 1960s, when America's manned spaceflight program needed the services of a proven communications provider, the call went out again to Western Electric. Here, amid much fanfare, the Hawthorne Works sends out a shipment of switching equipment to the NASA launch facility at Cape Canaveral, Florida. The Works manufactured an entire private branch exchange (PBX) to handle telephone traffic among personnel at the Cape.

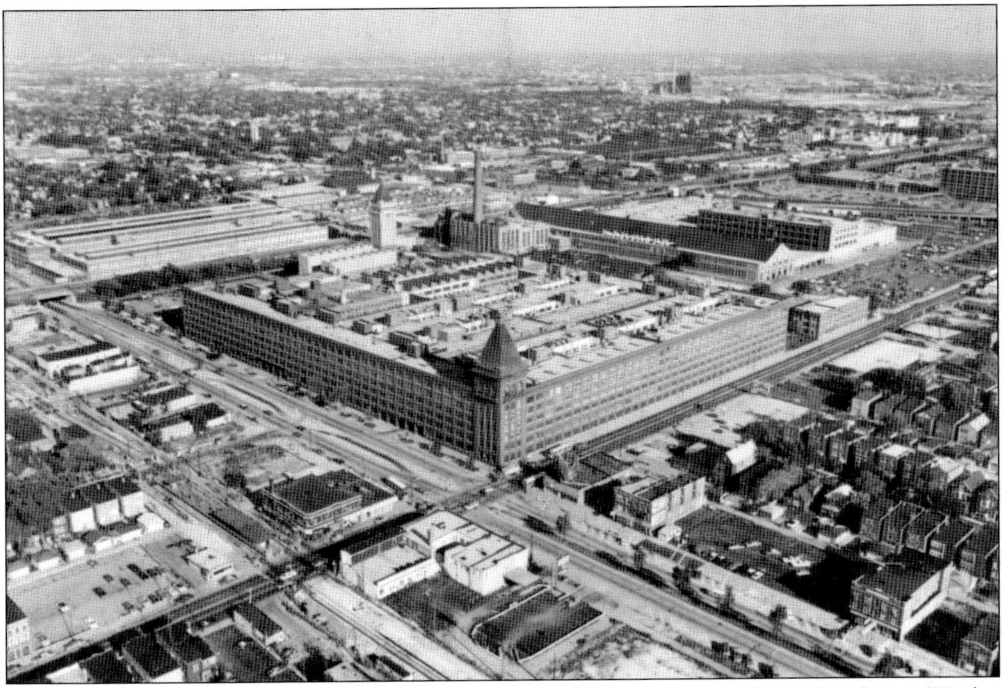

The aerial photograph above, taken in the 1970s, reveals the sheer size of the Hawthorne Works. The facade of the six-story main building stretches for two blocks down Cermak Road and Cicero Avenue. The Western Electric property extends from the cable plant beyond the railroad viaduct on the left to the buildings half a mile south on Twenty-sixth Street, on the right. The old foundry building (below) along Cicero Avenue was removed in 1975, reflecting the reduced need for metals in telecommunications equipment. By the time this photograph was taken, the complex had reached its greatest physical size, but its workforce was already in decline. Gradual decreases brought the number of employees down to about 23,000 by 1970.

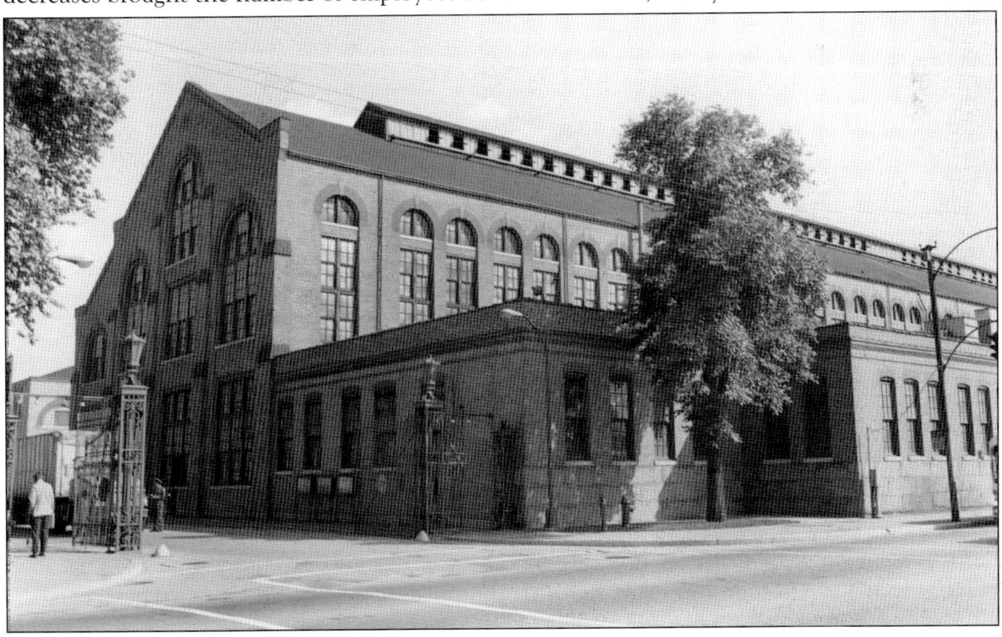

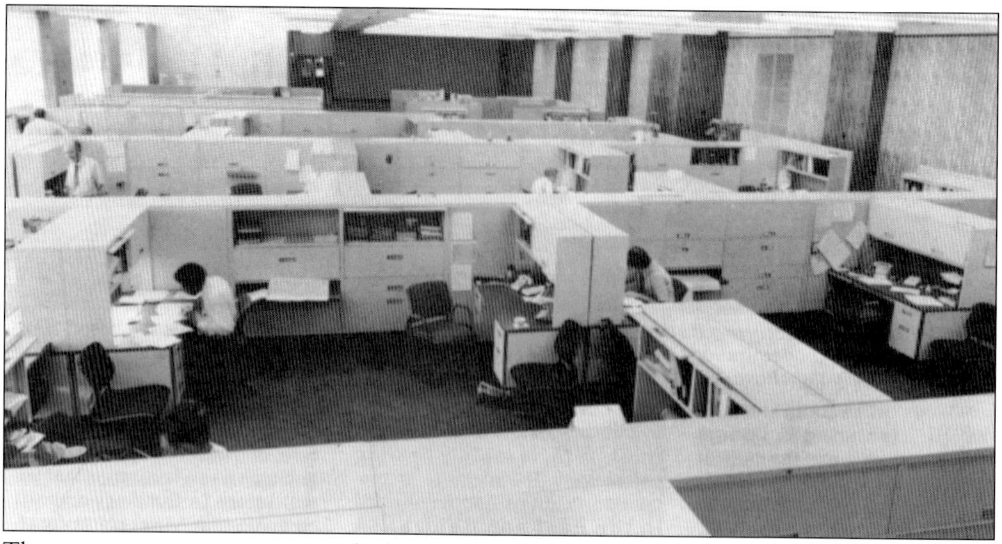

These capacitor engineers enjoy a little privacy and elbow room in their redesigned offices in the central manufacturing buildings. Completed in the late 1970s, the central manufacturing units absorbed more than 2,500 workers from the old east and central telephone apparatus buildings. The clean, well-lighted spaces must have seemed luxurious compared to the warehouse-like chambers of the original structures. The new, efficient layout saved the company over $2 million in the first two years. (Courtesy of the *Hawthorne Microphone*.)

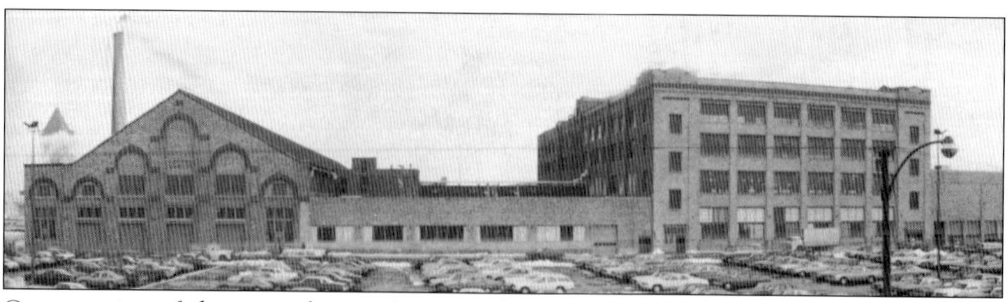

Construction of the central manufacturing buildings allowed Hawthorne to consolidate manufacturing in a compact, adaptable space. The one-story unit connected the refurbished general merchandise building, on the left in this 1980 photograph, and the four-story warehouse. Company officials described the upgrade as a "significant investment and expression of confidence in the future of Hawthorne." (Courtesy of the *Hawthorne Microphone*.)

Hawthorne produced 25 million capacitors per year by 1960, doubled that amount in four years, and then doubled it again by the 1970s. In 1978, Hawthorne churned out one million units per day and shipped $54 million worth of the components. Even as other segments of the Works slowed, Hawthorne invested in the new machinery seen here and anticipated output of 400 million capacitors by 1985. (Courtesy of the *Hawthorne Microphone*.)

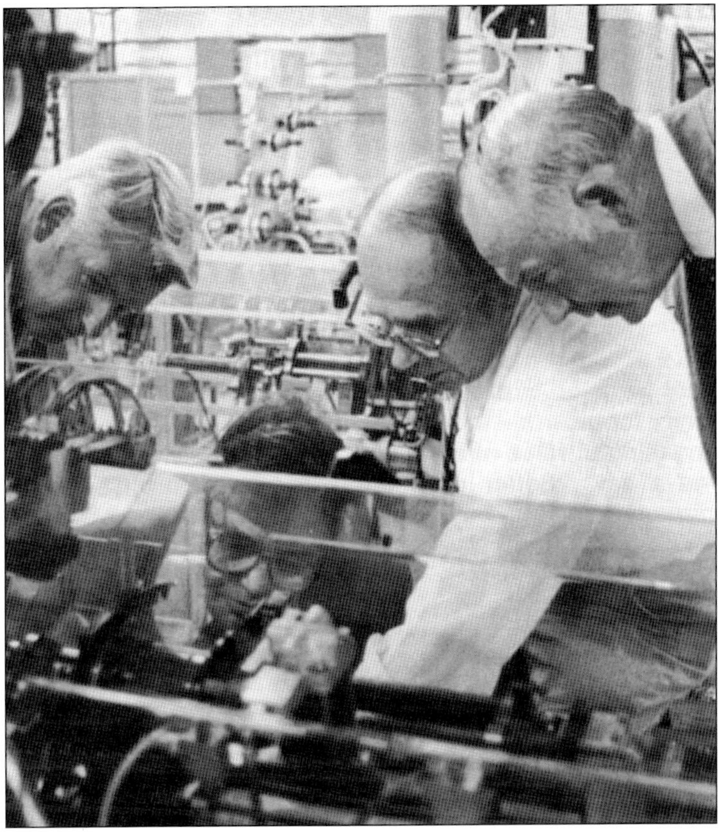

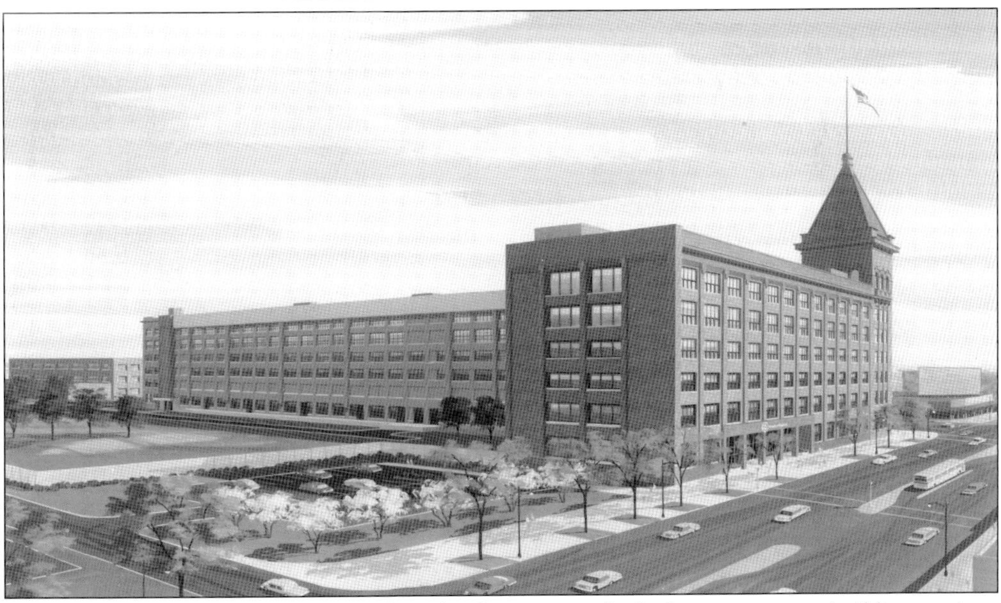

This is an artist's rendering of 1980 plans for the revamped telephone apparatus buildings, minus their east and center sections. With these modifications, which were carried out in 1981 and 1982, the company hoped to keep the aging structure competitive. The project removed more than one million square feet of excess floor space by erasing some of the oldest portions of the plant.

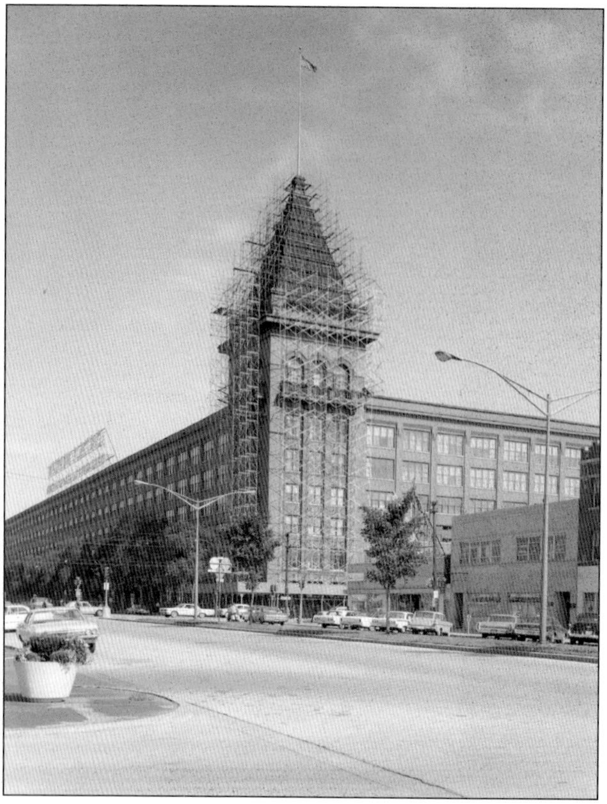

Seven decades of constant human traffic and extreme Chicago weather took its toll on the Works. At left, the executive tower undergoes a facelift in the 1960s. Maintenance expenses squeezed dollars from tight budgets and factored into decisions to move production elsewhere. Below, a powerhouse smokestack shows its age in the 1970s. Conversion to cleaner natural gas in 1969 increased operating costs by $250,000 a year. Skyrocketing energy prices led Works officials to consider buying electricity or converting back to cheaper coal, but both options presented obstacles. Rewiring for outside power would have been time-consuming and expensive, while a return to coal required costly upgrades to meet tighter anti-pollution regulations. Hawthorne's size, once an asset, became a serious liability.

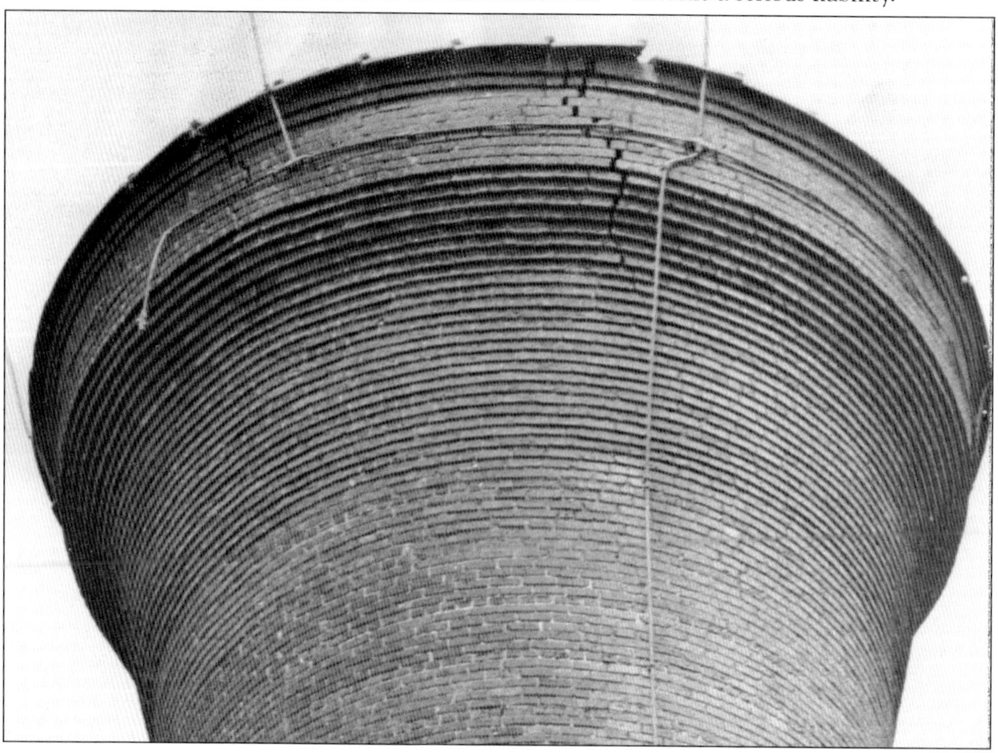

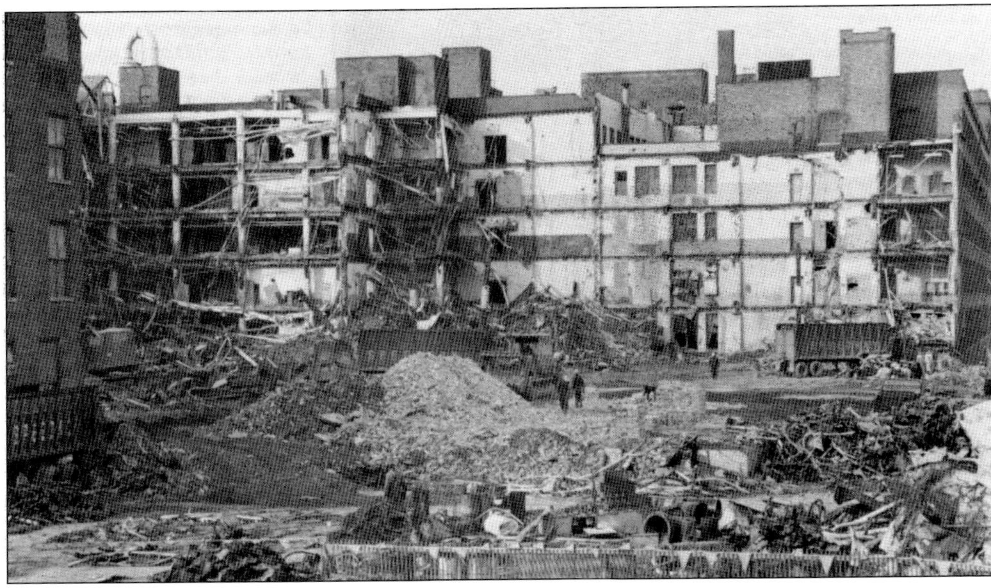

Through its first three decades, the Hawthorne Works' nonstop building spree doubled its floor space and kept its equipment updated. By the 1980s, the Works reversed the process, leveling sections of the factory left empty by staff reductions. A major demolition project in late 1981 brought down the eastern section of the telephone apparatus buildings, facing Cermak Road. These had been among the first buildings erected at Hawthorne, back in 1905. In 1982, the center sections of the telephone apparatus buildings were demolished. The vacated land was cleared of debris and landscaped. Company officials hoped this contraction would save money by reducing property taxes and energy expenses, but, like every other attempt to keep the Works viable, it proved to be too little too late. (Both courtesy of the *Hawthorne Microphone*.)

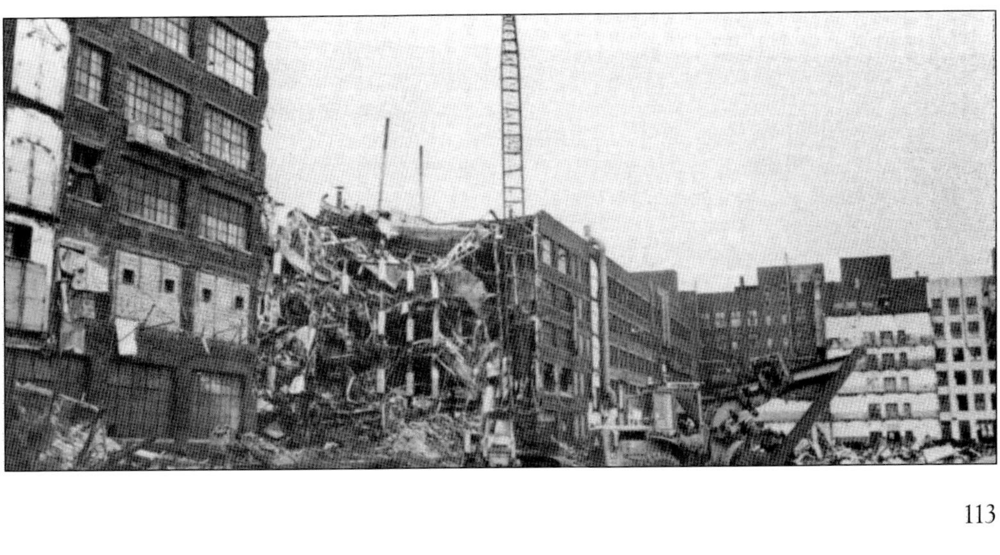

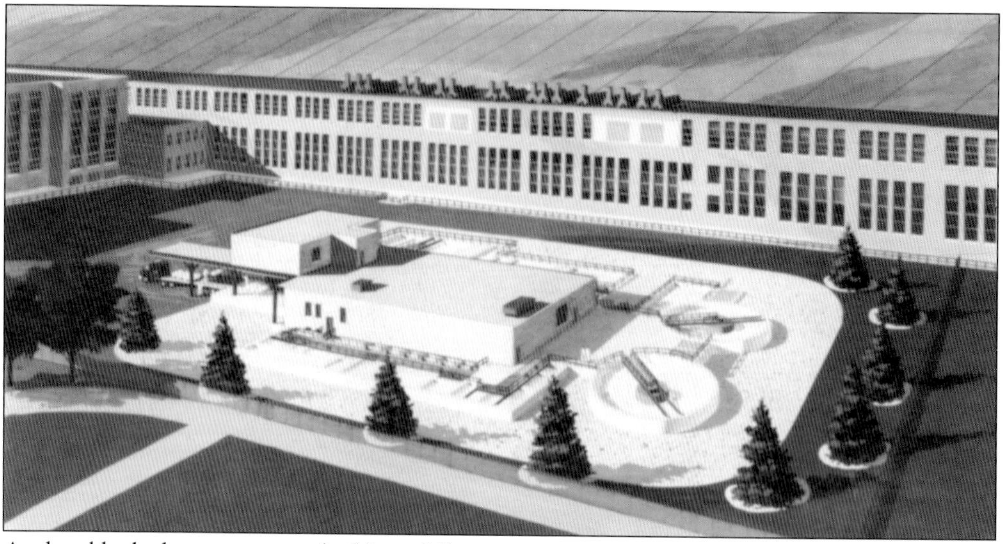

As the old telephone apparatus buildings fell, construction commenced on one last upgrade to the Hawthorne facilities. Revised Environmental Protection Agency chemical waste standards were set to go into effect in May 1983, so, in 1981, the Works broke ground on an updated treatment plant, seen here in an artist's rendering. The plant was designed to break down chemicals from the central manufacturing buildings before release into the public sewers. (Courtesy of the *Hawthorne Microphone*.)

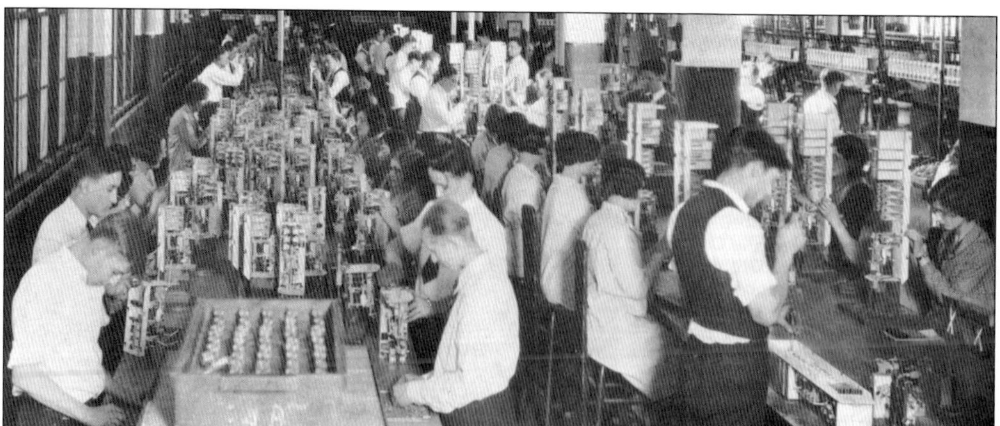

In 1980, after 54 years, Step-by-Step switching assembly at Hawthorne came to an end. Production of the durable system peaked in the early 1970s when 2,500 workers turned out 78,000 units. The Works delivered a total of over two million "shelves," but demand declined rapidly after the introduction of electronic switching. (Courtesy of the *Hawthorne Microphone*.)

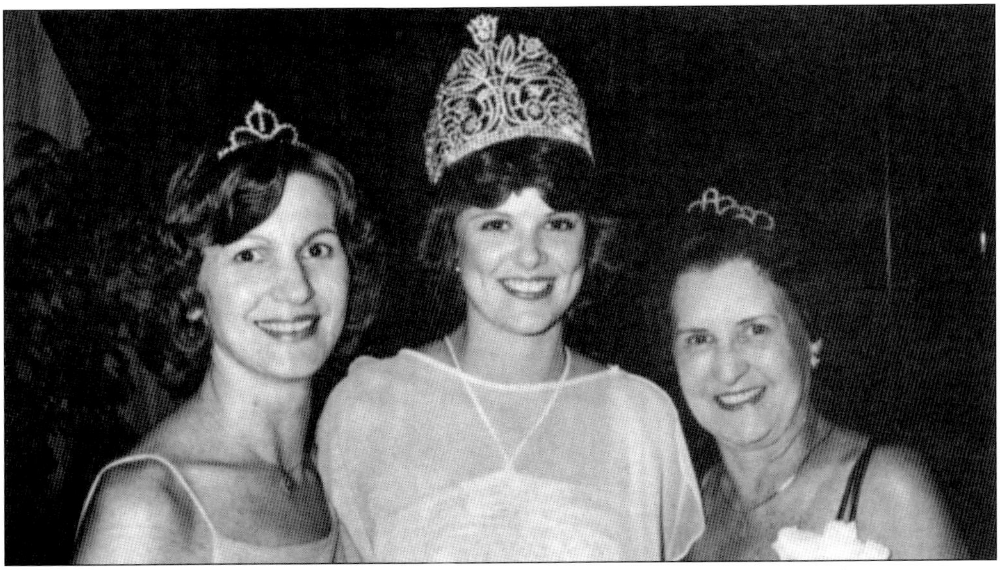

Above, the first Hello Charley Girl, from 1930, Jean O'Rourke Smith (right), crowns her counterpart Terri Frietch (center) 50 years later, joined by outgoing queen Genevieve Mokrzyckic (left). For the coronation ball, volunteers prepared a display of plaques depicting all the previous winners (below). The Charley Girl tradition ended in 1981 when company officials announced the cancellation of the pageant, citing the cost of the event and changes in the role of women that made such programs "no longer appropriate." Whether the cancellation was a mark of raised social consciousness or yet another belt-tightening measure was debatable, but no one could deny that times were changing for the Hawthorne family, and an institution that had weathered world wars and economic depression was facing yet another storm. (Both courtesy of the *Hawthorne Microphone*.)

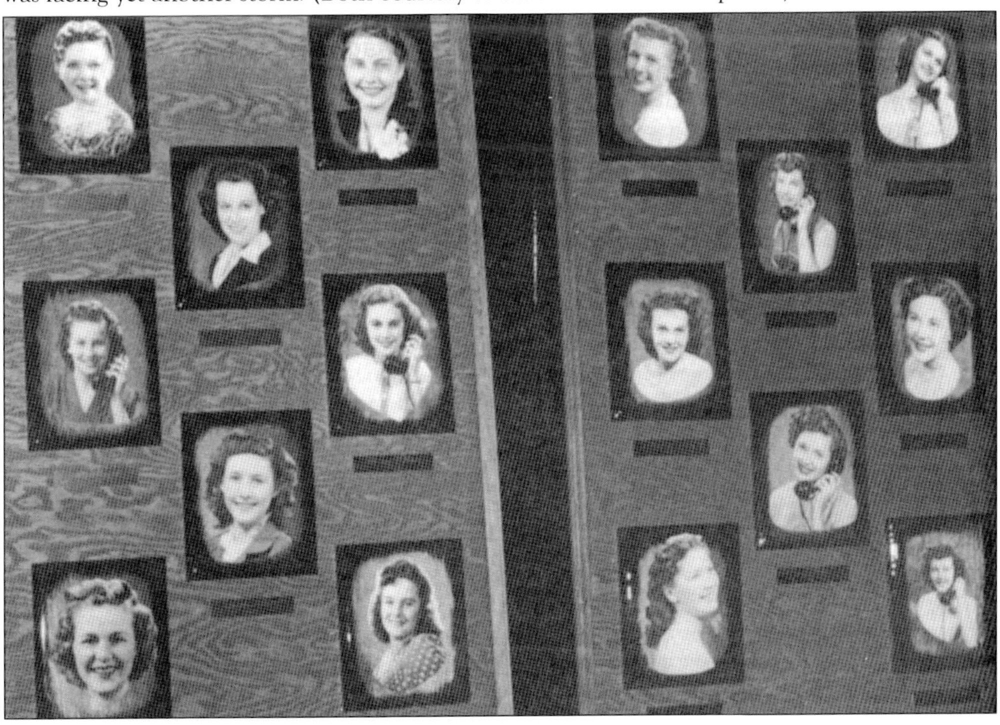

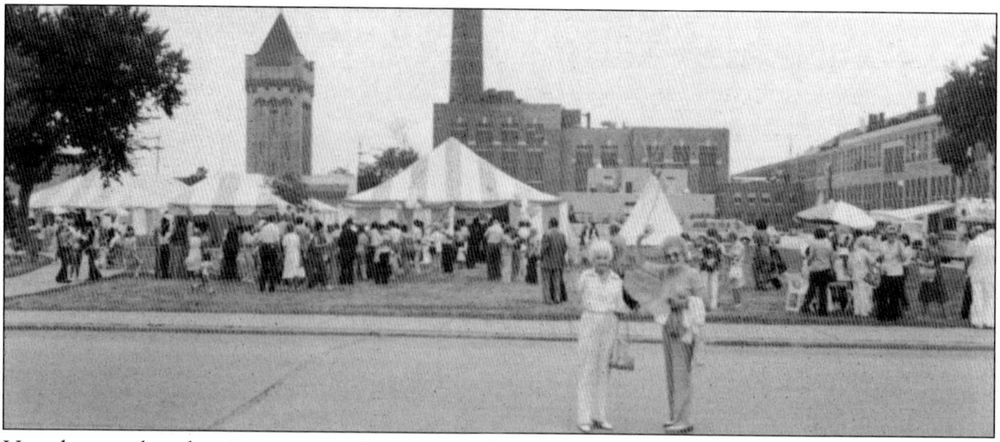

Hawthorne played an important role in its employees' lives, but as years passed and many moved miles away, fewer participated in Works-sponsored activities. Staff reductions and layoffs impacted workers' feelings about their jobs. A 1981 survey revealed increasing concerns about job security. A growing number (35 percent) felt less certain about their positions, and 83 percent believed management shared too little information. (Courtesy of the *Hawthorne Microphone*.)

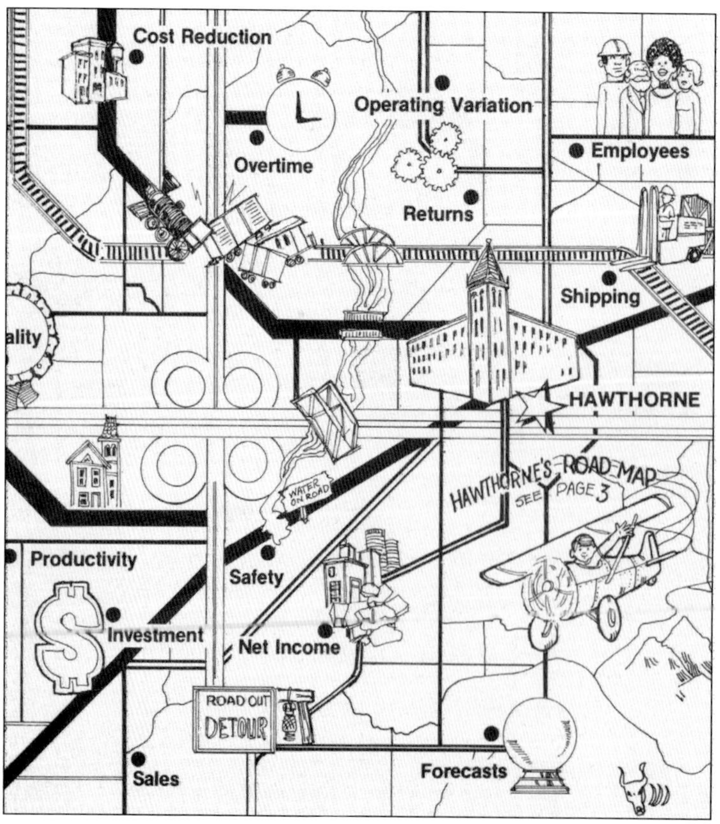

The 1981 survey exposed concerns about the company's methods. Nearly half of respondents believed employee morale had worsened, and only 39 percent gave their supervisor a positive rating. Almost 60 percent believed promotions were based on connections rather than merit. Despite these complaints, 83 percent felt that their efforts made a difference, while 91 percent still said "the company is a good place to work." (Courtesy of the *Hawthorne Microphone*.)

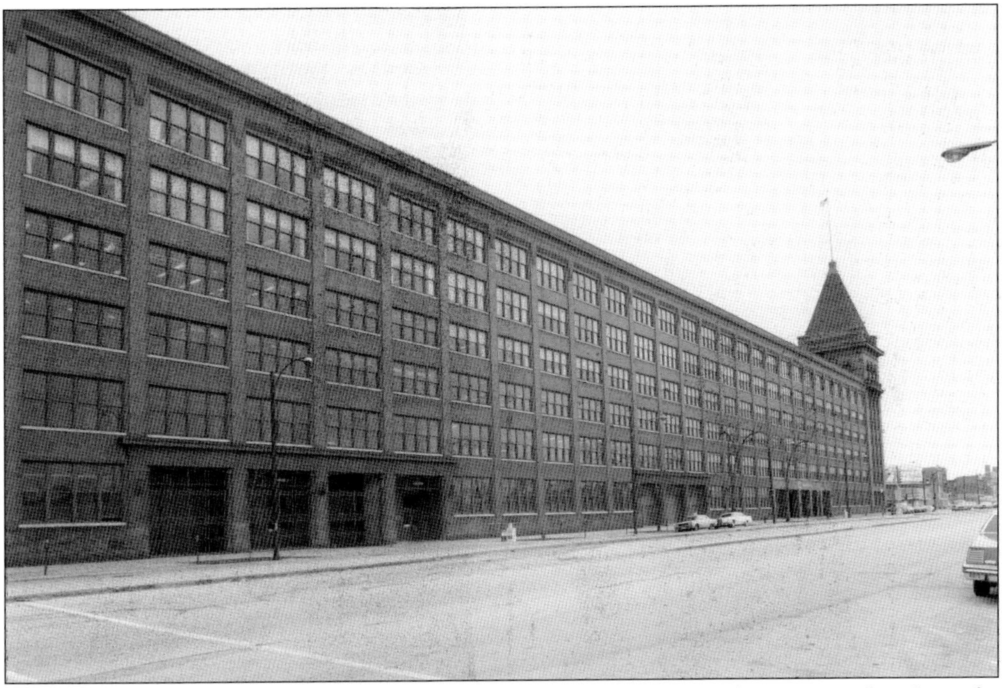

Seen here with its gates locked, the empty shell of the Hawthorne Works awaits its fate. It is a far cry from the glory days of the past, when shops stayed aglow 24 hours a day. In June 1983, Western Electric announced plans to close the Works gradually over the next three years. The remaining employees were offered buyouts, transfers, or jobs at other Western Electric locations. The plant succumbed to a reshaping of the world economy that battered American heavy industries. The town of Cicero lost jobs and property tax revenue ($300,000 annually from Hawthorne) as employers like Sunbeam, Hotpoint, and General Electric relocated. The disappearance of good-paying work also gutted Chicago's Lawndale neighborhood, to the east of Hawthorne, adding high unemployment to the list of chronic urban problems. Hawthorne's absence affected the community as much as its presence. (Below, courtesy of John Diaz.)

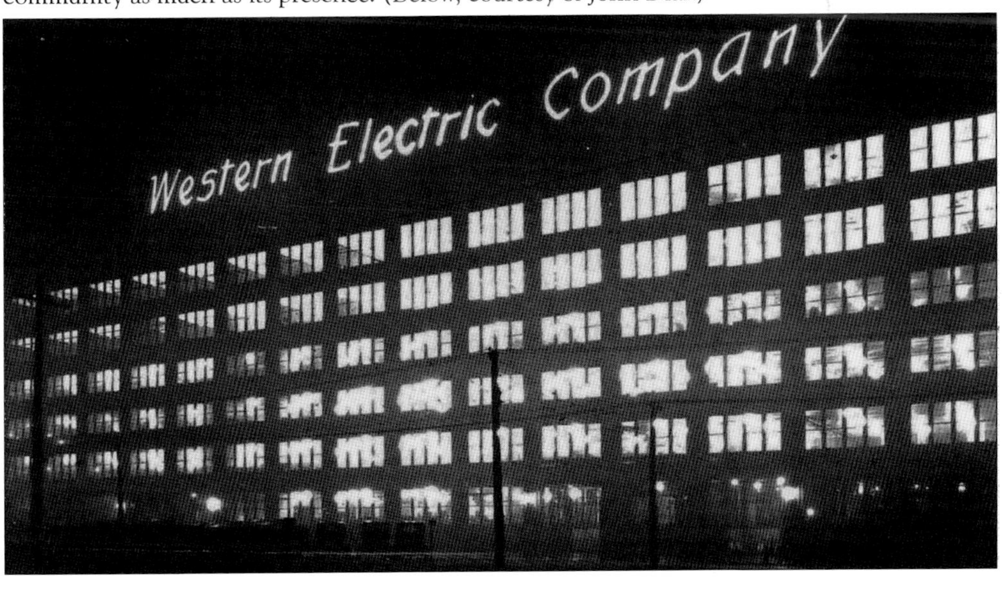

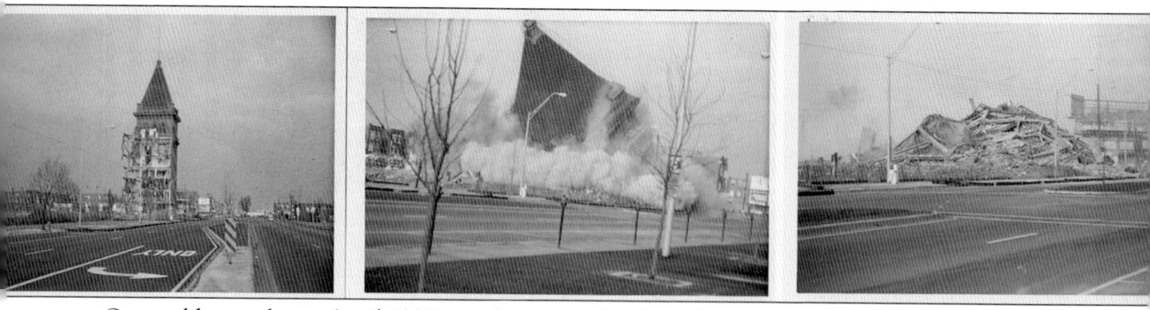

On a cold, gray day in April 1987, wreckers completed the demolition of the Hawthorne Works by bringing down the executive office tower, reducing to rubble what had been, just decades before, one of the largest employers in the Chicago area. Real estate developers who had purchased the land intended to leave the trademark tower standing, but the six-story structure proved unstable without the supporting building around it. The rod and wire mill was sold to another company and remained in operation. Hawthorne was just one of many large Chicago-area industrial plants shuttered in the 1970s and 1980s. In Cicero alone, close to 20,000 jobs were lost between 1972 and 1981. The busy factories made prosperous by the efforts of generations stood empty, leaving a changed community adjusting to a challenging new global economy.

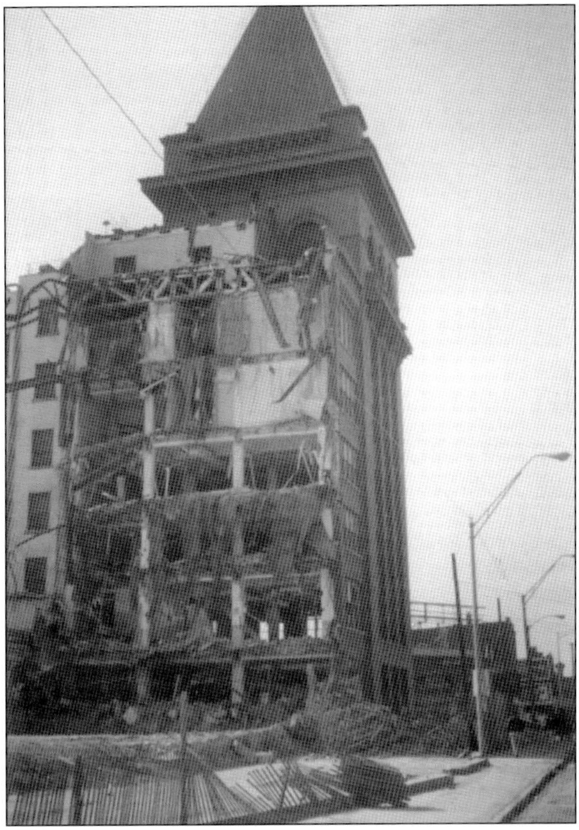

In April 1987, a security guard departing the old building for the last time found a crumpled piece of paper in a trashcan. On it was written this anonymous final tribute: "Countdown: As the buildings felt the heavy blows of the mighty ball impacting upon their sides, they fought back to resist the blows, showing that although age has crumpled some of their mortar, they were not that old to 'give in' to other forces. The walls around Hawthorne typified the strength of each of the many people who for decades had lived within . . . Now man has found that time no longer requires those walls as time no longer requires its inhabitants." (Images courtesy of the Brandsness collection; text courtesy of John Diaz.)

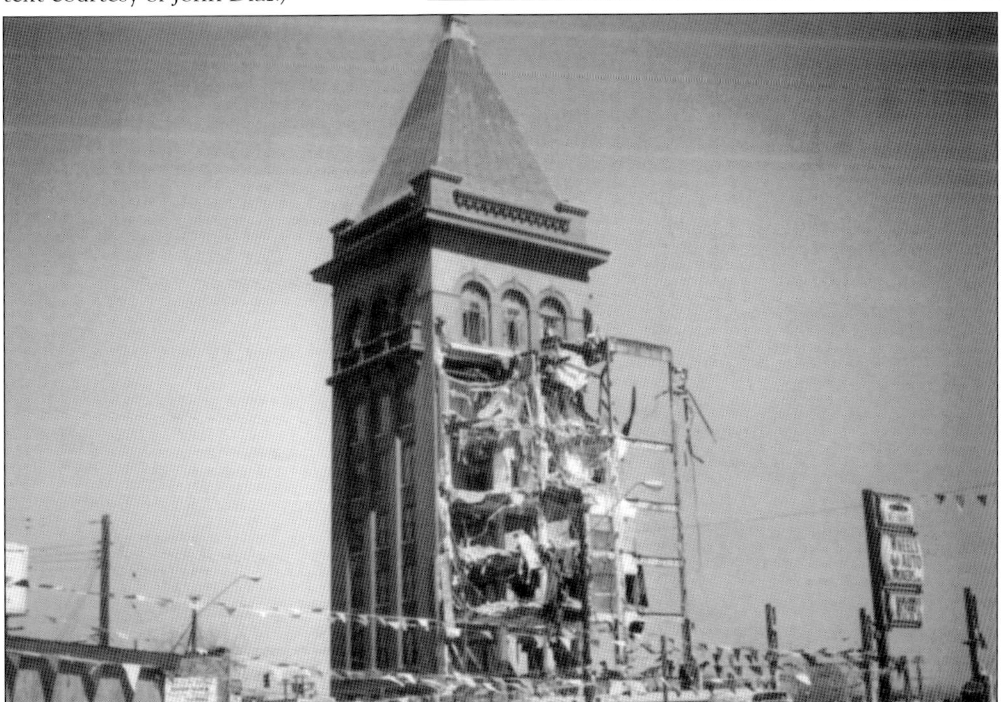

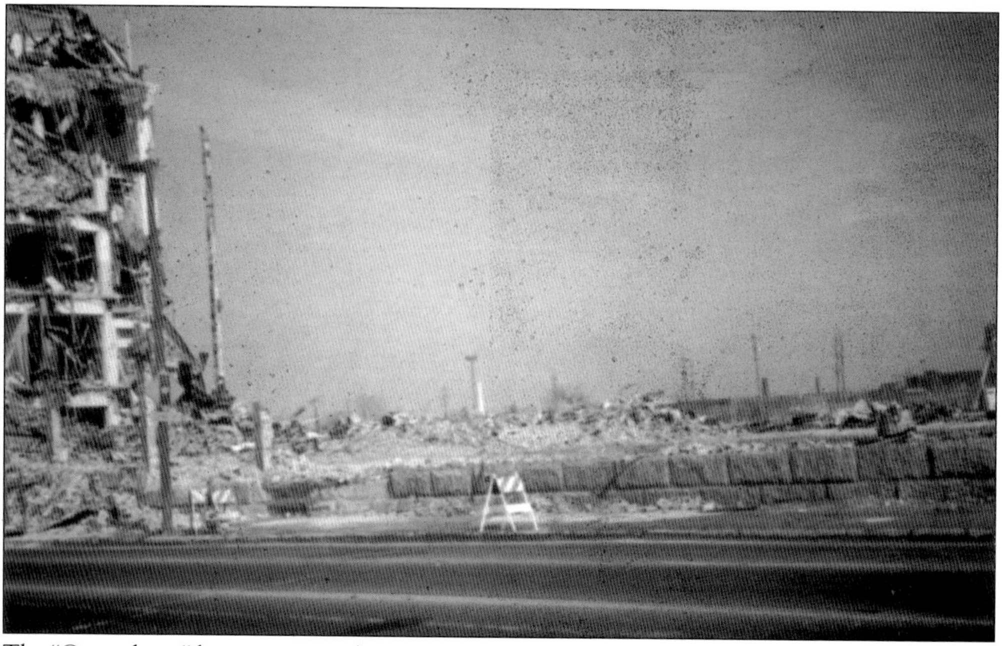

The "Countdown" letter continued: "As you stand there watching the mighty ball, feel the ground shake. Even though you are physically a distance from the happening, you are not so distant in your heart—the wall has become part of you and you hope it can and will resist the blows brought upon it. You realize forever that the wall can resist only so many blows—much like you and I—before it succumbs. Just then you see another massive chunk of wall begin to fall to earth and you turn away slowly and begin to walk, shoulders bent from the happening, and as you look back down at the ground, you see other signs of the end, for you are standing on weeds among dirt and stone which in the past was a lush carpet of dark green grass." (Images courtesy of the Brandsness collection; text courtesy of John Diaz.)

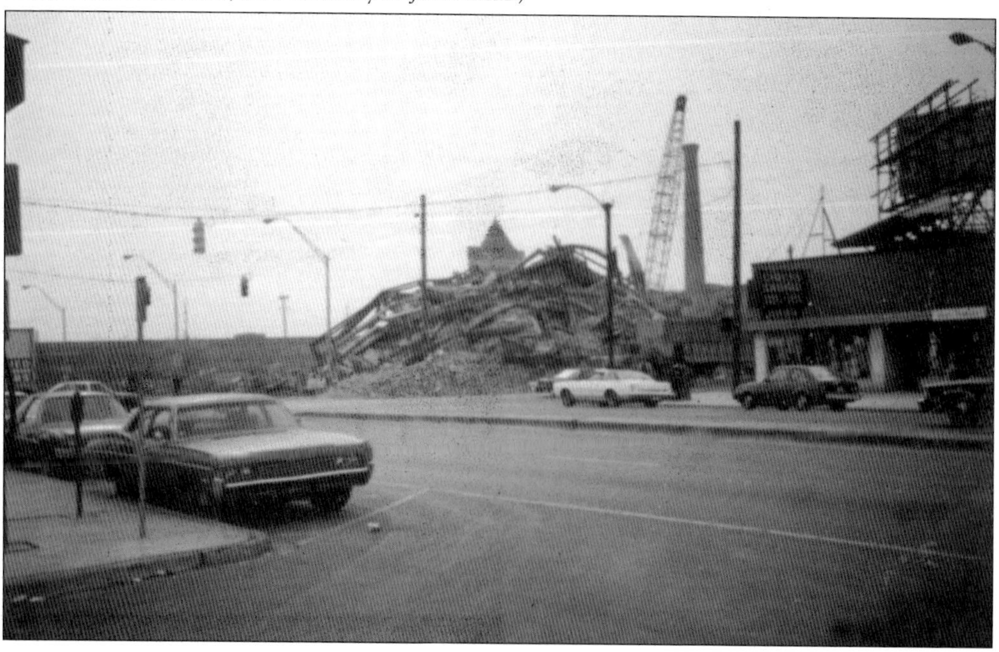

Nine

Legacy

Artifacts

On its 56th anniversary, in 1925, Western Electric published an advertisement in Chicago newspapers highlighting the company's accomplishments and looking forward another 56 years to 1981. The ad predicted confidently that "one landmark at least will still be here —the Western Electric Hawthorne Works . . . a solid, enduring factory."

The Hawthorne Works did make it to 1981, but just barely. A few years later, what had seemed so permanent, so solid, disappeared into the dust. Only a handful of relics remain, sitting in museum display cases and on archive shelves. What once covered more than 200 acres now occupies a single room and assorted file cabinets scattered across the country. Researchers from around the world still visit, curious about this vanished industrial Land of Oz they have read about in their textbooks. Retirees seek memories, but virtually all physical reminders of America's Electrical Capital have disappeared.

The museum at the Hawthorne Works opened in 1980 and included examples of the plant's handiwork accompanied by a slide presentation detailing the Works story. After the Works closed, a mere three years later, some items found their way into the collection of the Cicero Historical Society, housed at Morton East High School. The Hawthorne Works Museum at Morton College in Cicero opened in 2006, with artifacts drawn from the dispersal of the Cicero Historical Society collection and supplemented with pieces donated by the Alcatel/Lucent Archives and by individuals.

Those who recall the Hawthorne Works firsthand grow fewer each year. Their descendants have moved on to new hometowns, their upward mobility enabled by Hawthorne's might. A new generation buys shoes and snacks on its grounds, unaware that a century of accomplishment has been paved over for parking lots. But the Hawthorne Works lives on through them. For each time they pocket a hard-earned dollar, every time they savor the satisfaction of a job well done, each time they hold their child's hand and dream of a better future, they carry on the Hawthorne spirit, not one of bricks and steel and humming machinery, but one of the spirit of dignity earned through honest labor.

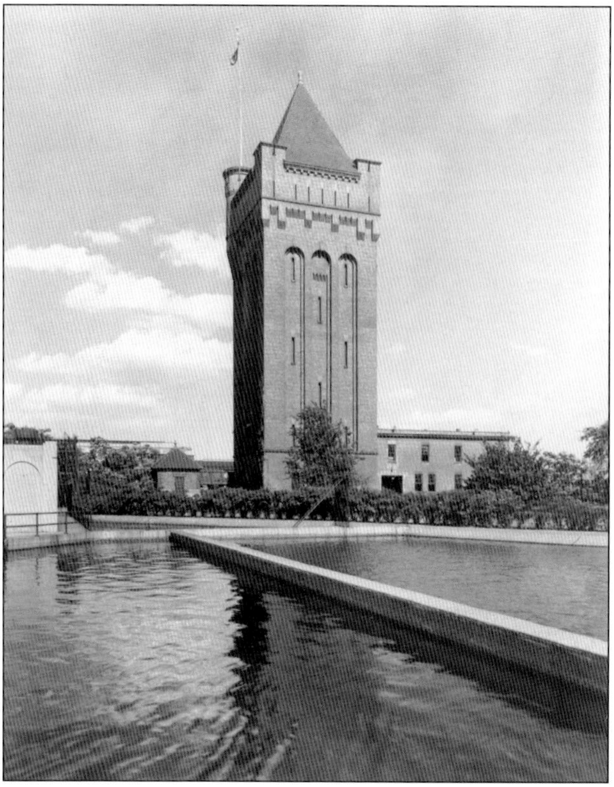

Time and "progress" have transformed the Hawthorne Works site, seen in these two images. Little remains of the sprawling Western Electric complex today. The space is now occupied by a busy shopping center where a shoe store has replaced the landmark six-story executive office tower. Acres of asphalt cover the cooling reservoir, courtyard, bandstand, hospital, and power plant. The former water tower, boarded up and inaccessible, stands as the solitary reminder of the decades when Cicero was home to one of the most vibrant and innovative enterprises in American industrial history.

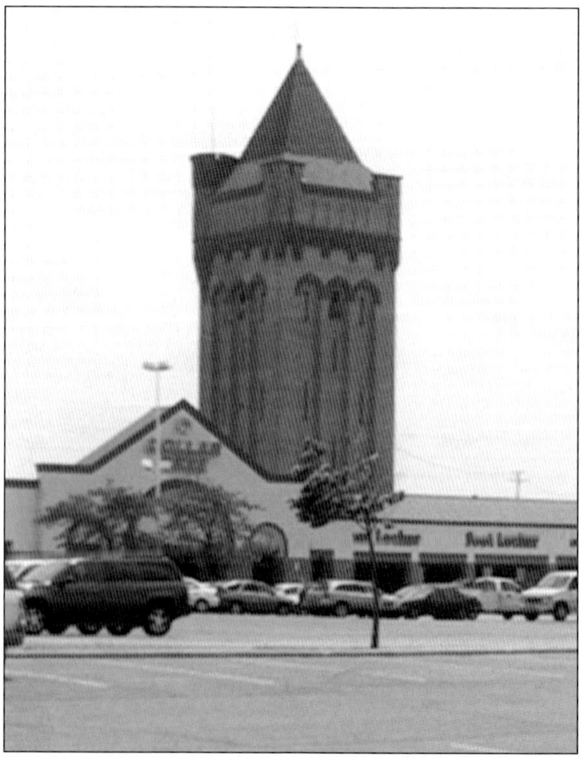

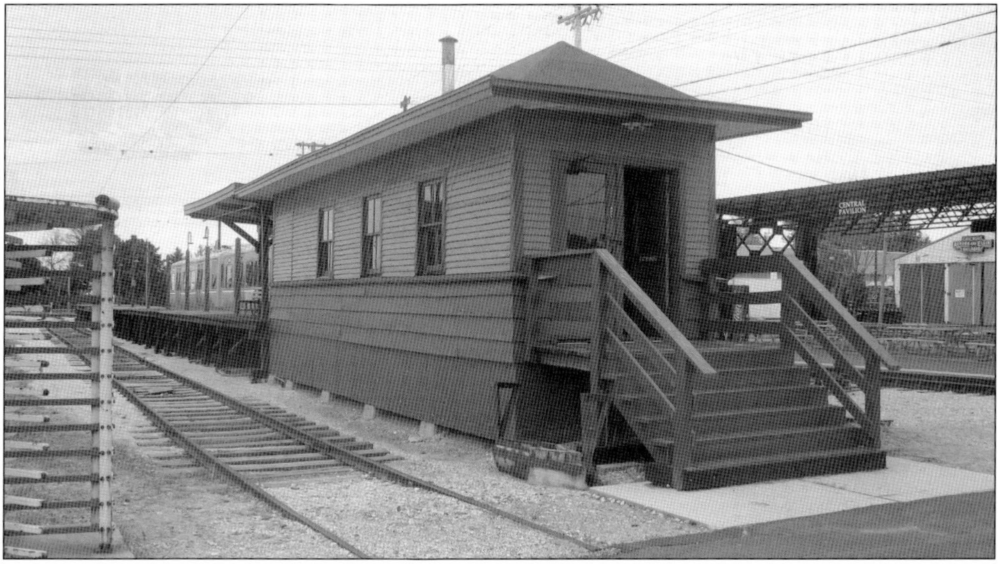

Visitors to the Illinois Railway Museum in Union, Illinois, can view reminders of the lost Hawthorne Works. The commuter train station that once stood at Fiftieth Avenue near Cermak Road, across the street from the Albright Gymnasium, has been salvaged and rebuilt on the museum grounds. For decades, thousands of Hawthorne employees poured through the station on their way to and from work.

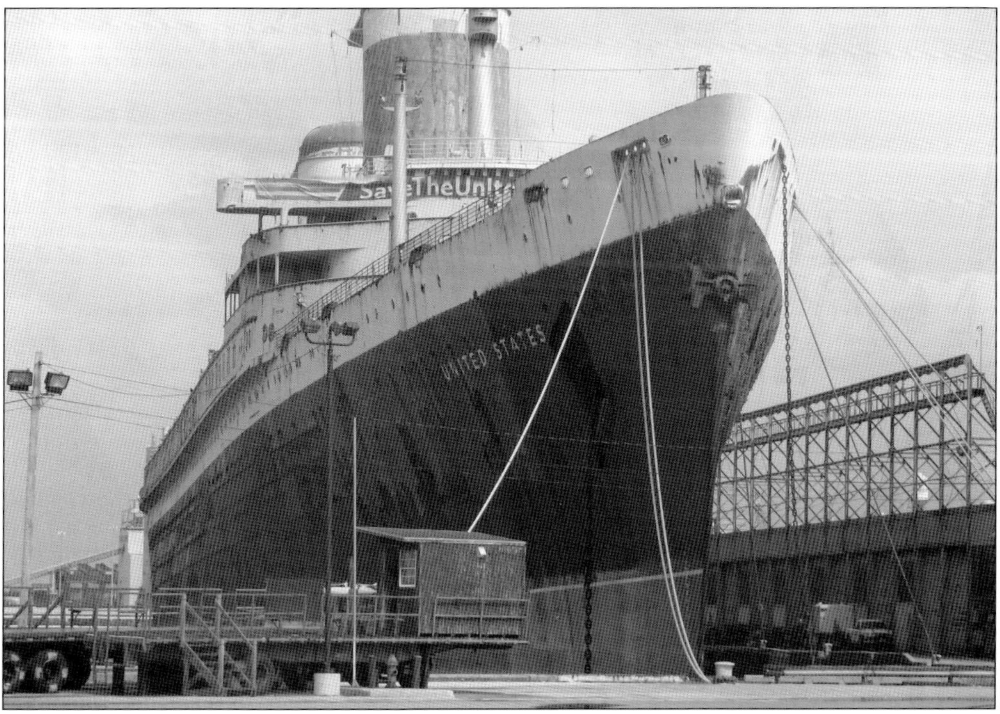

In 1953, Western Electric built the world's largest floating telephone system for the luxury liner SS *United States*. But the golden age of transatlantic travel ended in the 1960s, and now the "Big U" sits rusting at a Philadelphia pier and is in danger of being sold for scrap, another relic of a bygone era. The ship's owners sold the telephone system's copper wiring to salvagers in the 1990s.

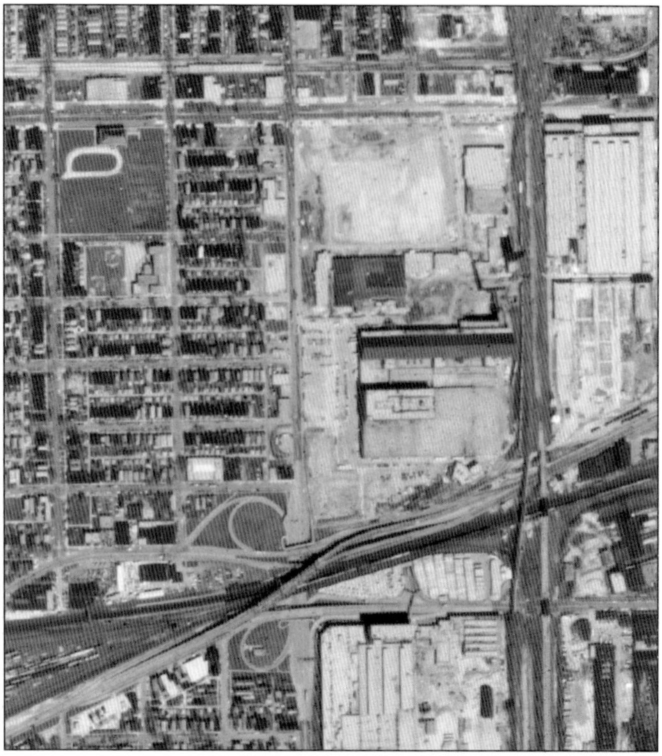

The 1988 aerial photograph at left shows the Hawthorne site a year after demolition. The telephone apparatus buildings are gone, their rubble cleared away. New stores already occupy what used to be the landscaped courtyard. The shadow of the spared water tower can be seen in the right center, and the Albright Gymnasium is in the top left. By 2002 (below), more stores and a parking lot further erased the footprint of the old Works. The Albright Gymnasium (top left) still stood, but was without its running track and tennis courts. The former cable plant (top right) was used as a warehouse by Cook County. (Both courtesy of historicaerials.com.)

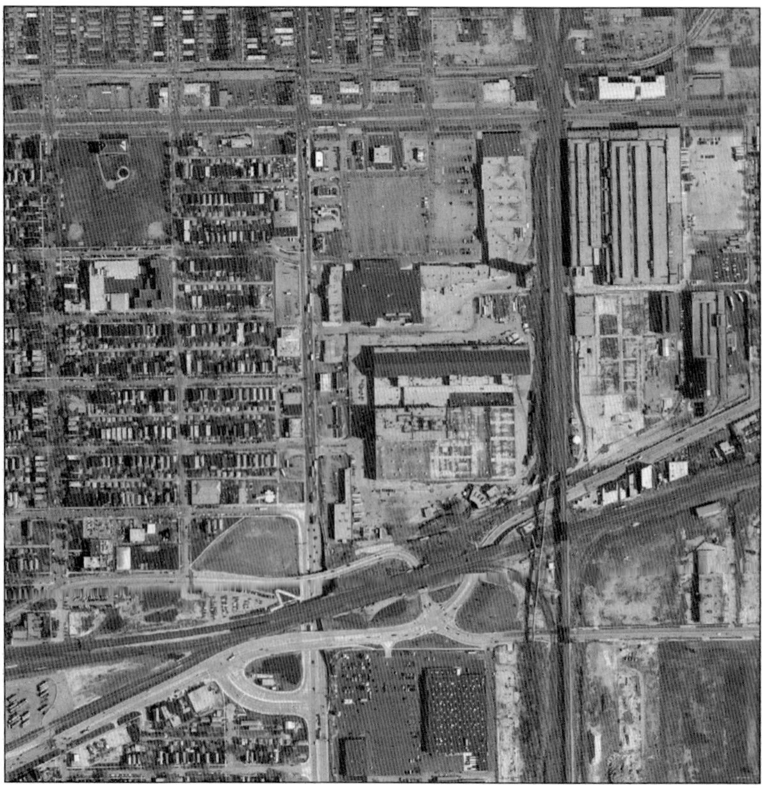

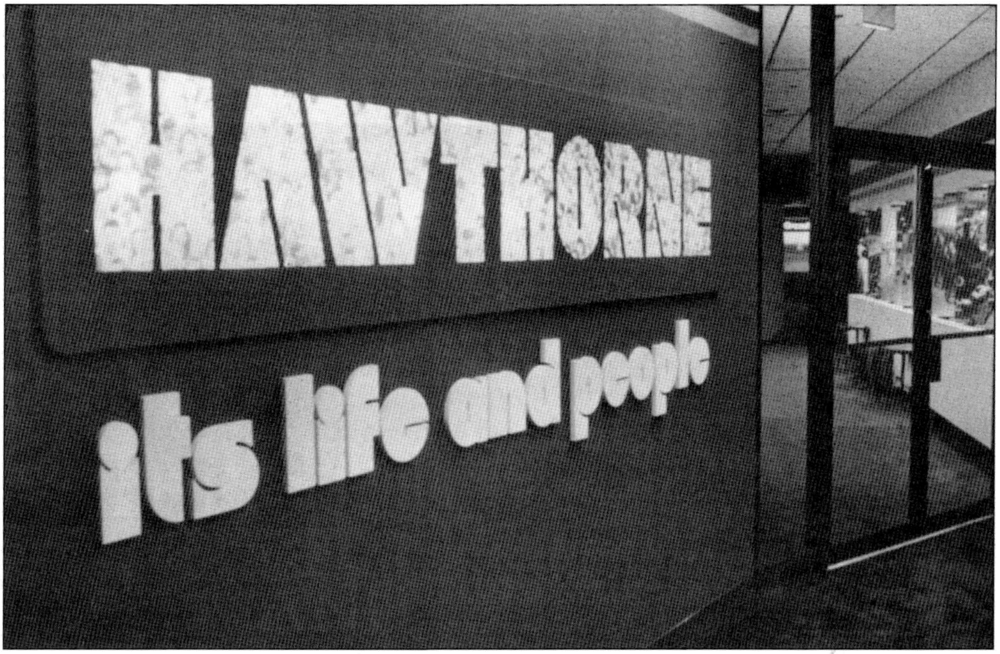

An exhibit from Hawthorne's 75th anniversary evolved into an official on-site museum that opened in September 1980. Products manufactured at Hawthorne throughout the decades were displayed, as well as numerous historical photographs. The first museum also included a library of plant literature and a theater featuring the slide presentation "Hawthorne: Its Life and People." The museum was open daily for staff but was also toured regularly by student, industry, and community groups. (Both courtesy of the *Hawthorne Microphone*.)

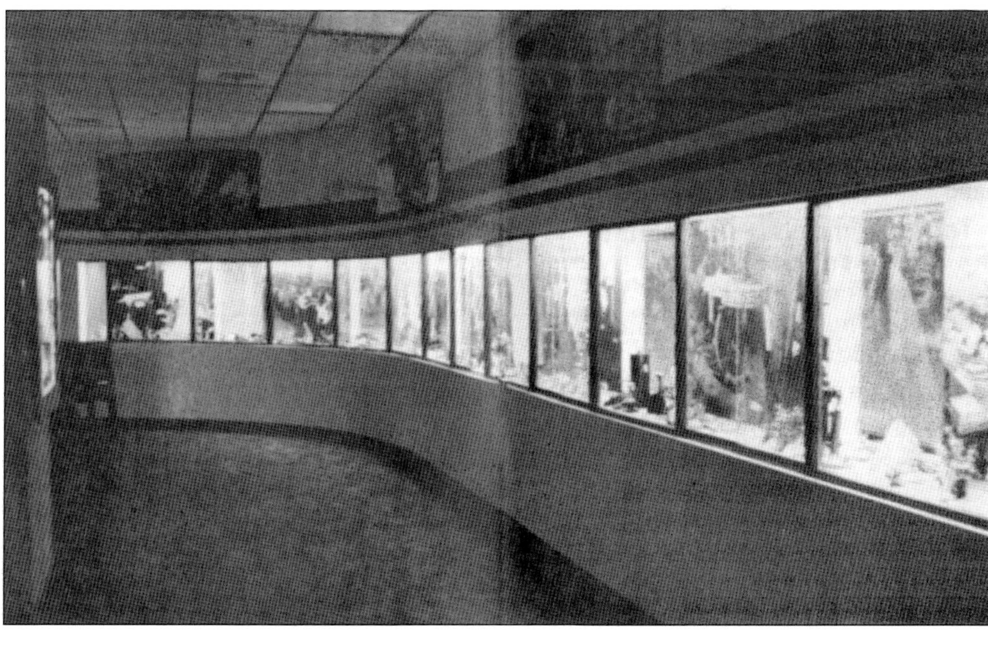

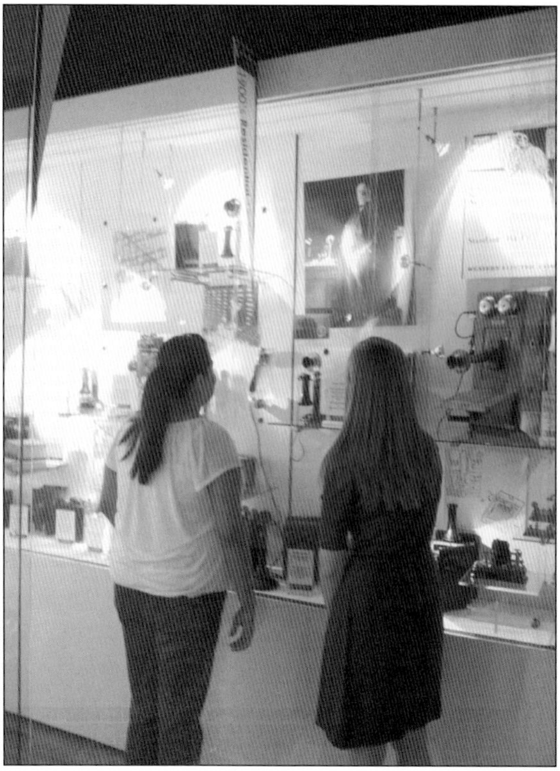

In 2006, a new museum space opened on the campus of Morton College. Lucent Technologies, one of the spinoff companies formed from the demerger of AT&T, donated artifacts and photographs to the museum. The Cicero Historical Society, steward of the Hawthorne Collection from the original museum, also contributed many pieces. Today, hundreds of students, researchers, and other visitors tour the museum each year to learn about Hawthorne's unique contribution to history. Generations of Hawthorne workers and their descendants continue to visit the museum to share their stories.

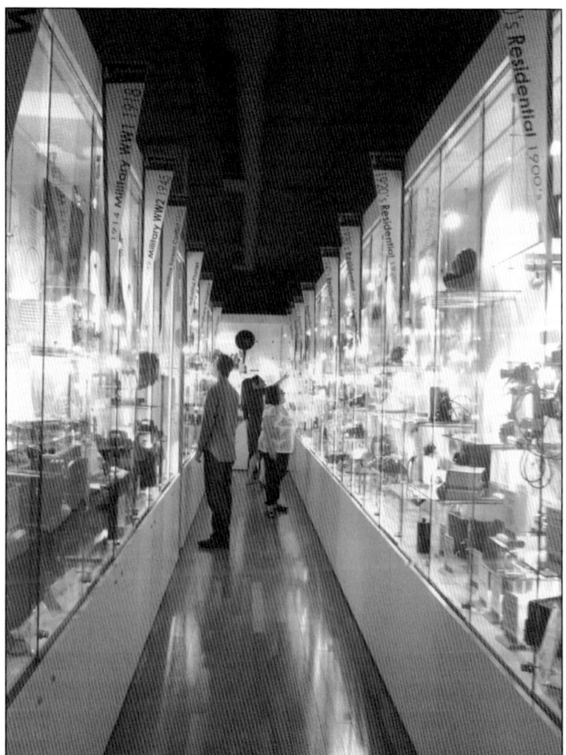

Bibliography

Adams, Stephen B. and Orville R. Butler. *Manufacturing the Future: A History of Western Electric.* Cambridge, UK: Cambridge University Press, 1999.

Brooks, John. *Telephone: The First Hundred Years.* New York: Harper & Row, 1976.

Cohen, Lizabeth. *Making a New Deal: Industrial Workers in Chicago, 1919–1932.* Second Edition. Cambridge, UK: Cambridge University Press, 2008.

Eig, Jonathan. *Get Capone: The Secret Plot That Captured America's Most Wanted Gangster.* New York: Simon & Schuster, 2010.

Gertner, John. *The Idea Factory: The Bell Labs and the Great Age of American Innovation.* New York: Penguin Press, 2012.

Gillespie, Richard. *Manufacturing Knowledge: A History of the Hawthorne Experiments.* Cambridge, UK: Cambridge University Press, 1991.

John, Richard R. *Network Nation: Inventing American Telecommunications.* Cambridge, MA: Belknap Press of Harvard University Press, 2010.

Lundy, Bert. *Telegraph, Telephone and Wireless: How Telecom Changed the World.* Monterey, CA: Booksurge, 2008.

Mayo, Elton. *The Human Problems of an Industrial Civilization.* Boston: Harvard University Graduate School of Business Administration, 1946.

Roethlisberger, F.J. *Management and the Worker: An Account of a Research Program Conducted By the Western Electric Company, Hawthorne Works, Chicago.* Cambridge, MA: Harvard University Press, 1967.

Stewart, Matthew. *The Management Myth: Why the Experts Keep Getting It Wrong.* New York: W.W. Norton & Co., 2009.